AF674694

PRAISE FOR THE BOOK

'Winning is a habit every one cherishes, whether on a playing ground or in a corporate boardroom. Great organizations/sporting teams, visionary leaders/outstanding players in both the arenas have displayed the same enduring characteristics consistently to maintain a sustained high performance. In *Pitch It!* Dev Prasad used fascinating stories from the cricketing world to piece together strategies that could be put to good use in a corporate warfare. An easy to read book, *Pitch It!* is a great compilation of winning strategies. In a country where cricket is a religion and the players demigods, any analogy with cricket is bound to draw crowds and make comprehension easy and intimate. Greatly enjoyed following winning habits through the lenses of two different arenas I love.'

—K. Srinivas, President, Consumer Business,
Bharti Airtel Limited

'*Pitch It!* takes a refreshingly different route to bring home to the reader, invaluable lessons in management and leadership, by delving generously into events—some well-known and some less—that have shaped the corporate and cricketing worlds over the years. Pearls of wisdom have been neatly woven into a pleasing necklace that offers answers, ideas, and inspiration! Each pearl is a significant incident involving famous cricketing personalities placed in front of the corporate mirror, to relate to an equally significant business situation. The author deftly compares the sporting and the business worlds to draw invaluable lessons for the aspiring business leader. The real life situations and their lessons—spanning the gamut of leadership challenges—have been chosen with care and presented lucidly, to make *Pitch It!* an engrossing and inspirational read!'

—D.V. Jagadish, Former Executive, GMSI and ASL, Asia Pacific, SW Group, IBM

'I have read many books on management and leadership and many on the game of cricket. This bold book of Dev captures in a succinct way the parallels in the game as it plays out in business. Rich in anecdotes and examples that have an ease of reading and absorbing as well, it is a great assembly of vignettes of the game and its relevance in business. Loved each chapter…makes you want to go back to it each time! Unputdownable!'

—S.V. Nathan, Director, Deloitte

'After having hit a century on debut, with his earlier book *Krishna*, Dev is well on his way to become the "Man of the series" for enthralling us with his *Pitch It!* This book can well pass off as a cricket historian's and a corporate management historian's delight, with the amount of research which has gone into the fact finding and stories woven around the facts. Dev, with his unique style of writing has managed to co-relate incidents of similar nature with awesome accuracy and deep insight of the dynamics of these incidents. As a corporate manager myself, I could easily relate to most situations depicted in the book, and almost did a quick recap of my MBA course during the reading. I spent one month to read this book—slowly, but surely, like a Rahul Dravid innings, building my thoughts around and savouring each incident, and giving each one the merit it deserves. The ease with which he slices and punches the stories through the field and finds the boundaries, reminds me very much of the master blaster in action, and to coin one of Dev's own idea, very similar to a Microsoft or an Apple in winning in the corporate space.'

—Girish Krishnamurthy, Global Manager, Enterprise Customer Assurance Imaging and Printing Group, Hewlett-Packard Co.

'This is a book of many delights. As a die-hard cricket fan who happens to be in the management field, I found *Pitch It!* to be very interesting, relevant, and insightful. The parallels between incidents on the cricket field and the world of business are well developed. It is a book that will draw you in and keep you hooked.'

—Shyam Vembar, Vice President, Mahindra & Mahindra Ltd

'The best leadership lessons are from sports. *Pitch It!* is an aggregation of interesting stories from cricket and the parallel drawn to a leadership trait that is so important to be successful in today's corporate world. The stories are truly compelling and well-narrated. Cricket being another religion in India, this book can be handy for leaders to connect, inspire, and motivate the young workforce of today. I would like to congratulate Dev for this unique approach of connecting with the readers through short stories on cricket and leadership.'

—M.R. Srinivas Prasad, Head of Healthcare R&D, Philips Innovation Campus, (Former Karnataka State and India cricketer)

PITCH IT!

PITCH IT!

INSPIRATIONAL STORIES FROM THE CRICKET DRESSING ROOM TO THE CORPORATE BOARDROOM

DEV PRASAD

PORTFOLIO
PENGUIN

An imprint of Penguin Random House

PORTFOLIO

USA | Canada | UK | Ireland | Australia
New Zealand | India | South Africa | China | Singapore

Portfolio is part of the Penguin Random House group of companies whose addresses can be found at global.penguinrandomhouse.com

Published by Penguin Random House India Pvt. Ltd
4th Floor, Capital Tower 1, MG Road,
Gurugram 122 002, Haryana, India

Penguin Random House India

First published by Random House India 2013
This paperback edition published 2019

Copyright © Dev Prasad 2013
Illustrations copyright © Anupama Ajinkya Apte

All rights reserved

10 9 8 7 6 5 4 3 2

The author of this book has, with due care and caution, undertaken the compilation of information and analysis from various sources. However, he does not guarantee that such information is accurate, verified, sufficient, updated, or comprehensive.

ISBN 9788184004458

Typeset in Electra LT by R. Ajith Kumar

Printed at Repro India Limited

This book is sold subject to the condition that it shall not, by way of trade or otherwise, be lent, resold, hired out, or otherwise circulated without the publisher's prior consent in any form of binding or cover other than that in which it is published and without a similar condition including this condition being imposed on the subsequent purchaser.

www.penguin.co.in

FSC www.fsc.org MIX Paper from responsible sources FSC® C047271

This is a legitimate digitally printed version of the book and therefore might not have certain extra finishing on the cover.

To JRD Tata

who taught me integrity, values, principles, and humility

CONTENTS

ACKNOWLEDGEMENTS

Cricket is a team game where contributions from each of the eleven players might be varied but all are equally important and significant. Each has to play a specific role for the success of the team. Here is my Team XI to whom I owe deep gratitude:

1. **Uma Rao:** My cousin, who is herself an eminent author in Kannada literature, was the first person to read my article in the newspaper and see the potential to adapt it into a management book. Initially I thought her idea was impractical and not feasible—how could I convert a one-page article into a book? Uma is a very strong-willed lady and knows how to put her points across. After a two hour chat over lunch with her, I decided that it was worth a try. She gave me no choice! Had it not been for her, this book would never have been written.
2. **My friends:** Kiran Mirle is an exceptionally creative guy who is wasting his time in the IT industry. He was the one who gave the brilliant idea of adding corporate studies to the cricketing anecdotes. I protested: 'How can I get so many corporate case studies? Sounds like mission impossible to me!' He coolly replied: 'talk to Balaji.' Balaji Vembar is a 'walking encyclopedia'. Call him anytime during the day and he can solve your problems by narrating an interesting

anecdote. Never short of ideas, his inputs are invaluable to me. Ajit Shenvi has been my sounding board throughout this project. With ruthless honesty, he can rip apart any great idea or work. He graciously agreed to read my manuscript and gave very valuable suggestions.

3. **Kiran Mazumdar-Shaw:** I am greatly indebted to her for agreeing to write the 'Foreword' for this book. Despite her frequent business travels and meetings across the globe, she had the enthusiasm and time to read my manuscript. I would also like to thank Seema Ahuja, head of corporate communications, Biocon. She always responded to my mails and phone calls promptly and was a great support.

4. **Venkatesh Prasad:** I met Venky, as he is popularly known, at a management workshop where he was one of the speakers. During the lunch break, I spoke to him about my upcoming book. He found the concept very unique and interesting and immediately agreed to write the 'Epilogue'. Though he is still very actively associated with the game and travels constantly, he managed to find time for me.

5. **The reviewers** – K. Srinivas, D.V. Jagadish, S.V. Nathan, Girish Krishnamurthy, Shyam Vembar, and M.R. Srinivas Prasad. They took time off their busy schedules to review the manuscript. There were occasions where they read the manuscript in hotel rooms, flights, and even departure lounges!

6. **Urmila Dasgupta:** My literary agent from Purple Folio. She reminds me of John Wright, one of India's most successful cricket coaches. She won't suffocate you with too many changes but can tell you what works and what doesn't. Within three months of signing the contract with her, she had got me the contract with my dream publishing house.

7. **Team Random House:** Milee Ashwarya, the Editorial Director, reminds me of Sachin Tendulkar. She shares the same passion and high energy levels as the 'Little Master'. My first meeting with her was scheduled for one hour but we talked for over two and a half hours! By the time I was driving back home, I had already decided that my next book should be for Random House, even if it was something as tough to write, as *Don't Lose Your Mind, Lose Your Weight* or *Kitchen Clinic*—that's the kind of impact she has on you! Anukriti Sharma, who is a mix of MS Dhoni and Rahul Dravid. She can be unflappable like 'Captain Cool' even under crunch times and pressure cooker situations, and at the same time she is a perfectionist and technically very sound like 'The Wall'. Her meticulous and diligent editing reminds you of some of the glorious innings played by Dravid. There were numerous instances when I showed her editing skills to my sons and exclaimed, 'Now, that's what I call Queen's English!' Shruti Katoch and Caroline Newbury from the Publicity team have recently come to the batting crease and in their brief innings, they have already shown the aggression and shrewdness of Yuvraj Singh and Steve Waugh, the best 'finishers' of the game who were always there to guide their team to many memorable victories.

8. **My family:** I would like to thank my father who, despite his frail health, took time to read my manuscript and provided insightful comments. I would like to thank my parents, wife, and children for giving me the space and time to write this book. Without their care and sacrifices, it would have been impossible. While other families would rush to malls for shopping and watching movies during the weekend, my wife and children were willing to stay back at home to watch me pound my laptop's keyboard.

9. **JRD Tata:** My relationship with him is akin to that of Ekalavya with his guru Dronacharya in the epic *Mahabharata*. Like Ekalavya, without having met my guru, I too have tried my best to imbibe some of JRD's great qualities. Compared to the legend, I am just an insignificant drop in the ocean. It is to him that this book is dedicated.
10. **Companies that I worked for:** These provided me with many invaluable insights while writing this book. Many of the anecdotes are based on what I had seen, heard, and experienced during my corporate life.
11. **Readers**: To the millions of readers across India. Like the thousands of spectators thronging the picturesque cricket stadia across the vast country, you play an important role in the ecosystem. It is only because of you that the game is alive and kicking!

FOREWORD

Cricket is often seen as a metaphor for life. Whether it is an account of winning or losing, or playing in the spirit of the game, cricket exemplifies the best and worst of human behaviour. From batting on a sticky wicket to being on the back foot, the game is full of stories of courage, astute strategy, and sheer doggedness. There are also several examples of errors of judgement and character flaws that have helped teams snatch defeat from the jaws of victory.

Corporate life is probably closer to cricket than many of us realize. Both focus intensely on winning. Players in both are imbued with a sense of mission and a desire to succeed. In cricket, as in business, there are strategy and review sessions, teamwork is key, and leadership is critical. Perseverance at every level and effective decision making stands between you and failure.

Extrapolating lessons learnt from cricket to corporate life, Dev Prasad, in his book *Pitch It!* offers instructive and inspirational anecdotes on how to succeed in the corporate arena. Refreshingly devoid of management jargon, what sets this book apart is that anyone can relate to it—from a corporate trainee to a mid-level manager to the CXO.

In India, cricket permeates all walks of life, and the corporate world is no exception. As followers of the game, all of us have applauded Sachin Tendulkar's approach to batting, celebrated Anil Kumble's spirit, and agonized whenever the Indian team loses the plot and the game. As the stories in the book unfold, we learn what made the difference between success and failure in cricket and juxtapose these lessons with a corporate situation. The management lessons learnt through cricket are simple yet impactful, and they resonate since they are based on rigorously researched vignettes of a game that captures our interest as well as imagination.

Dev Prasad takes on various dimensions of corporate life—leadership, attitude, ethics, teamwork, and execution to name a few—and draws parallels between a cricketing situation and a corporate one. We read about the importance of risk-taking as reflected by India's captain MS Dhoni and Wipro's Azim Premji, tenacity as an important determinant of success for Australia's Steve Waugh and Nirma's Karsanbhai Patel, and the leadership lessons of former West Indies captain Clive Lloyd, India's former captain Saurav Ganguly, and Infosys founder Narayana Murthy.

As this book takes us through various lessons, it reflects certain management principles that have guided me in my entrepreneurial journey. As the experience of leading corporate personalities and cricketers show, success is not the result of a one-off effort but a continual, persistent process. To succeed, we need to sense trends and give strategic direction in response to the changing situations.

Taking calculated risks when faced with challenges and accepting failures and learning from them are important lessons we must learn. After all, challenges are intrinsic to the growth of any company or individual. They can either spur us towards growth when tackled boldly or defeat us when handled ineptly. As the case study in the book demonstrates, Biocon grew even when we faced hurdles because we thought our way through them by reinventing ourselves—moving from our enzymes-driven business to a biopharmaceutical business. When we started Biocon, our resources were limited, the available infrastructure was primitive, and we had to function in a fairly hostile business environment. But we succeeded against all odds because we believed in ourselves and our ability to succeed. We leveraged our existing resources in the most creative manner possible and took acceptable risks to grow towards our goals; much as Martin Crowe, Clive Lloyd, Chris Harris, and Larry Gomes did while playing for their teams.

I have always believed that the more challenging the environment the greater the opportunities. A chapter in this book illustrates this by showcasing the attitude of MS Dhoni and ICICI Bank's Chanda Kochhar. Biocon's journey has helped me realize that there are no shortcuts to success. Hard work, clear vision, and the courage of conviction can help you reach your goals, no matter how difficult they might seem at first. Failure provides the experience that success cannot guarantee. I am not suggesting that one must seek failure, but if and when it comes, learn from it instead of running away. MS Dhoni has converted failures into success through a resolute approach that has earned him the apt title of 'Captain Cool'. We must be passionate about work and have a sense of ownership and purpose, acting in accordance with a deep sense of integrity. Sachin Tendulkar's attitude to the game is an illustrative example of all these factors at work as a champion cricketer.

Corporate success is not about climbing the ladder but about being able to inspire people, empower them, earn their respect, and motivate them to be and do their best. A sense of self-confidence, determination, and hard work are critical in winning and inspiring others. In the end, success is all about making a positive difference. The stories of individuals, companies, and cricketers featured in this book serve to tell us just how we need to 'play the game'.

Kiran Mazumdar-Shaw
Chairman and Managing Director
Biocon Limited

PROLOGUE

Just like the game of cricket, this book too evolved slowly before taking its final shape. A couple of years back, the organization that I worked for introduced a monthly e-newsletter. This newsletter was meant to be the senior management's communication to all employees. Every month, one management team member had to write an article that would be of interest to the employees—it could range from recent happenings in the company, update on the latest products and technologies, people-related topics to general industry trends. Soon it was my turn to contribute to this newsletter. My colleagues requested me to write an article that should encompass all aspects of management but in a manner that could be appreciated right from the CEO to the junior-most engineer in the organization. 'No management jargons please!' they had joked.

This sounded like a herculean task. How was I supposed to write a management article devoid of management jargons? I realized that the article had to be unique and innovative since it was meant to address a wide spectrum of audience with varied levels of corporate experience. I pondered: What was that one thing that binds us all together? I didn't have an answer.

A few days later, one sunny morning while driving to office, I passed through a narrow lane where I found a bunch of urchins playing cricket using a makeshift bat, a ball, and stumps. A few kilometres ahead, I passed by the playground of a renowned public school. I noticed a few schoolboys playing cricket using the finest cricketing gear. Soon I was stuck in traffic because the KSCA Stadium was issuing tickets for an India-Pakistan cricket match. Thousands of cricket-crazy spectators had braved the chill of the night and were waiting patiently for their turn.

I had found my answer. The single important factor that binds billions of Indians together is cricket!

Cricket and corporate life have many similarities. Though the final goal is to win, both strongly emphasize strong leadership, attitude, team building, teamwork, ethics and principles, flawless execution, innovation, and agility to the ever changing conditions.

If the cricketing world has the humble and unassuming Sachin Tendulkar as its biggest icon, the corporate world has a colossus like JRD Tata—the epitome of humility and grace. Both cricket and the corporate world has seen people with humble beginnings rise to the highest echelons. If Dhoni, who started his career as a ticket collector at the nondescript Kharagpur Railway Station, could go on to become the Indian captain, so could Dhirubhai Ambani, a clerk at A. Besse & Co, form the multi-billion dollar Reliance empire.

For every Rahul Dravid who always put his team ahead of himself—whether it was opening the innings on a seaming track or donning the wicket keeping gloves to accommodate an extra bowler—we have corporate head honchos like Anu Aga who came out of retirement and took the reins of her company when the situation demanded. If the importance of teamwork and synergy is emphasized by Rajasthan Royals winning the inaugural IPL Tournament, the lack of this trait has also shown the downfall of many high-profile IT mergers.

Cricket has shown us that top performing players and teams have always shown a willingness to adapt to the changing demands of the game. Not only IT companies like Apple and

Facebook but even those in the food industry like Kellogg's and McDonald's have been highly successful. This is because of their innovativeness and ability to judge the market needs much better than their competitors.

Both cricket and the corporate world have been rocked by scandals. The Australian Cricket Board had no hesitation in showing the door to its star leg spinner when he used a banned diuretic. Similarly, one of the top American IT companies sacked its high performing CEO on ethical grounds. It didn't matter if the leg spinner was the highest wicket taker for his nation nor the fact that the corporate CEO had turned around the company and doubled its share value at the stock market.

I thought: Why not write an article that has interesting anecdotes from cricket and draws management lessons from them? Would such a commentary be palatable to my colleagues?

When my article was published in the e-newsletter, it became one of the most read articles of the quarter. I received many appreciative mails, with some of the readers even asking me to send the article to a newspaper. I got in touch with one of the leading newspapers in Bangalore and within a fortnight, they published my article. Once again, I was fortunate enough to receive lots of appreciation. My cousin Uma, who is an eminent author, suggested that I convert it into a book. One of my friends asked me to add corporate case studies to make the book more interesting. Thus *Pitch It!* was born.

Pitch It! is an innovative book that consists of sixty inspirational stories from cricket and draws analogies with corporate scenarios. Each cricketing anecdote is linked to a corporate case study.

The book consists of ten chapters covering different aspects like leadership qualities, traits required to be successful, team building and people development, importance of teamwork, ethics and values, attitude needed to be successful, how to realize one's vision through flawless execution, the importance of continuous innovation, the need to know the market, and the challenges that even successful companies face.

This book is not meant to be read in a single sitting. Neither is the reader expected to read the book sequentially. One can read a few episodes from a specific chapter and then jump to another chapter—the entire book can be read in that manner. This is because the sixty episodes, spread across ten chapters are quite independent of each other. Read this book slowly as if you are sipping a glass of vintage wine or a steaming cup of coffee, allowing the flavour to sink in rather than gulping it all in one go!

This book is not intended to glorify or belittle cricketers, corporate leaders, or organizations. It is purely meant to narrate different situations of cricket and the corporate world that can work as useful lessons for the readers. Hence the reader might notice an occasional contradiction—in one anecdote an individual's or an organization's strength might be depicted but in another, the same individual's or organization's weakness may be mentioned. This is because I have focused on situations rather than individuals or organizations.

This book would be of interest to not only the lovers of the game but also to those who like to read management case studies. It has case studies of cricketers, corporate leaders, and organizations from India and different parts of the world.

India is a country where cricket is a religion and a child learns the names of the cricketing idols before he knows his own name; a nation whose mood is dictated by the fortunes of its cricket team; a land where cricket is played and watched throughout the year. When a match is over, we switch off the TV and get back to other mundane tasks that we had deferred simply to watch 'that final over'. From the cosy comforts of the living room, it is back to the daily grind. However, occasionally, it would be good to pause and ponder over the lessons that we can learn from the most loved game of our nation.

1

LEADERSHIP

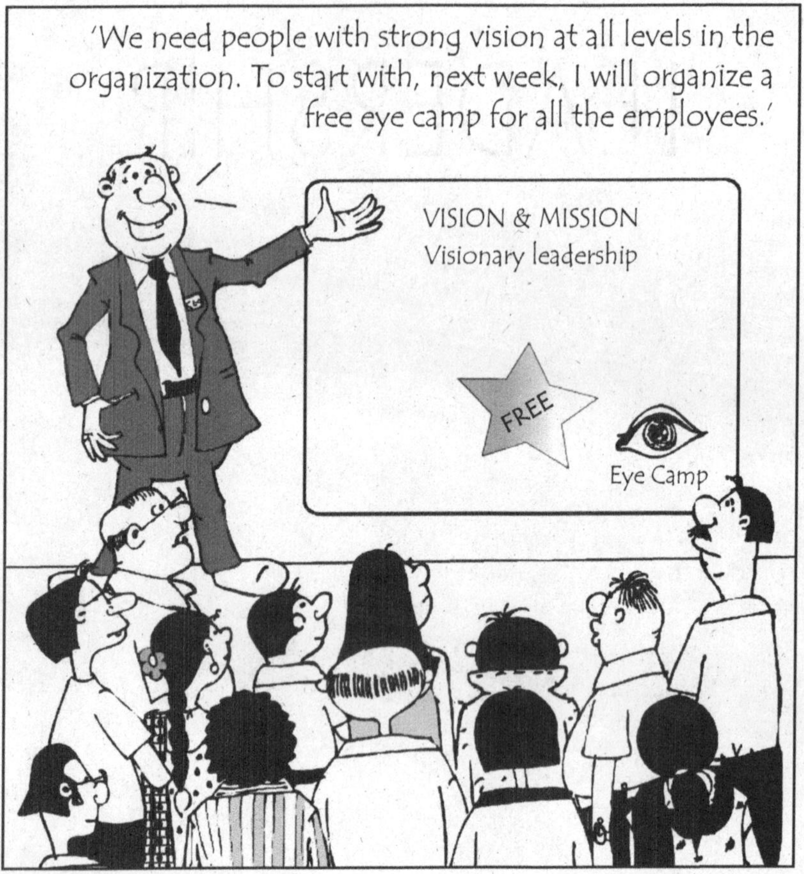
'We need people with strong vision at all levels in the organization. To start with, next week, I will organize a free eye camp for all the employees.'
VISION & MISSION
Visionary leadership
FREE
Eye Camp

Humility and Modesty

(SACHIN TENDULKAR–JRD TATA, TATA GROUP)

'Lives of great men all remind us we can make our lives sublime; and, departing, leave behind us, footprints on the sands of time.'

—Henry Wadsworth Longfellow

When I began writing this book, I had a tough time deciding who should feature in the first chapter and what attribute of theirs should I describe first. Luckily, a management workshop that I conducted solved my quandary. During one of the sessions, I distributed a sheet of paper to all the participants with just two questions:

1. Which cricketer and corporate leader do you consider as the greatest of all times?
2. What is their most important attribute?

To my first question, more than 80% of the participants had written Sachin Tendulkar and JRD Tata. This was not surprising since Indians consider Tendulkar as the 'God of Indian cricket' and JRD Tata as one of the greatest visionaries of the Indian industry.

However, the answer to the second question stumped me!

I had expected the participants to pick from Tendulkar's and Tata's numerous enviable traits like competency, passion, dedication, people management skills, communication skills, and self-belief. Surprisingly, none of the participants chose any of these qualities. In fact, everyone had used the same attribute to describe the two great men—'humility'!

Later, while driving back home, I thought about the proceedings of the workshop. Tendulkar has excelled in cricket for more than two decades. He holds practically every cricket record. Similarly, JRD Tata's qualities and achievements can fill an entire book. However, none of the participants cared about the number of runs Tendulkar had scored, nor the centuries he had hit. Neither did they care about the numerous companies that JRD Tata had established and led successfully.

What mattered to everyone in the room was their humility.

After some retrospection, I asked myself, 'Why am I surprised? If I too was a participant, wouldn't I have mentioned exactly the same characteristic of theirs?'

Of course I would!

When I think of Tendulkar or JRD Tata, the first word that comes to my mind is 'humility'.

Sachin Tendulkar has been considered one the greatest cricketers in the world and is often compared with the legendary Donald Bradman of Australia. The debate regarding who is the better of the two never ends. Tendulkar has broken almost every cricketing record, be it in Test or One Day matches.

It is a cliché to say that in a country where cricket is a religion, Sachin is considered a God, and is worshipped by over a billion Indian fans. In fact, it is a cliché to say that this is a cliché!

Every sports writer and cricket commentator says that each time Sachin goes out to bat; he carries the hopes of a billion Indians on his shoulders. What differentiates this diminutive genius from other cricketing giants is his humility. He is known to have his feet firmly planted on the ground and head firmly on his shoulders. Whether he is speaking at a post-match ceremony, as a chief guest at a social function, or playing with underprivileged children at an orphanage, his humility comes shining through.

One of the oldest fans of Sachin is 87-year-old Saraswathi Vaidyanathan, a resident of Chennai. Despite her old age and failing health, she stays awake late at night and watches all his matches. She had also maintained all important statistics and records related to the Little Master. In 2010, she had the opportunity to meet the cricketing legend during one of his visits to Chennai. It was an emotional meeting for both of them. The old lady had difficulty in walking, so Sachin himself walked to her and seeked her blessings with folded hands.

His voice was choked with emotion when he said, 'I read that you have followed all my innings and know all my records. I need your wishes.'

Saraswathi too was overcome with emotions and said, 'I am so lucky to meet you.'

Sachin, in all his humility, was quick to reply, 'No, I am lucky to meet you.'

She affectionately called him her fourth grandson and gifted him an idol of Lord Ganesha. The batting genius touched her feet and once again sought her blessings.

In his 22 long years of cricketing career, there has never been a single instance of Sachin getting involved in any kind of controversy—be it throwing tantrums, sledging players, confronting umpires, or rebelling against the cricketing board. There have been many other cricketers who have remarkable batting or bowling records but they do not evoke the kind of respect Sachin does—probably because people respect the man and not just his records.

There was an instance when Sachin was batting and the Australian players tried to sledge him, hoping to make him lose his concentration. It is believed that Brett Lee, one of Australia's fastest bowlers, walked to his teammates, and asked them not to sledge the Indian batting genius. He told them that Sachin is the greatest cricketer ever and deserved to be shown respect worthy of his stature. It is also believed that Brett Lee told his teammates that they were better off watching and learning from his game.

In the corporate world, Jehangir Ratanji Dadabhoy Tata, popularly known as JRD Tata, is the epitome of humility and humbleness. JRD Tata was the chairman of Tata Group of Companies which comprises over 100 operating companies in seven business sectors: communication and information technology, engineering, materials, services, energy, consumer products, and chemicals. The group has operations in more than 80 countries across six continents. The total revenue of Tata companies, taken together, was approximately $100.09 billion in 2011–12. Founded by Jamsetji Tata in 1868, Tata's early years were inspired by the spirit of nationalism. It pioneered several industries of national importance like steel, power, hospitality, and airlines. Later it made forays in the areas of automobiles (Tata Motors) and Information Technology (TCS). JRD, as he is popularly known, was one of the pioneers of Indian aviation industry and went on to become India's most famous businessman. He won numerous awards, the most prestigious ones being Bharat Ratna, India's highest civilian award, and Legion of Honour from the French Government.

Under his leadership, the Tata Group grew from $100 million to over $5 billion. He increased the number of companies from 14 to 95. Tata became the most famous industrial house in India and a household name across the country. However, JRD was unaffected by all this. Till his death, he remained the most affable and humble celebrity of India. He had numerous great qualities worth emulating but the greatest of all was his humility.

In 1932, JRD founded India's first commercial airline 'Tata Airlines'. It started as a mail service between Bombay (Mumbai) and Karachi and later extended its operation to Madras (Chennai) and Trivandrum (Thiruvananthapuram). In 1946, it became a public limited company and was renamed 'Air India'. After independence it was acquired by the Government of India. Despite JRD Tata being the founder of India's aviation industry and owner of the first airlines of the country, he travelled like a commoner. Pyarelal, of the music director-duo Lakshmikant–Pyarelal, fondly recollects an anecdote related to JRD. Pyarelal was at the airport, catching a flight to Tirupati. He noticed JRD Tata standing in the security-check queue in front of him, holding a briefcase in his hand. Pyarelal turned towards his son, Gautam and gave him his first lesson in humility. He pointed towards JRD Tata and said, 'This entire airport is his. He can walk into any of his private jets if he wants. But he still stands in queue like everyone else.'

This was so refreshingly different from the way today's politicians and celebrites behave, assuming it is their birth right to flout all rules and procedures at the airport and be pampered as VIPs!

JRD's Tata Group also owns the world famous Taj Hotels Resorts and Palaces, a worldwide chain of hotels and resorts located in more than fifty destinations. They own hotels, palaces, private islands, and resorts around the world. However, JRD Tata's simplicity and humbleness made him behave like any normal traveller. He would personally walk to the reception and sign at the registration desk even while staying in his own hotels.

What a stark contrast if compared to the current day celebrities who come to the hotels with their coterie and announce their arrival by their rude, boorish, and loud behaviour!

Once, JRD Tata went to Wankhede Stadium in Mumbai to watch a cricket match. Since the stadium was under his ownership at that time, he walked up to the gate without a ticket. Seeing him dressed in simple attire, the guard failed to recognize him. He did not allow JRD to enter the stadium since he did not possess a ticket. The great man, without speaking a word, quietly went around the gate and stood near the fence to watch the match. When one of the organizers noticed him, he rushed out and apologized to him. He wanted to fire the guard but JRD asked him not to do so since the guard was merely doing his duty.

I wonder how we would have reacted if we were in JRD's shoes!

Tendulkar had his share of detractors too but that has rarely affected his attitude and approach towards the game and his fans. Whenever India has lost a match, his critics have held him responsible, forgetting that cricket is a team game where everyone needs to contribute. Similarly, whenever he has played well, he has received lots of accolades from his fans. However, he remains unaffected by brickbats and accolades. Humility has always been his hallmark. Similarly, JRD Tata too is best remembered for his humility and values. He has instilled ethics and values in thousands of Indians who swear by him even today. On his death, the Indian Parliament was adjourned—an honour not normally given to citizens.

TURNAROUND SPECIALIST

(KAPIL DEV — CARLOS GHOSN, NISSAN, RENAULT)

'Whenever a situation develops to its extreme, it is bound to turn around and become its opposite.'

— Frank Capra

Tunbridge Wells. Does it ring a bell?

This small town in southern England was witness to one of the finest innings ever played in the history of cricket World Cup. India played against Zimbabwe in one of the qualifying matches of the 1983 World Cup at this venue. Having fared very poorly in the 1975 and 1979 World Cup tournaments, where the team was eliminated in the qualifying rounds itself, it was imperative for India to play well to have any chance of qualifying for the semi-finals. However, the moment India went in to bat, disaster struck. Within no time, the team was reduced to 17 runs for the loss of 5 wickets.

In walked Kapil Dev, skipper of the Indian team. Any other batsman would have been extra cautious and done his best to block all the good balls and defend his wicket, even at the cost of the scoring rate dropping down. However, Kapil had other thoughts. He was completely undaunted by the grim situation. With controlled aggression, he carted the Zimbabwe bowlers to all corners of the park and scored a blistering 175 off 138 balls. His aggressive knock consisted of 16 fours and 6 sixes. This was the highest individual score by an Indian for many years to come. India finished at 266 for the loss of 8 wickets and in response, Zimbabwe made 235 and lost the match by 31 runs. This performance of Kapil is considered as one of the best ODIs that completely changed the game.

Cynics have been quick to belittle Kapil's performance, saying that minnow Zimbabwe was no Australia or West Indies. However, we should remember that in the same tournament, the mighty Australians lost to Zimbabwe. It is also important to understand that while playing in such a critical World Cup match, the score of 17 for 5 can be worrisome against any kind of opposition.

Carlos Ghosn is the chairman and CEO of Japan based Nissan and Paris based Renault, two of the leading car manufacturers in the world. From childhood, he underwent a lot of transition. He was born in Brazil but was Lebanese by race. He studied in Lebanese schools and later went to France for his graduation. Having spent his formative years in different countries, he always considered cultural differences interesting rather than intimidating. No wonder he became the CEO of two automobile companies—one Japanese and the other French.

In 1996, Renault hired Ghosn as its executive vice president and made him responsible for advanced research, car engineering & development, car manufacturing, and purchasing and supervision of the company's activities in South America. In 1999, Renault purchased a 36.8% stake in Nissan. While maintaining his role at Renault, Ghosn joined Nissan as its COO in June 1999, became president in June 2000, and was named the CEO in June 2001.

When Carlos Ghosn joined Nissan, it had a debt of $20 billion and only 3 of its 48 models were generating profits. No one ever thought that the company's sinking fortunes could be reversed. Ghosn promised to resign if the company did not reach profitability by the end of the year, and claimed that Nissan would have no net debt by 2005.

He defied Japanese business etiquettes by taking many decisions which were relatively alien to Japanese culture during those days. He cut 21,000 jobs which was around 14% of the total workforce. He also shut the first of the five domestic plants, and auctioned off prized assets such as Nissan's aerospace unit. His radical methods made him quite unpopular in the initial days.

However, in one year, Nissan's net profit climbed to $2.7 billion from a loss of $6.1 billion in the previous year. Within three years, Ghosn transformed Nissan into one of the industry's most profitable automakers, with operating margins consistently above 9%—more than twice the industry average. Nissan's operating profit margin increased from 1.38% in FY 2000 to 9.25% in FY 2006.

He also made major structural changes at Nissan, dramatically altering the corporate culture. He ended its reliance on an interwoven web of parts suppliers with cross holdings in Nissan—a Japanese operating model called 'Keiretsu'. The dismantling of Keiretsu earned Ghosn the nickname 'Keiretsu killer'. He changed the company's official language from Japanese to English, and included executives from Europe and North America in key global strategy sessions.

While most people would feel comfortable with their own country, culture, and people, Ghosn was different. He believed that differences in religion, race, colour, sex, and age made work more challenging and interesting. He felt that if he met someone who was different from him then he had a lot to learn from that person. According to him, the only way to grow stronger was to confront oneself.

Ghosn was instrumental in orchestrating one of the most aggressive downsizing campaigns of the century and spearheading the turnaround of Nissan from near bankruptcy. After the Nissan financial turnaround, he achieved celebrity status. Despite being the chariman and CEO of an automotive company in a country like Japan, which is so deep rooted in tradition, he was able to go against the existing culture and turn around the company's fortunes. During a poll in Japan where the citizens were asked whom they would like to see as their next leader, Carlos Ghosn received more votes than their current Prime Minister!

In May 2005, Ghosn was named the president and CEO of Renault. In the business and corporate circles, Japan and France are considered the toughest frontiers for foreigners because both these countries take great pride in their native language and culture. In these countries, foreigners find it difficult to climb the ladders of corporate success. Ghosn's greatness lies in the fact that he was simultaneously the CEO of a Japanese as well as a French automotive company. He also became the world's first person to be the CEO of two Fortune Global 500 companies simultaneously. He was voted Man of the Year 2003 by *Fortune* magazine's Asian edition. In October 2006, Ghosn became an Honorary Knight Commander of the Order of the British Empire.

Kapil Dev and Carlos Ghosn achieved one of the best turnaround of fortunes in their respective fields. When Kapil walked into the middle, his team was precariously placed at 17 for 5. When a team loses quick wickets, the batsmen at the middle focus on rebuilding the innings. Though it is essential that no further wickets are lost, it should also be ensured that there is no drop in the run-rate. Kapil had a twofold strategy of keeping his wicket intact and at the same time being aggressive enough to keep the run-rate high and not allowing Zimbabwe's bowlers to dominate.

The situation was no different for Ghosn when he joined Nissan. Ghosn cut down costs aggressively but he did not lose focus on innovation and introduction of new products. Though the prevailing business situation forced him to cut thousands of jobs, he was a people oriented person and a democratic leader. He always empowered his team members and listened to their suggestions. What differentiated him from other CEOs were his listening and observation skills. When he was asked to name a business leader whom he respected and had read about, he candidly admitted that he did not think much of them and his lessons were learnt from his own employees. He said that when his employees narrated their experiences, it had a great impact on him—even if that employee was a shopfloor worker or a junior technician. He believed that the best way to understand and appreciate people was by understanding the difficulty they were going through in a given situation.

When a company performs badly, in most of the cases, the CEO indulges in a knee-jerk reaction. He often fails to differentiate between expenses and investments. The emphasis on keeping the bottom line low can result in chopping off even those activities that are needed for the company to grow. For example, cutting budgets on innovation, research, and improvements can prove detrimental to the long-term growth of a company. Both Kapil and Ghosn combined aggression with the right degree of caution and never lost focus on their final objective.

Power of Communication
(Mike Brearley—Louis Gerstner, IBM)

'The art of communication is the language of leadership.'
—James Humes

John Michael Brearley, OBE, popularly known as Mike Brearley, has become one of the most outstanding cricket captains ever. He was also considered as a 'thinking captain' primarily because he was a brilliant academician blessed with a sound cricketing mind. Though his team had very few stars, he was a very successful captain because he could 'out-think' the opposition.

Even as a young child who accompanied his father to watch cricket matches, Brearley knew the importance of being a good listener. His father was a club cricketer himself. Mike would listen to the endless analysis and comments that his father would share regarding batting, bowling, fielding, and the pitches.

Mike Brearley's thirst for knowledge, understanding his players, and learning their viewpoint continued even after he became the skipper of England's cricket team. He had high level of interaction with each and every member of his team. His conversations were not just centred on the ongoing series or their current form but also included issues like the hotel where they stayed, the food that they ate, etc. These were not formal meetings but informal chats—some of them during tea breaks, lunch breaks, or even on the field. These chats put his players at ease and they were able to openly express themselves. He understood each player's self-assessment, strengths, weaknesses, likes, and aversions.

Each and every conversation that he had would get deposited in his mind like a data bank. At the time of crisis, he could access his data bank and withdraw learnings quickly and turn seemingly hopeless situations into incredible ones.

During the third test between England and Australia at Headingly, Leeds, in the famous 1981 Ashes series, Australia needed merely 130 runs to wrap up the match. The turning point of the match came when Brearley, knowing Bob Willis' favourite bowling end, made him switch ends. The rest, as they say, was history. Bob Willis in a remarkable spell of fast bowling took 8 wickets for 43 runs and helped England register an improbable victory.

During the same series, in the fourth test at Edgbaston, Birmingham, he faced a similar situation. Australia needed just 151 runs to win with 5 wickets still in hand, and they were comfortably coasting towards victory. Brearley knew that Ian Botham's confidence had been high since he was once again back amongst the runs. He threw the ball at Botham who was initially reluctant but took up the challenge that his skipper had given him. In one of the best spells of fast bowling, Ian Botham took 5 wickets for 1 run and fashioned England's win against the mighty Aussies.

Mike Brearley studied at Cambridge University and pursued academics for long enough to cultivate the habit of thinking, analysing, and developing good listening skills—all attributes vital to academics. He later used all these skills in cricket as well.

In one of the management workshops that I attended, the speaker highlighted the importance of being a good listener. He said, 'everyone loves to talk. Those who are not talking are not listening; they are just waiting to talk!'

Some of the most respected leaders of the world are great orators. This has led to the wrong perception that to become a good leader one just needs to have good speaking skills. Very few realize that great leadership is also about having good listening skills. Any communication can be effective only if it is a two-way process. Every conversation that you have is a lesson in learning. Every word that you listen should go into your memory bank as a repository for future use.

Louis V. Gerstner was the chairman of the board and CEO of IBM from April 1993 till 2002. When IBM's chairman and CEO John Akers resigned, the directors first looked within the computer industry for his successor. However, when they could not find anyone suitable, they hired Gerstner who was an outsider to the computer field.

Gerstner is credited with reviving IBM's fortunes and saving it from bankruptcy in early 1990s. Some of his decisions and changes resulted in one of the most remarkable turnarounds in business history.

When Gerstner joined IBM, he soon realized that he had to tackle many challenges apart from the usual ones related to sales and revenues. He had to prevent the company from being split into different business units and focus on computer services. Many products like IBM PCs and the operating system OS/2 needed a 'relook' because they were not faring well. Apart from all this, he also had to change the culture and remove multiple layers of bureaucracy.

Gerstner was well aware that the best weapon to implement all these changes would be to initiate good two-way communication. He realized that it was important he met not only his management team members but also other levels of the organization to get first hand information about the products, market, competitors, and customers. He began to meet his employees on a periodic basis and gathered all the relevant information. He spent hours listening to what his employees had to say about any topic related to IBM.

Gerstner also shared his views, decisions, and changes that he planned to do with his employees. The company was lacking an effective communication structure with its employees and customers. The existing form of communication was very formal so people didn't feel involved in the decision making process—they felt it was more of a diktat. Gerstner established informal communication by simply writing out a friendly email to all the employees. His informal emails, sent to all IBM employees became popular as 'Dear colleagues' emails. He wrote his first email within a week after he had joined the company.

Gerstner was extremely transparent in his communication and kept his employees updated about the challenges that the organization faced and sought their views. His emails touched the hearts of thousands of employees. They all stood by him during the hour of crisis and backed him fully in all his decisions. It was a masterstroke from Gerstner—by involving his employees at all stages, he made them feel as if they were a part of the decision making process. Their level of involvement was so high that they began looking at IBM's problems as their own and not that of a CEO's or the board of directors'.

Each time he faced a problem, he discussed it with different people within the organization and customers; he ensured that he communicated his final decision to every appropriate employee. This way, he always had a 'closed loop' communication channel. Gerstner not only narrated the company's challenges and problems but also the future strategy and areas of focus. He wrote about setting up IBM services organization and spoke about the importance of being closer to the customers and product innovation.

Both Mike Brearley and Louis Gerstner showed that to become a great leader you need to have excellent communication skills. Domain knowledge is not very important. Mike Brearley's record as a batsman was quite ordinary—his batting average was just 22.88 runs in 39 Test matches and he didn't even manage to score a single century. However, his excellent leadership and people management skills made Australian fast bowler Rodney Hogg to comment that he has 'a degree in people'! Similarly, Louis Gerstner was neither a computer engineer nor from the IT industry. He had earlier worked at RJR Nabisco and American Express.

Brearley made the most of his short cricketing career. Even at the highest level of cricket, his natural flair for captaincy was recognized and therefore it is not surprising that he captained England in 31 of the 39 test matches that he played. He won 17 and lost only 4 test matches. In 1985, he published his book *The Art of Captaincy*. Gerstner too had a very successful career. When he joined IBM in 1993, the company had accumulated losses of approximately $16 billion and the stock price had crashed to a low $40 per share. But by 1999, it was once again one of the most profitable computer companies in the world.

What Brearley and Gerstner had done was not rocket science, they just did the basics right with amazing results. Both used the power of communication to their advantage. In today's world of Internet, Facebook, Twitter, etc. where any news can reach the other end of the world in a matter of seconds, communication has become even more important than ever. In a multinational company that has operations all around the world; an incident that occurs in its US office will be known to its Singapore office within a matter of minutes. This necessitates that the organization should communicate the news to its employees before they hear it from external sources. A CEO loses credibility when his employees get to know company related news from an outside source, before he tells them. This can be avoided if a leader is constantly in touch with his people and communicates with them on a periodic basis. Communication can be done either by modern means like emails, blogs, e-newsletters, Intranet or through traditional methods like town meeting, 'all hands' meeting, etc. For any great leader, the key to success is communication which should always be a two-way process.

VISIONARY LEADERSHIP

(ANIL KUMBLE — STEVE JOBS, APPLE)

'Do you want to sell sugar water for the rest of your life, or do you want to come with me and change the world?'

— Steve Jobs to John Sculley

Anil Kumble, one of the greatest leg spinners the world has ever produced, made his debut in the year 1990. Though he was a great thinker, strategist, and one of the shrewdest cricketers in the game, surprisingly captaincy came to him very late in his career. He became the captain of the Indian Test team in November 2007 and his tenure lasted exactly 12 months till he announced his retirement after the third Test against Australia in November 2008.

In August 2008, India won against Sri Lanka at Galle by 170 runs. It is a match best remembered for Virender Sehwag's double century off just 230 balls and Harbhajan Singh's match haul of 10 wickets. What many don't know about is the event that happened immediately after this match.

It is quite common for a team to celebrate their victory. Sri Lankans are an extremely strong side on their home soil and to beat them on their home turf would send any victorious team into a tizzy. However, Indian captain, Anil Kumble had set his feet firmly on the ground. He knew that the Galle Test victory was just a small step towards becoming the No.1 Test team in the world. For an army general, it was just one more day's battle and not the war.

Kumble did not want to lose the momentum; so he immediately called for a team meeting, even while his team members were still savouring their fantastic victory. He knew that the best time to motivate a team is when they are on a roll. Stars like Sachin Tendulkar, Rahul Dravid, Sourav Ganguly, VVS Lakshman, MS Dhoni, Gautam Gambhir, Harbhajan Singh, Virender Sehwag, and Zaheer Khan were a part of the team meeting.

Kumble had made a road map to prepare the team as the best cricketing team in the world. He shared his vision and explained how they could achieve this within the next two years. He focused on the need to study the opposition by analysing their strengths and weaknesses and also said that the workload should be distributed since each member had a specific role to play. He made it clear that the best of oppositions would have to be taken upon if this dream was to be achieved.

As Harbhajan Singh fondly recollects, 'the plan was to work towards becoming the best. I still remember when Kumble spoke and everybody listened.' Time and again, Virender Sehwag also talked of Kumble's inspiring words.

At the outset, this looked like a herculean task because of various factors. Virender Sehwag and Gautam Gambhir were just recovering from injuries. Saurav Ganguly was not in his best form and was inching towards the end of a brilliant career. Zaheer Khan, India's best fast bowler was also struggling with frequent injuries. Kumble himself was a few months away from retirement. However, all of them were motivated by Kumble's vision and the plan to work towards becoming the best team in the world.

India defeated Australia 2–0 in a home series. This was the series where Kumble announced his retirement. Dhoni, who was already the captain of the country's ODI and Twenty20 teams, succeeded Kumble as the Test captain, thus making him the captain in all forms of cricket. India next played England at home in December 2008 and won the series 1–0. A home series win by a margin of 2–0 against Sri Lanka in December 2009, catapulted India to No.1 Test ranking.

India managed to retain its numero uno status by not losing any series for the next few years. It beat Bangladesh in January 2010. This was followed up with a home series against South Africa where India drew with the visiting team. India also managed to draw the series against Sri Lanka, who are known to be very strong on their home ground. Next, India beat the mighty Australians in October 2010 and a couple of months later, the hosts drew the series against South Africa.

Though Anil Kumble had retired in November 2008, a year before India achieved its No.1 ranking, his dream continued to inspire the Indian team. England and Sri Lanka toured India and were beaten. Bangladesh was also defeated when India stepped across the border. India continued to hold its No.1 rank till August 2011. The players still cherish that team meeting held by Kumble because the seeds of success were sown there.

Steven Paul Jobs, popularly known as Steve Jobs, is one of the most famous names in the corporate world. He was the co-founder and former CEO of Apple Inc. In the late 1970s, Steve Jobs along with Steve Wozniak and others designed and manufactured the first commercially successful personal computers, known as Apple II series. In early 1980s, Jobs created Macintosh using mouse-driven graphical user interface which changed the world of personal computers.

In 1983, Steve Jobs lured John Sculley away from Pepsi to come and join as Apple's CEO, asking: 'Do you want to sell sugar water for the rest of your life, or do you want to come with me and change the world?' This is the kind of passion and vision that Steve Jobs had.

Though Jobs was a great inventor and a visionary, he was also an eccentric manager. This caused deterioration in Jobs's working relationship with Sculley, and at the end of May 1985—following an internal power struggle and an announcement of significant layoffs—Sculley relieved Jobs of his duties as the head of Macintosh division.

Jobs founded NeXT, a computer platform development company specializing in higher-education and business markets. Apple's subsequent 1996 buyout of NeXT brought Jobs back to the company he co-founded, and he served as its CEO from 1997 to 2011. He was responsible for many visionary products like iMac in May 1998, iPod in October 2001, iPhone in January 2007, iPad1 in January 2010, and iPad2 in March 2011.

Jobs always aspired to position Apple and its products at the forefront of the information technology industry. He was a great visionary who could foresee and start trends with innovation and style. He also had the ability to foresee the potential of great products that even its creators sometimes did not see.

The first Apple computer was built by Steve Wozniak who wanted to give it to Homebrew Computer Club. Steve Jobs was quick to recognize the potential of Wozniak's product, and persuaded the latter to manufacture it and start their own company. The rest, as they say, is history. It is also believed that Xerox was the first to develop a computer that had Graphical User Interface and a mouse in 1973. Unfortunately, the company did not capitalize on the innovation. Six years later, Steve Jobs visited Xerox PARC and saw the product. He incorporated the GUI and mouse into his products—Lisa and Macintosh. Xerox realized its mistake after Apple's products took the world by storm. It tried to build commercial products with GUI and mouse, but its expensive workstations were unable to compete with Apple's products. Eventually, Xerox had to quit the workstation market. The iconic iPod too was built on Portal Player's reference platform.

During his keynote speech at the Macworld Conference and Expo in January 2007, Steve Jobs quoted the famous ice hockey legend Wayne Gretzky, 'I skate to where the puck is going to be, not where it has been.' He added, 'we have always tried to do that at Apple, since the very beginning. And we always will.'

One of the most important qualities of a great leader is the vision and mission that he has for his team or organization. There are many teams that win a Test match or a Test series but are unable to maintain that position, and soon the team slips in its rankings. This is not because of deterioration in the quality of the players but due to lack of vision and the desire to be in the No.1 position. Pakistan and West Indies have extremely talented players but they are highly inconsistent—they win or lose by a mile.

Anil Kumble not only created a vision for Team India but also shared it at the appropriate time. If a team has just been beaten at a Test match or an ODI, then sharing a vision to a bunch of demotivated players is of no use. Kumble shared it when the team was on a high—after winning the Galle test. Whenever the team went through difficulties, the players always remembered Kumble's vision and that motivated them to perform to their best potential. His vision of India becoming the No.1 team in the world was achieved in 1 year and 4 months, which was 8 months ahead of his plan.

Steve Jobs was one of the greatest visionaries in the corporate world. Each time people tried to write him off, he came up with new innovations. He was the person who gave the world its first computer that had a mouse and an extremely simple GUI. He invented iPod that revolutionalized the music industry and the way people listened to music. His later inventions like iPhone and iPad changed the way the world communicated.

In his autobiography, John Sculley, successor of Steve Jobs at Apple, said, 'Apple was supposed to become a wonderful consumer products company. This was a lunatic plan. High-tech could not be designed and sold as a consumer product.'

How wrong Steve Jobs proved John Sculley!

Leverage Capabilities

(Martin Crowe, Clive Lloyd, Chris Harris, Larry Gomes — Kiran Mazumdar-Shaw, Biocon)

'Once we accept our limits, we go beyond them.'

—Albert Einstein

It is a misconception that you can win only if you have a highly talented team and favourable working conditions at your disposal. Nothing can be farther from truth than this.

Everyone knows how talented Brian Lara and Sachin Tendulkar are; so their success is not surprising. Any captain will consider himself fortunate to have such talented teammates. However, just their presence cannot guarantee success because cricket is a game of team effort and only the best team wins. Similarly, the absence of such players should not discourage or demotivate the captain. A good captain is one who can make the best use of his teammates and succeed.

Chris Harris, a former New Zealand cricketer and one of the finest all-rounders, was a left-handed middle order batsman and a right-arm medium pace bowler. He was neither the best batsman nor the best bowler in the New Zealand team but his contribution was invaluable. There were numerous occasions when he would walk in to bat at a time when his side had suffered a batting collapse. He would play a match saving or a match winning innings. Similarly, there have been plenty of occasions when he would be asked to bowl against a rampaging opposition and he'd quickly oblige the captain—either by taking wickets or by restricting the run-rate.

One of the reasons why Chris Harris was so successful was because he never tried to emulate his talented teammates. He understood the game and played within those constraints. Interestingly, his captain too understood his strengths and limitations and used him accordingly. In 250 ODI matches, he scored 4,379 runs and took 203 wickets. He became the first cricketer from New Zealand to take 200 wickets and that too, at an economy rate of 4.28. He was also a brilliant fielder with more than 90 catches and many impressive run-outs.

Another cricketer who achieved great success despite the lack of flamboyance was West Indies player, Larry Gomes. In a star studded team of highly talented players like Gordon Greenidge, Desmond Haynes, Vivian Richards, and Clive Lloyd, he managed to hold on to his own style and game. During the Packer era, many regular West Indies players were dropped and Larry Gomes was inducted into the team. However, when the Packer issue was resolved, the dropped players returned to the West Indies team but Larry Gomes managed to retain his position. Like Chris Harris, Larry Gomes too played within his limitations. He never tried to emulate his illustrious teammates and match their aggressive and flashy stroke play. He was happy to play a supporting role, allowing the more talented players to take centrestage. In Larry Gomes's case too, the captain was well aware of his strengths and weaknesses and used him accordingly.

Unlike Clive Lloyd and Gordon Greenidge, Larry Gomes was slightly built. Even though he lacked Vivian Richards's flamboyant batting style, he possessed an efficient technique. His batting did not have the repertoire of Alvin Kallicharan when it came to hook and pull shots. He would nudge and push the ball towards covers or midwicket and run his singles well. Unlike

Gordon Greenidge or Vivian Richards who signalled their arrival at the crease with a flurry of strokes, he was happy to gently push the ball and run for ones and twos. Before the opposition realized, he would have scored a half century!

Larry Gomes was not the most exciting West Indian batsman to watch since he avoided flashy stroke play and preferred to leave alone anything pitched wide off the stumps. But his methods were highly effective and drove the opposition to despair. Just when the opposition would feel thrilled for having triggered a collapse in the powerful West Indian batting line-up, Larry Gomes would walk in and with his inimitable style would guide his team to safety. He scored six centuries against the mighty Australians—the best being the century on the hard and bouncy track at Perth. In 60 test matches, he scored 3,171 runs at an average of 39.63. In 83 ODIs, he scored 1,415 runs at an average of 28.87 runs and also captured 41 wickets. He was named 'Wisden Cricketer of the Year' in 1985. He also has a stadium in Malabar, Arima, named after him.

Kiran Mazumdar-Shaw is the chairman and managing director of Biocon. She was born in Bangalore and studied at Bishop Cotton Girl's High School and later completed her BSc (Zoology) Honours from Mount Carmel College. She then did her post-graduation in Malting and Brewing from Ballarat College, Melbourne University.

She started her career as a trainee brewer in Carlton and United Breweries, Melbourne. She also worked for some time as a Technical Consultant at Jupiter Breweries Limited, Calcutta, and as a Technical Manager at Standard Maltings Corporation, Baroda.

In 1978, she joined Biocon Biochemicals Limited, Cork, Ireland as a trainee manager and also started Biocon in the garage of her rented house in Bangalore with a seed capital of ₹10,000. Apart from the numerous problems that are faced by any start-up, she also had to overcome credibility problems because of her youth and gender. Women entrepreneurs were quite rare in the 1970s. Being a young 25-year-old lady made it even tougher. She found it difficult to get financing from banks and to recruit people who would be willing to work for a start-up.

She also faced infrastructural problems such as non-availability of uninterrupted power, good quality of water needed for Biotech work, sterile labs, research equipment, and skilled human resources. She was interested in doing pioneering work and chose Biotech which was unheard of in those days. It allowed her to apply her knowledge of fermentation science to do something innovative. While Biopharma at the higher end of the spectrum guided her aspiration, she chose to start with fermentation technology based specialty enzyme business, keeping in mind the challenging regulatory environment. She chose to capitalize on her core knowledge, working on a model with a relatively low entry barrier.

She is responsible for taking Biocon to great heights over the years. Within a year of its inception, it became the first Indian company to manufacture and export enzymes to the US and Europe. In 1989, Biocon became the first Indian Biotech company to receive US funding for proprietary technologies. In 2001, it became the first Indian company to get approval from US Food and Drug Administration for the manufacture of a cholesterol lowering molecule.

Till the arrival of Kiran Mazumdar-Shaw, Biotech was an unknown area in most parts of India. Her exemplary work in this relatively unknown sector earned her the Padma Shri Award in 1989 and Padma Bhushan Award in 2005. She was named among *Time* magazine's 100 most influential people in the world. She also featured on the Forbes list of world's 100 most powerful women.

A major part of credit for the success of Chris Harris and Larry Gomes should go to their respective captains because they were aware of the capabilities of these players and played them accordingly. Clive Lloyd, the West Indian captain never tried to make Larry Gomes into a Gordon Greenidge or a Vivian Richards. He was happy to see Larry Gomes play the waiting game. This not only had a calm influence on the rest of the team but also helped West Indies wriggle out of tight situations on more than one occasion. Chris Harris started his ODI career under the captaincy of Martin Crowe. Like Clive Lloyd, Martin Crowe too was blessed with a sharp cricketing brain and leadership acumen. He knew that Chris Harris's game was most suited for ODIs. He allowed Chris Harris to bowl at gentle pace which was difficult to put away by the batsmen on the New Zealand pitches. He never tried to convert Chris Harris into a tearaway fast bowler like the great Sir Richard Hadlee nor a pinch hitter like Greatbatch.

On a similar note, one of the reasons for the success of Kiran Mazumdar-Shaw and her company was the fact that she understood the ground realities and leveraged on the available resources and infrastructure very well. When she started Biocon, she was well aware of the fact that India was neither a leader nor reputed for research in the area of Biotechnology. She knew that the only way she could make headway in this field was by making forays in those products that would be accepted in the west.

The key lesson for a leader is—know yourself and leverage on the resources and capabilities that are available at your disposal. There are certain companies that start off on a very ambitious note. Though their intentions are noble, they fail to make much headway because the senior management is not aware of ground realities. The vision of the CEO and the board of directors remain unfulfilled dreams. We also have companies on the other end of the spectrum—those that kick-start operations by executing low-end work and never moving up the value chain. They are better known for their low cost products or services rather than cutting-edge technology.

This is where Kiran Mazumdar-Shaw struck the right balance

between the two—generating revenues and pursuing her dreams. She knew that it would be very tough for a start-up company like hers to make headway in research. Hence, during the initial years, she focused on those products that were acceptable from a start-up Indian company like Biocon. However, the good thing was, she never forgot her long cherished dream. As Biocon grew in revenue, size, and credibility, she introduced a more diverse set of products and also fulfilled her dream of bringing in a research focus to diabetes, oncology, and auto-immune diseases. In 1990, she scaled up Biocon's proprietary solid substrate fermentation technology developed in-house, from pilot to plant level.

She was inspired by Indian software companies and thought that if they could succeed then so could she. This inspired her to set up Syngene in 1994 to provide development support services for discovery research. In 1997, she focused on human healthcare through a dedicated manufacturing facility. Three years later, she established Clinigene to cater to clinical development services.

This chapter is not meant to undermine the talent of Chris Harris or Larry Gomes but it highlights how they played within their limitations and went on to become highly valuable players for their respective teams. And more importantly, Martin Crowe and Clive Lloyd, their respective captains knew how to make best use of their abilities to win matches. Similarly, Kiran Mazumdar-Shaw too made best use of the available resources to make Biocon into a winner in the field of Biotechnology.

In today's world where creating a vision is the buzzword, she emphasized the importance of a short-term specific mission that enables you to move in the direction of your broader vision. Her mission was twofold—to build a Biotech company that would be respected all over the world, and to change the world's perspective about India's capability in the field of research. She succeeded in accomplishing both and that too in style!

Challenges as Opportunities
(MS Dhoni – Chanda Kochhar, ICICI)

'The best executive is the one who has sense enough to pick good men to do what he wants done, and self-restraint to keep from meddling with them while they do it.'

– Theodore Roosevelt

After India's shocking exit from the 2007 World Cup in West Indies, three Indian stars: Sachin Tendulkar, Rahul Dravid, and Saurav Ganguly expressed their desire to skip the inaugural T20 ICC World Cup Tournament. MS Dhoni, the new captain of the Indian team, had barely got into his new role when he was confronted with this news. Any other leader would have been crestfallen and written his team off. He might have participated in the World Cup, but only as a ritual that had to be completed. Moreover, the tournament was being played in South Africa that has one of the fastest tracks in the world. The Indian team had always fared badly in the past despite playing there with star studded teams.

However, MS Dhoni was unfazed by their past performance in South Africa. Neither was he worried about the absence of senior members in the team. He knew that what his boys lacked in experience, they made up with ample self-belief and confidence. He told them not to get overawed by the quality of the opposition, and instead, just focus on the immediate game. 'One game at a time' was his mantra.

Dhoni had many youngsters in the team, some of them travelling to South Africa for the first time. This also proved to be beneficial because the young boys had no 'past baggage'. Young legs also meant being agile on the field, something that Indian players lacked. In a Twenty20 match, this made a huge difference.

The young guns went about their task—defeating Pakistan, England, South Africa, and Australia to reach the finals. They defeated their old nemesis Pakistan once again in the finals and won the T20 Championship in its inaugural year, sending the entire nation into mass hysteria.

Attrition!—the most dreaded word, especially in the world of IT and ITES!

In today's fast-paced world, no article would be complete without talking of attrition. In the IT industry, it is a fashion to change jobs like changing clothes. Gone are the days when people would join a company and stay there till retirement. Companies no longer reward 35 years of loyalty with a ₹200 HMT watch, to be proudly displayed on a wrinkled wrist.

Since the past decade, Indian economy has opened up and the job market is booming. Every year, thousands of new jobs are created and there is a severe dearth of good and competent resources. The growth figures are mindboggling. Newspaper reports mention Company X's plans to add another 10,000 in the next quarter or about Company Y's plans to grow by 50% by end of the year.

This kind of rapid growth has led to a too many jobs for too few skilled people. Since the demand far outnumbers the supply, it has resulted in high attrition. The IT Industry has an attrition figure of 15–20%. The situation is far worse in the ITES/BPO industry which has attrition in excess of 30%.

In certain cases, attrition can be mitigated by doing a few basic things right—like providing stimulating work environment, good work culture, people friendly policies, exciting work content, challenging roles, etc. However, we should also accept the fact that attrition cannot be completely avoided even if all the basic needs are fulfilled. In such cases, it is important to have robust contingency plans to tackle it.

In the corporate world, there are lots of instances where a leadership change at the top position can churn the senior management. Even as the new CEO is grappling with his new role, he has to manage top level attrition, and yet meet the objectives of the organization. His situation is akin to that of a sailor who has to not only keep the ship afloat in a stormy sea but also steer it safely to the harbour.

In recent times, one of the best examples of managing attrition is Chanda Kochhar. She is currently the managing director and CEO of ICICI Bank, India's largest private bank and overall second largest bank in the country. She also heads the corporate centre of ICICI Bank.

Chanda Kochhar joined ICICI Ltd as a management trainee after completeing her masters in 1984. She had a meteoric growth as she became the deputy general manager in 1996 and general manager in 1998. In 2001, she took over as executive director, and in 2006, she was appointed as deputy managing director of ICICI Bank. From 2007 to 2009, she was the bank's chief financial officer and joint managing director. When she succeeded K.V. Kamath as the bank's MD and CEO, she had to face lot of turmoil and attrition among the senior management and leadership of the company.

A fortnight before Chanda Kochhar took over as the MD and CEO, Renuka Ramnath, MD and CEO of ICICI Venture (I-Venture) put in her papers after working there for over 20 years. Soon, ICICI Prudential Life Insurance's managing director and CEO, Shikha Sharma and Sanjoy Chatterjee too put in their papers. When V. Vaidyanathan, managing director and CEO of

ICICI Prudential Life Insurance resigned, it was the fourth senior management resignation after Chanda Kochhar had taken over the reins of ICICI.

However, despite the churn among top management, Chanda Kochhar was able to provide sustained leadership to make ICICI bank one of the biggest brands in Indian financial sector.

Challenges were never new to Chanda Kochhar and her favourite mantra has always been to treat every challenge as an opportunity. She had imbibed this quality from early days of her career at ICICI. At one point in time, she was handling the corporate side of the bank which accounted for almost 50% of the business. One day, her CEO moved her to consumer credit business which was less than 1% of the business. The goal for her was to make it more than 50% of the bank's business. Chanda grabbed this opportunity with both hands and came out with flying colours.

Chanda also faced many other challenges during her long stint at ICICI. One of them was in 1998 when she successfully setup cross functional teams to service the bank's top 200 clients. The other major challenge came in the year 2000 when ICICI entered the retail industry. Here too she was extremely successful in making ICICI one of the biggest players. These early experiences proved to be very useful for her when she took over as the MD & CEO of ICICI. Despite losing four of her top managers, she was able to weather the storm and succeed in her endeavours.

Under her leadership, ICICI Bank won the 'Best Retail Bank in India' award and 'Excellence in Retail Banking Award'. She had already won the 'Retail Banker of the Year 2004; Asia-Pacific region', 'Business Woman of the Year 2005', and 'Rising Star Award' for Global Awards. She also consistently figured in *Fortune*'s list of 'Most Powerful Women in Business' since 2005. In 2009, she was ranked at No.20 in the Forbes 'World's 100 Most Powerful Women' list. She was honoured with Padma Bhushan

Award, the third highest civilian honour by the Government of India, in the year 2010 for her services to the banking sector.

A good leader should not only manage tough challenges but also come out winning—as seen by the examples of MS Dhoni and Chanda Kochhar. Both faced severe attrition of senior members in their respective teams at a time when they were still grappling with their new roles. However, their strong leadership skills ensured their success. Dhoni and his boys won the Twenty20 World Cup and Chanda made ICICI one of the biggest banks in the country.

Leadership by Chance

(Mike Brearley—Kumar Mangalam Birla, Aditya Birla Group)

'The teacher is the one who gets the most out of the lessons, and the true teacher is the learner.'

—Elbert Hubbard

These days most companies invest heavily on career planning and succession planning for their employees. In majority of the cases, especially for leadership and senior management positions, the horizontal and vertical transitions are done in a well-planned manner. However, there are certain situations where the succession planning is either not well-defined or it is weak in terms of deployment.

How does an organization handle a situation where there is an unexpected change at the top level?

More importantly, how does the newly crowned leader succeed in a scenario where the leadership position is given to him in the most unexpected manner?

Former England captain Mike Brearley was an excellent cricketer even during his days at St John's College, Cambridge, but he made a late entry into Test cricket because of his busy academic career. He made his debut for Cambridge University in 1961, and even during those days his potential as a captain was recognized. Three years later, he became the captain of

Cambridge University. He toured South Africa during 1964–1965 as a member of MCC. Here too, his inherent potential for captaincy was recognized and he was made the captain of MCC (Under-25) team in 1966–1967.

However, Brearley took up an academic career, teaching Philosophy at Newcastle, England. He played for his Middlesex county team only when he had term breaks at college. He decided to pursue cricket as a full time career only in early 1970s. He was selected for the England cricket team in 1976 at a ripe old age of thirty-four, an age when most cricketers would be contemplating retirement!

Australia visited England in 1981 for a six test Ashes series. Since Australia and England have been traditional rivals, the Ashes series always invoke a lot of passion and enthusiasm in both the countries. Players from both sides invariably reserve their best performances for the Ashes series.

Ian Botham, the star England all-rounder was named the England skipper, despite his poor track record as a captain. Australia won the 1st Test match by 4 wickets at Trent Bridge, Nottingham. Though England drew the 2nd Test at Lord's, there was a lot of hue and cry in the media regarding Ian Botham's captaincy and his own performance as a player—he had just scored two ducks in the 2nd Test.

Unable to bear the pressure and not being able to live upto his own high standards, Ian Botham stepped down from captaincy for the remaining part of the series. The English selectors had to quickly elevate one of their players as the new captain. There was no time for any succession planning or training. Mike Brearley was made the England captain for the 3rd Test at Headingly, Leeds. Before he could even get familiar with his new role, the 3rd Test had commenced. It started off disastrously for England and Australia piled a mammoth 401 for 9 and in reply, England could manage a meagre 174. England was asked to follow-on with an arrear of 227 runs. In their 2nd innings, England was precariously placed at 105 for 5, still trailing by 122 runs. In walked Ian Botham and scored 149 runs. Despite his heroics with the bat, Australia needed to score a paltry 130 runs to win the match. Australia was well placed at 56 for 1, needing just 66 runs for victory with 8 wickets in hand.

Brearley had enough knowledge about the wicket and Bob Willis' kind of bowling to make him switch ends. Willis didn't disappoint his skipper. He bowled a superb spell of 8 for 43 to dismiss Australia for 111 and pave way for an English victory. England became the only second team in Test match history to win a match after being made to follow on. Ian Botham was a completely rejuvenated man and played a major role in England's famous victory—he had scored 50 runs and taken 6 for 95 in the 1st innings and scored a brilliant 149 not out in the 2nd innings. He openly acknowledged the role of Brearley's captaincy that helped him turn around his performance.

England kept up the winning momentum and went on to win the next two Test matches at Edgbaston, Birmingham and Old Trafford, Manchester thus ending the Ashes series with a 3–1 victory. Mike Brearley was hailed as the world's best captain.

Aditya Vikram Birla, popularly known as AV Birla was one of the most famous Indian industrialists. Born into the famous Birla family, he had diverse businesses in the areas of textiles, cement, aluminium, fertilizers, and petrochemicals. He died quite suddenly at the age of 52. His son, Kumar Mangalam Birla, then aged 28, took over the reins of the Aditya Birla group.

When Kumar Mangalam took over the Birla empire, he noticed that the focus on performance management was low. As in the case of many 'family owned Indian companies', his companies too were plagued by the fact that some of the senior managers were holding key positions based on caste rather than merit. The young Birla strongly believed in meritocracy and wanted to make his company look professional in its outlook. Hindustan Lever was renowned for its HR practices, so he hired a senior HR professional from there to head the HR function for his group. In a major clean-up operation, the company had to get rid of hundreds of senior managers.

Birla also wanted to get rid of the 'yes man' culture by encouraging honest and constructive feedback. He introduced a 360 degree feedback concept for everyone, including himself. His 'first line' reportees were given an opportunity to give feedback about his performance. Birla realized that for his companies to compete with global companies, he had to not only attract the best talent but also nurture and develop them. This resulted in the setting up of 'Gyanodaya'—The Aditya Birla Institute of Management, to strengthen the management capabilities of its managers. When Birla took over the Aditya Birla group, there were lots of 'doubting Thomases' about his tender age and his ability to carry forward the multi-billion dollar empire left by his deceased father. However, the young Birla more than met the expectations of the customers, shareholders, and employees. Within a short time, he not only consolidated the existing businesses but also moved into new areas like cellular communication, BPO, asset management, and software. He introduced radical changes into the organization structure, strategies, and professionalism in the functioning of the group leading to a turnover of around $40 billion dollars.

Kumar Mangalam Birla has been named 'CNN-IBN Indian of the Year 2010', NDTV's 'Global Indian Leader of the Year', World Economic Forum's 'Young Global Leader', 'The Ernst & Young Entrepreneur of the Year' and received many other awards. Extraordinary, for a man who had not even been groomed into the role and had leadership thrust on him under tragic circumstances.

Though it is always good to plan for proper transition especially at senior positions, there are many occasions when this is not possible. In the case of Mike Brearley, Ian Botham was the captain of the English team. Botham was one of the stars of the England team. He was a consistent performer, young and far away from retirement. Hence no one had anticipated a change in leadership. However, Botham, on his own will, decided to step down from captaincy, and the English selectors had to scramble for an immediate replacement. When Mike Brearley was asked to lead the team, he had absolutely no time to prepare. England was already engaged in a tough series against the mighty Australians. What made matters worse was the fact that his side had just lost the 1st Test and were trailing in the ongoing series.

The case of Kumar Mangalam Birla was also similar. His father was heading the huge Birla empire and no one had expected him to die so suddenly and that too at such a young age. Due to his father's untimely death, Kumar Mangalam Birla had no chance to have a proper transition from his predecessor. He was young and inexperienced and had to take over a huge industrial empire, most of it headed by very senior people. However, like Mike Brearley, Kumar Mangalam too had to learn quickly and take control of the conglomerate. If a leadership position is given in a sudden, unexpected manner then you have to be a quick learner. You will neither have the time to ramp up slowly nor will you have an oppurtunity to experiment. Like a drowning man thrown into a whirlpool, you have to learn to swim fast for survival.

Leadership Diplomacy

(Anil Kumble — Ratan Tata, Tata Group)

'Diplomacy is more than saying or doing the right things at the right time, it is avoiding saying or doing the wrong things at any time.'

—Bo Bennett

One of the most important qualities expected in great leaders is the art of diplomacy and interpersonal skills. It is not enough if a leader is competent and leads from the front—he should know how to conduct himself in public and have proper communication skills.

During India's tour to Australia in 2007–2008, it lost the 2nd Test at Sidney by 122 runs. The match was full of umpiring errors—Rahul Dravid was given out though he had not edged the ball, Andrew Symonds was not given out though he had nicked the ball. Towards the end of the match, Saurav Ganguly slashed the ball towards Michael Clarke. Though the fielder didn't collect it cleanly, his skipper Ricky Ponting claimed that the catch was 'clean'. Ganguly's wrong dismissal signalled the collapse of the Indian innings and India lost the match. Even though India had lost the Sydney test primarily because of many umpiring errors, Anil Kumble was extremely graceful even in defeat.

However, the biggest controversy of this match occurred when Andrew Symonds accused Harbhajan Singh, the Indian off spinner, of racial abuse. Harbhajan Singh while batting alongside Sachin Tendulkar exchanged a few words with Symonds, who complained to the umpires that Harbhajan had called him a monkey. This was seen as a racial abuse and soon snowballed into a huge controversy, famously known as 'Monkeygate'. It caught media's attention across the world because it involved two cricketing giants, Australia and India.

ICC Match Referee Mike Proctor was quick in handing a three match ban to Harbhajan for his alleged racial abuse. This created a huge furore not only in India but all over the world. The general perception was that Mike Proctor had hastily given his judgement without proper hearing and was himself dubbed a racist! Soon, this snowballed into a huge controversy with the Indian and Australian media doing their bit. BCCI threatened to pull out of the Australian tour if Harbhajan was not given a proper hearing. Subsequently, a special tribunal was held in Adelaide where John Hansen cleared Harbhajan Singh of all racism charges and lifted the three match ban.

During all these controversies, accusations, and counter accusations, one man who stood like a rock was the Indian skipper, Anil Kumble. He was completely unfazed by the numerous meetings that he had with the players from the teams, the match referee, Indian cricket officials, Australian Cricket Board officials, and the media. He remained composed and never spoke a controversial word that could ignite the matter further. Though India lost the Sydney test, the Indian skipper won respect from all over the world. He showed that a leader can be assertive without being abusive or aggressive. During the post-match interview of the Sydney Test match, despite emotions running high in both teams, he merely said, 'only one team played the match in the true spirit of cricket.'

Ratan Tata became the chairman of Tata Sons and Tata Group in 1991. He was also the chairman of many Tata companies such as Tata Motors, Tata Steel, Tata Consultancy Services, Tata Power, Tata Chemicals, Tata Tea, Tata Teleservices, and The Indian Hotels Company. He has been credited with many global acquisitions like Tetley, Jaguar, Land Rover, and Corus. This has given Tatas a global footprint since 65% of the group's revenue comes from abroad.

Ratan Tata announced to the world that he would launch a car worth ₹1 lakh ($2,500 approximately). The objective of this car, named Nano, was to make four-wheelers affordable to the common man in India. The Nano project was one of the most prestigious projects not only for Tatas but for the entire nation because the entire global automobile industry was watching its progress.

West Bengal government promised 997 acres of land at Singur for its manufacture. Tatas started the construction of the factory in January 2007 and the car was scheduled to roll out by October 2008. Unfortunately for Tatas, the Singur project faced stiff opposition from many farmers and political parties. There were many agitations led by various organizations to halt the work at Singur.

Despite these agitations, Tatas went ahead with their project and in July 2008, the company had begun the trial production. It was all set for commercial production by October 2008; however, the situation began to rapidly deteriorate from July onwards. The agitators began to block the roads leading to the Nano plant, so commuting to the factory became a nightmare for the Tata employees. In August, the agitators stopped the employees from leaving the factory in the evening. Frequent police intervention was required to diffuse the situation. Politicians from various opposition parties too joined in to extract their pound of flesh.

Tata realized that the Nano plant at Singur was no longer safe for its employees. Being an employee-friendly company, it felt that the only viable option was to move out from West Bengal. A month later, in September, the company decided to halt the work at Singur, and on 3rd October 2008, Ratan Tata announced his decision to shift the project out of West Bengal. It is believed that Narendra Modi, Chief Minister of Gujarat, was quick to realize the dynamics of the situation. He probably sent a text message to Ratan Tata with just one word, 'Suswagatham' (Welcome). It was an invitation to Ratan Tata to move the Nano factory from Singur (West Bengal) to Sanand (Gujarat).

The entire nation sighed with relief because this meant that the unrest at Singur would soon end. However, for the Tatas, this was the beginning of another major headache of shifting their factory from West Bengal to Gujarat—a distance of more than 1,500 kilometres! What made it even more challenging was the fact that they could not afford to delay the launch of the much awaited Nano.

The company estimated fourteen months as the lead time to shift the plant and start the production. The most critical task was to shift the equipments safely from Singur to Sanand. Any damage to the equipments meant a delay in the project. Different routes were studied between Singur and Sanand and the best road was selected. Each truck was equipped with security guards to provide security to the employees and machinery.

The dismantling of the plant at Singur and the construction activity at Sanand happened simultaneously. By May 2009, the entire machinery from Singur was shifted to Sanand and it was installed there by October 2009. By November 2009, trial production began at Sanand, one month ahead of schedule! The plant was formally inaugurated by Narendra Modi in June 2010.

Anil Kumble won the Arjuna Award in 1995, and a year later, he was one of the Wisden Cricketers of the Year. In 2005, he won the Padma Shri Award from the Government of India. He is known for his hard work, dedication, and never-say-die attitude. He is also known as the 'smiling assassin' because he believes that aggressiveness should not be through sledging but must come from a desire to take a wicket in every ball. There have been numerous instances in Tests and ODIs when he won matches for India. However, to me, the best example of his leadership was seen during the 'Monkeygate' scandal. The way he handled his teammates, the Australian players, the media, and the cricket boards of both the countries was a lesson that every aspiring leader should learn.

Ratan Tata has won the first Award for Responsible Capitalism. He was also awarded the 26th Robert S. Hatfield Fellow in Economic Education by Cornell University. He received Carnegie Medal of Philanthropy by Carnegie Endowment for International Peace in 2007, and the NASSCOM Global Leadership Award in 2008. He also received Padma Bhushan in 2000 and Padma Vibhushan in 2008. He is renowned for excellent leadership qualities. People often talk of his vision to make Tata group a global conglomerate. Ratan Tata is also known for empowering his group companies unlike some of his Indian counterparts who tightly control the groups. His values and principles are a benchmark in the Indian industry. Though he is known for many exemplary leadership qualities, what stands out is the manner in which he handled the Nano controversy at Singur. It is one of the best case studies on how a leader should handle a crisis and come out of it successfully.

In the 'Monkeygate' episode, Anil Kumble lost the Sydney Test match but inspired his boys to come back strongly and win the next Test match at Perth. What makes the victory admirable is the fact that Perth has one of the fastest tracks in the world and has always favoured the home team. Harbhajan Singh getting acquitted worked as an icing on the cake.

In the Singur incident, Ratan Tata had lost out to West Bengal politics but he instilled enough confidence in his Nano project team to shift the factory to Sanand. What makes this creditable is that the factory was ready one month ahead of schedule.

In both these incidents, Anil Kumble and Ratan Tata drew admiration for the manner in which they diplomatically handled extremely volatile situations. In both cases, they were in seemingly hopeless situations, but they were victorious in their endeavours.

2

TEAM BUILDING AND PEOPLE DEVELOPMENT

'My company strongly believes in career progression, growth, and people development of the employees. Our employees start their career as clerks in the groud floor department and they retire as clerks in the top floor department of this building.'

Build on Your Strengths

(West Indies Cricket Team — Dr Wiedeking, Porsche)

'Build upon strengths, and weaknesses will gradually take care of themselves.'

—Joyce C. Lock

In 1975, West Indies team led by Clive Lloyd won the first Cricket World Cup by defeating Australia in a thrilling match. However, their subsequent trip to Australia was a disaster. They lost the series 5–1 and their nemesis were fast bowlers Dennis Lillee and Jeff Thomson of Australia. At the end of the series, Clive Lloyd realized that the only way to combat Australia and other cricketing nations was to develop a battery of fast bowlers. He also knew that West Indians were strongly built and athletic so that would make his task simpler.

Lloyd was instrumental in developing a team consisting of express fast bowlers like Andy Roberts, Michael Holding, Colin Croft, and Joel Garner. By the time Andy Roberts was reaching the end of his career, Malcolm Marshall was inducted into the squad. Lloyd not only built a devastating bowling attack but also supplemented it with a very strong batting line-up. Desmond Haynes and Gordon Greenidge were the most consistent opening pair in the world. And when you have Vivian Richards, Alvin Kallicharan, and Clive Lloyd to follow, you can surely imagine the plight of the opposition!

This strong batting and bowling line-up helped Clive Lloyd become one of the most successful Test captains of all times. During his captaincy, the side had a run of 27 matches without defeat, which included 11 wins in succession.

In today's competitive world, our obsession to address our areas of improvement often makes us forget looking at our strengths and capitalizing on them. Knowing our strengths and using them to our advantage is as important as working on our areas of improvement. Part of the blame also rests on the numerous surveys that are conducted in every organization. We have surveys for everything—customer satisfaction, employee satisfaction, facilities and administration, and even canteen surveys!

All these surveys invariably focus on the 'areas of improvements'. The moment the survey results are declared, the management gets busy in putting actions to address the identified improvement areas. Very few care for the identified strengths, even if they are the pillars of the organization. How many times have we not seen great organizations busy addressing their weak areas but neglecting their strengths till it is too late?

There are also companies that were initially victims of 'herd mentality' but when they found that it didn't work for them, they were quick enough to make amendments. One such company is Porsche, a German automobile company with its headquarters in Zuffenhausen, Stuttgart.

During 1950s and 1960s, Porsche was a well-known brand, producing high-end sports cars. People were willing to pay extra dollars for its quality and performance. Unfortunately, the company went through a difficult phase in 1970s and 1980s.

Porsche made a mistake which is extremely common in the industry—it became a victim of 'herd mentality'. Porsche studied what the successful Japanese automobile companies were doing and decided to emulate them. The Japanese car industry was focusing on low cost fuel-efficient cars, something they were really good at. Porsche felt that it too needed to manufacture cheap cars to compete with its Japanese counterparts.

Instead of focusing on its strengths, Porsche started making inexpensive models. It did not meet great success because making inexpensive cars was not its core competence. By late 1980s and early 1990s, Porsche was on the verge of bankruptcy. This is when its newly appointed CEO, Dr Wendelin Wiedeking understood the mistake and decided to reverse it.

Dr Wendelin Wiedeking began his professional career in 1983 in the production and materials management department at Porsche AG. After a stint at Glyco AD, he returned to Porsche in 1991 as the head of production and two years later, became the CEO of the company which was struggling to stay afloat.

Wiedeking recruited many new employees because he felt his organization needed people with fresh thoughts. He was also willing to take unpleasant decisions. He decided to drop unprofitable models like 928 and 968 but retained and overhauled the 911 model because that represented the true Porsche quality and brand. He did not want to build cars which were similar to the Japanese, but he did have high regard for the Japanese style of manufacturing. He studied these car manufacturers and realized the importance of having good supply chain management practices and a highly productive workforce. He hired consultants to help him reduce inventory levels by outsourcing major components and assemblies, and he also focused on reducing the fixed costs and improving the overall productivity of his workforce.

Apart from refurbishing the 911 model, he also introduced two new models: Boxster and Cayenne. Wiedeking's strategy worked and people once again began to buy Porsche because its models were very distinctive and classy. The customers took pride in telling their friends that they owned a Porsche. By 2004, Porsche became one of the most profitable automobile companies in the world. Its CEO, Dr Wiedeking stayed on as its president and CEO till July 2009.

Wiedeking won many awards for himself as well as his company. He won the 2002 German Images Award, the 2003 CICERO Speaker Prize, and 2005 Peter Stihl Prize. In 2006, Porsche was awarded the title of the most prestigious automobile brand by Luxury Institute, New York. It was also awarded the 2006, 2009, and 2010 J.D. Power & Associates award.

The example of Clive Lloyd and Porsche indicate the importance of recognizing and building on strengths rather than following the herd. Clive Lloyd studied the past performance of West Indies and realized that the success of West Indies in 1950s and 1960s was closely linked to the performances of its fast bowlers Roy Gilchrist, Wes Hall, and Charlie Griffith. These bowlers had performed very well against India, Australia, and England. On more than one occasion, the opposition found them to be unplayable. Lloyd wanted to bring back those glorious days of West Indies cricket when their fast bowlers intimidated the opposition batsmen with a barrage of fast and hostile deliveries. Apart from skill and talent, one of the major requirements to become a good fast bowler was to have a strong and athletic physique, something that the West Indies players genetically possessed. Lloyd made use of their strong physique and developed their cricketing skills and made them the most fearsome fast bowlers in the world.

What Wiedeking did was also similar. When he took over as the CEO of Porsche, the company had lost its focus and was struggling. It had introduced many inexpensive cars to compete with its competitors but without much success. He studied the past performance of Porsche to understand what had worked for the company and what had not. He realized that Porsche was well-known for its cars in the premier segment. People looked at Porsche for its high-end cars that were renowned for excellent quality and performance.

Though the above corporate example is about an automobile company, it is equally relevant for other industries. Since the past couple of decades, Indian companies have done well in the global software industry. One of the prime reasons for this is the low cost for software development. However, we should realize that this cost advantage will not last long. The annual hike of Indian software engineers is slowly negating the cost advantage that we have over the US and Europe. It is time for us to look at our inherent strengths and build on them. We need to develop 'centres for competence' in different technologies and domains. This is the only way to remain competitive in a global market. Multinational companies from other countries should be willing to come to India for its competence in specialized areas and skills, irrespective of our development cost.

Good Infrastructure: A Foundation to Success

(Australian Cricket Team—Toyota)

'The loftier the building, the deeper must the foundation be laid.'

—Thomas Kempis

As in the case of any other country, Australia too had the problem of most great cricketers retiring almost at the same time. Despite this, Australia has won the World Cup championship on four occasions and that too over a span of twenty years—1987, 1999, 2003, and 2007. One of the reasons for Australia's consistent success is the robust infrastructure that supports Australian cricket.

Australia has 5 major test venues—Perth, Brisbane, Adelaide, Melbourne, and Sydney. Each of these venues is completely different from the other. Perth has one of the hardest and bounciest surfaces in the world; Brisbane's wicket offers a great deal of swing to the fast bowlers. Melbourne and Sydney are slow in nature and assist the spinners. Because of this, when a budding Australian cricketer begins his cricketing journey in domestic matches, he is exposed to different kinds of surfaces. Thus, when he enters the international arena and plays in other countries, he is able to adapt himself very quickly. His performance at Perth can help him tackle the bounce on South African pitches. His matches at Brisbane would have taught him to face swing bowling under English conditions. Similarly, playing at Melbourne and

Sydney would help him face the Indian spinners on the dust bowls of India and Sri Lanka.

Contrast this with the Indian situation. Most budding Indian cricketers hone their cricketing skills on featherbeds of Ferozshah Kotla, Wankhede, Eden Gardens, Chepauk, or Chinnaswamy Stadium. The ball rarely rises above the waist on these pitches. It is quite common to see Ranji Trophy and Duleep Trophy matches posting scores of 500 plus. However, once these lads enter the international arena, their techniques are found insufficient, especially on the hard surfaces of Australia and South Africa. Their inability to tackle swing bowling under English conditions is one more chink in their weak armour.

Each time India returns home after a whitewash at the hands of South Africa, Australia, or England, the Indian fans and media make disparaging remarks about the cricketers. Everyone admits that Indians are a very good team under favourable home conditions but they get exposed on faster tracks. Unfortunately very little is done to improve the pitches and make them more 'bowler friendly'. A disastrous tour to Australia would be followed up with a home series against a weaker nation where our team performs well and everything is quickly forgotten.

The other difference between Australia and the Asian teams is the importance given to domestic cricket. The Australian cricket infrastructure is exactly opposite to that of Pakistan's. If Pakistan has a practically non-existent domestic cricketing infrastructure, Australia has one of the finest infrastructures in the game today. Though India has a good domestic cricket structure 'on paper', it is not effective because of many reasons. Firstly, as mentioned above, Indian pitches are batsmen friendly so the batsmen never get tested in domestic matches. Secondly, the quality of the players who play domestic cricket in India is grossly different from the international scene.

In Australia, domestic cricket is taken very seriously. If a test player loses form or is out of the national team due to an injury, he is expected to play domestic cricket and prove his worthiness before being inducted into the national team. The presence of their international stars participating in domestic matches has resulted in high quality of the game. This has ensured that the budding cricketers get an opportunity to play against the best Australian players, and in turn, resulted in high quality domestic players and very good bench strength, something that we have always lacked. Unfortunately, in India, the moment a cricketer dons the Indian colours, he is exempted from all domestic matches. There have been very few instances where a player recovering from injury or loss of form has gone back to domestic cricket.

Toyota Motor Corporation is a multinational automobile manufacturer, headquartered in Aichi, Japan. What differentiates it from the other automobile manufacturers is the sound manufacturing processes and supply chain infrastructure that it has evolved over the past few decades. Toyota was one of the pioneers in adopting Kaizen for its core processes.

Kaizen is the Japanese name for 'improvement', or 'change for the better'. It basically refers to philosophy or practices that focus upon continuous improvements of processes in manufacturing, engineering, game development, and business management.

According to popular misconception, Kaizen can be applied only to the manufacturing processes involving the operators on the shopfloor. In reality, Kaizen refers to activities that continually improve all functions, and involves all employees, right from the CEO to the assembly line workers. It also applies to non-engineering processes such as administration, purchasing, logistics, and supply chain management. By improving standardised activities and processes, Kaizen aims to eliminate waste. It was first implemented in several Japanese businesses after the Second World War. Among the automobile manufacturers,

Toyota was one of the first companies to implement Kaizen.

The other revolutionary concept that was adopted by Toyota was JIT or the 'Just in time' concept. Conventional automobile manufacturers would order for raw material well in advance and this would result in huge pileup of inventory. This resulted in a large amount of money blocked in dead inventory. If a particular car model became obsolete or did not sell the expected volumes then the situation would become even worse. The organization would thus be sitting on huge amount of unused raw material which would adversely affect the operating income. For this reason, Toyota adopted and implemented the concept of JIT in which the purchase department of the company worked very closely with its suppliers. The raw materials and components were built and delivered by the suppliers just when Toyota needed them. This resulted in very low amount of inventory lying on the shopfloor and also mitigated the inventory losses if a particular model sold less than expected or was stopped. The amount of wasted inventory was thus practically zero.

In April 2001, Toyota adopted the 'Toyota Way 2001', an expression of values and conduct guidelines that all Toyota employees embraced. It defined its values and conduct guidelines with the following five principles:

1. Challenge
2. Kaizen (improvement)
3. Genchi Genbutsu (go and see)
4. Respect
5. Teamwork

The Toyota Way has helped the organization develop a sound infrastructure. Today, Toyota is one of the biggest and most respected names in the automobile industry. It is one of the largest companies to manufacture hybrid vehicles in the market and is also the first to commercially mass-produce and sell such vehicles.

It has grown into a large multinational corporation with factories in most parts of the world, manufacturing or assembling vehicles for local markets. It displaced GM and became the world's largest automobile maker in 2008.

Australia and Toyota have been leaders primarily because of the sound infrastructure that they have put in place. Australia has been one of the most formidable cricketing teams in the world since the last three decades. Players have come and gone but it has not impacted their game and rankings. Whenever they lose a match, even though it is rare, the news hits the headlines in all leading newspapers.

Toyota too faced stiff competition from its domestic and global markets. Companies like Honda, Suzuki, Ford, and GM were fiercely competing with it in the global automotive market. However, its strong shopfloor manufacturing and supply chain management practices ensured its success for a long time. In 2011, Toyota was the 3rd largest automobile manufacturer by production. In July 2012, it had manufactured its 200 millionth vehicle.

SUCCESSION PLANNING IS PLANNING FOR SUCCESS

(AUSTRALIAN CRICKET — GENERAL ELECTRIC)

'Failure to plan for succession is planning to fail.'

—J. K. Williams

There are two major aspects of a team that has been able to sustain its great performances for long periods of time—a sound succession plan and a robust bench strength. Succession planning is the process of identifying backups for all the critical people in the team. It is very important for any organization because it reduces risk and ensures business continuity when a key resource leaves. Bench strength denotes the number of people who are currently in the background but are ready to take over the role of frontline people when the situation demands. So in a way, both are interlinked.

As in any sport, in cricket too the professional life span is quite short. There are very few instances of cricketers playing for fifteen years or more. In majority of the cases, the typical tenure would be around 10–12 years. Typically, a batsman makes his debut at the age of 22–23 and contemplates his retirement when he reaches around 35 years. In case of a fast bowler, the professional life span is even less because of frequent injuries. His legs and shoulders will not generate the same amount of pace once he crosses 32 years. As in the case of other sports, cricketers too are not free from injuries.

In a scenario where there is a constant churn in the team, it is very important to have backup players who can quickly replace the retired or injured players. A great cricket team is not just about the highest number of victories; it is also about consistency and the ability to keep winning despite constant changes.

West Indies and Australia have been two of the greatest cricketing nations in the world but their ability to build and sustain match winning teams is a study in contrast. West Indies were invincible during late 1970s and 1980s. They boasted of a team that had some of the best batsmen in the world like Desmond Haynes, Gordon Greenidge, Alvin Kallicharan, Vivian Richards, and Clive Lloyd. These batsmen were supported by some of the fastest bowlers in the world like Andy Roberts, Michael Holding, Joel Garner, Colin Croft, and Malcolm Marshall. Unfortunately the West Indies Cricket Board did not focus on succession planning of these players. When most of their great players retired, they did not have sufficient number of talented youngsters to replace them. This resulted in a gradual decline in West Indies cricket. The team which was once the best in the world is currently not even among the top five. A team that once played 27 Test matches without even a single defeat; now loses to relatively weak teams like Bangladesh!

Let us now take a look at the other great cricketing side—Australia. Like West Indies, they too were invincible. During 1990s and 2000s, the Australian team boasted of world class players like Matthew Hayden, Justin Langer, Mark Waugh, Steve Waugh, Adam Gilchrist, Glenn McGrath, and Shane Warne. Australia too faced a similar problem when many of its great stars retired around the same time. Mark Waugh retired in 2002 and his twin brother Steve Waugh retired a couple of years later. Two of Australia's best bowlers, Glenn McGrath and Shane Warne retired in 2007. Adam Gilchrist, rated as the best wicket keeper-batsmen in the world, retired in 2008. Justin Langer and Matthew Hayden who formed the best opening pair for Australia retired in 2007 and 2009 respectively.

However, despite the upheaval in the Australian team in the 2000s, the impact was much less. Though Australia lost its No.1 position, it is still rated as one of the best teams in the world.

How was Australia able to handle the shake-up in the team better than West Indies?

It was due to its tremendous bench strength and excellent succession planning.

Having a sturdy cricketing infrastructure at domestic level helped Australia ensure that it would always have a strong bench strength. In Australia, it is mandatory that everyone plays domestic matches. This has two advantages—firstly, everyone takes these matches seriously; secondly, since even big stars play domestic cricket, the quality of cricket is outstanding.

Australia also does an excellent job of succession planning. They plan for the future and this is not just for the players but even for the captain. Even when its skipper Steve Waugh was performing consistently, the Australian selectors had decided that he would be succeeded by Ricky Ponting. Similarly, even when Ponting was at his peak, Michael Clarke was announced as his successor. The biggest advantage of having good succession planning is that the potential leader gets groomed into his future role. Ricky Ponting would have learnt a lot about captaining by watching Steve Waugh. Similarly, since Michael Clarke knew that he would take over Ricky Ponting as the skipper, he learnt by watching his predecessor's strategies both on and off the field.

General Electric is an American multinational company which operates in four segments—Energy, Technology Infrastructure, Capital Finance, and Consumer & Industrial. Headquartered in Fairfield, Connecticut, Jack Welch became its CEO in 1981 and held that post till 2001. A year before Welch became the CEO, the company's revenue was around $ 26.8 billion. A year before he left, it had grown to $130 billion! He became one of the most famous CEOs in corporate history and was named 'Manager of the Century' by *Fortune* magazine.

Jack Welch started his career in GE in 1960 and spent 21 years with the company before he became its CEO. The fact that a person who was fresh out of college could go on to become the CEO of the company speaks of the sound management practices that the company had put in place. Welch's predecessor was Reginald Jones who was himself one of the greatest CEOs of GE. Jones was due to retire in 1981 but he began succession planning seven years prior to his retirement!

In 1974, Jones created a document: 'A Road Map for CEO Succession'. He identified 96 employees of GE for the post of his successor. At the end of two years, he succeeded in pruning down the list to 12 and then finally to 6 candidates. He made each of them a sector executive and asked them to report to the corporate executive office. This was done to monitor their performance closely. During the next few years, the 6 candidates were subjected to different challenges, issues, evaluations, tests, etc. Finally, Jack Welch was chosen as the CEO of the American conglomerate.

The succession planning of Reginald Jones that resulted in Jack Welsh getting the top spot is one of the most famous examples in corporate history. However, only a few are aware that Welch too spent a great deal of effort and time to identify his successor. Though he was scheduled to retire in 2001, he too prepared a list of his potential successors in 1994, seven years prior to his retirement. He also developed a list of qualities that the future CEO should possess. The initial list that he submitted to the GE board had 23 names. By 1998, the list was cut down to 8 candidates. Finally, the race was between James McNerney,

Robert Nardelli, and Jeffrey Immelt. It was Immelt who finally succeeded Jack Welch in 2001.

In case of the Australian cricket team, Steve Waugh was one of the greatest captains, but his retirement did not create any ripples. The team continued winning and during the tenure of his successor Ricky Ponting, the team managed to win two more World Cups in 2003 and 2007. It remained among the top cricketing nations of the world. Similarly, Michael Clarke, taking over the reins from Ricky Ponting, did not cause any hiccups to the team.

Similarly, in the case of GE, Reginald Jones was considered one of the most admired CEOs of the US. He was twice rated 'The most influential person in business'. One year prior to his retirement, he was named 'CEO of the Year'. Any organization would have spent sleepless nights at the thought of his retirement, but not GE. The transition from Jones to Welch did not stop GE's march towards greatness. After Welch's retirement, his successor Immelt continued all the good work at the top. In 2011, GE was rated the 14th most profitable and the 6th largest company in the US. It was rated as the 5th best global brand by Interbrand and the 15th most admired company by *Fortune*.

TRUST YOUR INTUITION

(IMRAN KHAN, JAVED MIANDAD — BOEING)

'Good instincts usually tell you what to do long before your head has figured it out.'

— Michael Burke

Most decisions, whether in cricket or the corporate world, are taken based on past data and credentials. However, there are times when we need to depend on our instincts.

Imran Khan, the former charismatic Pakistani captain, was known for picking boys from his backyard and catapulting them to the highest echelons of cricket. During the 1992 World Cup, he plucked Inzamam-ul-Haq out of nowhere and made him play in the premier championship of world cricket. Inzamam was an unknown player at that time and unfortunately for him and for his skipper, he wasn't successful during the initial part of the tournament. The Pakistani media and critics were already baying for Imran's blood. Talks of favouritism were heard in the cricketing circles.

Luckily for Imran, his protégé had reserved his best performances for the most crucial part of the tournament. One of the semi-finals was played between Pakistan and New Zealand. While Pakistan had spluttered its way through, New Zealand had won most of its matches with highly clinical performances. The earlier wins in the tournament and the fact that the semi-finals was being played on New Zealand's home turf made them the firm favourites. They batted first and scored 262 for 7 wickets. Pakistan lost a few early wickets and when Inzamam walked in, his team was in a precarious position. However, he played brilliant innings and scored 60 runs off just 37 balls. This is regarded as one of the finest World Cup performances. Though Pakistanis were the underdogs at the beginning of the match, they won it with an over to spare.

Inzamam made an equally crucial contribution in the finals too. Pakistan batted first and was off to a sluggish start but he came in and scored a blistering 42 off just 35 balls to take the team to 249 for 6 wickets. In response, England could manage only 227 runs and lost the match by 22 runs. Even though Inzamam had hardly played any formal first class cricket, he showed his talent by single-handedly winning critical matches for them and was a key member of the Pakistani squad which won the 1992 World Cup.

Inzamam-ul-Haq proved that his innings during the 1992 World Cup was no flash in the pan. He had a very long cricketing tenure, playing 120 test matches and scoring 8,830 runs at a healthy average of 49.6 runs. His performance in the ODIs was equally good—he scored 11,739 runs at an average of 39.52 from 378 matches.

Wasim Akram, one of the best fast bowlers in the history of cricket with 502 ODI wickets, is second only to Sri Lankan off-spin bowler, Muthiah Muralitharan. He is considered to be one of the founders and finest exponents of reverse swing bowling.

Like Inzamam, Akram too made an entry into international cricket with hardly any credentials to back him. He was an unknown club cricketer who had failed to make it to his college team. When he came to the trials at Gaddafi Stadium, there were many famous players present. Akram didn't even get a chance to bowl on the first two days. On the third day, his performance was good enough to impress Javed Miandad. Since Miandad was already a star cricketer, he had enough clout to insist upon Akram's inclusion in the national team.

Thus Wasim Akram made his debut for Pakistan against New Zealand in 1985, without much domestic experience. Only in his second match, did he announce his arrival by claiming 10 wickets. Just like Inzamam, Akram too played a very important role during Pakistan's 1992 World Cup triumph. During the final match against England, Akram scored a swift 33 runs off 19 runs. When England came into bat, Akram took the wicket of star batsman Ian Botham. In his next spell, Akram produced two beauties to get rid of Allan Lamb and Chris Lewis off successive deliveries in one over. His stellar performance won him the Man of the Match.

Though Wasim Akram was known for his devastating swing bowling, he was also a very accomplished batsman. In 104 Test matches, he scored 2,898 runs and took 414 wickets. His ODI record is even more impressive—in 356 matches, he scored 3,717 runs and took 502 wickets. He was the first bowler in international cricket to take more than 400 wickets in both forms of the game—a feat equalled by Muthiah Muralitharan. He is also the only bowler to achieve four hat-tricks—two each in Test matches and ODIs.

Akram was awarded Wisden Cricketer of the Year in 1993. He was also one of five new members inducted into the ICC Cricket Hall of Fame in 2009.

Similarly, there are many decisions that happen in the corporate world that are based on intuition rather than past credentials. If the cricketing world saw the successes of Pakistan's greats like Inzamam-ul-Haq and Wasim Akram, the corporate world has seen the success of Boeing when it made its foray into the world of commercial aircraft.

Boeing is an American multinational aerospace and defence corporation, founded in 1916 by William E. Boeing in Seattle,

Washington. It is made up of multiple business units—Boeing Commercial Airplanes (BCA), Boeing Defense, Space & Security (BDS), Engineering, Operations & Technology, Boeing Capital, and Boeing Shared Services Group.

In March 1910, William Boeing purchased Heath's shipyard in Seattle, which later became the site for his first airplane factory. Boeing was incorporated in Seattle in 1916 as Pacific Aero Products Co. Boeing studied at Yale University and later worked in the timber industry where he acquired knowledge about wooden structures. This knowledge proved to be very useful when he later began to design and assemble airplanes.

In 1917, the company's name was changed to Boeing Airplane Company. In late 1917, during the First World War, Boeing knew that the US Navy would need sea planes for training. Boeing manufactured and provided this to US Navy and thus began a long journey for Boeing as one of America's biggest military aircraft manufacturers. During the Second World War, Boeing built a large number of bombers like B-17 Flying Fortress and B-29 Super Fortress. The Second World War saw Boeing provide supplies to the nation's military establishments.

Unfortunately, after the Second World War, most orders of the military aircrafts were cancelled and more than 50,000 people lost their jobs at Boeing. In order to make itself profitable, it developed a four-engine commercial aircraft, Stratocruiser, which was based on its bomber B-29. Unfortunately, this was not a big success as it lagged behind its rival Douglas in the field of commercial airplanes.

Despite all these odds, Boeing embarked on its journey to build commercial jet aircrafts. Many cynics wrote off Boeing and termed its latest venture as foolhardy. They could not be blamed because Boeing was known primarily for its military aircrafts. Its only commercial airplane, Boeing 377 Stratocruiser, had resulted in a $15 million loss to the organization. It was still recovering from the job loss of thousands of employees. Moreover, even its arch rival, Douglas had decided to continue making only propeller driven airplanes.

Boeing had its first flight of the 707-120 in December 1957, and it received FAA certification in September 1958. It was USA's first commercial jet airliner and very soon it overtook all its European rivals like the British De Havilland Comet and the French Sud Aviation Caravelle to become the leader in commercial jet manufacture. This was a success story of an organization that had pooled in all its resources and gambled on a product even when it had no history of past success.

The success stories of Inzamam and Akram are known to all cricket fans, however, not everyone knows the role played by Imran Khan and Javed Miandad. Imran was ready to go against conventional wisdom and select a young batsman with practically no domestic experience. Similarly, Miandad watched a rookie fast bowler at the nets and inducted him into the national team. It was fitting that both these youngsters were the stars of Pakistan's 1992 World Cup triumph.

Boeing's success story rings a similar bell. It had no success in commercial airplanes. Its own rival Douglas took the safer path of continuing to manufacture propeller based airplanes. However, Boeing embarked on a difficult journey by deciding to put its faith and money in an unknown technology. Just like Imran and Miandad, Boeing too felt its stance vindicated when its gamble paid off. These incidents teach us that apart from making decisions based on past data, once in a while we must listen to our inner voice. If you have the conviction that your hunch is going to be right, go ahead with it.

Say No to Favouritism

(Cricket Team Selection—Yash Birla, Yash Birla Group)

'Leaders who practice favouritism in the workplace have no chance to build a culture of trust.'

—Robert Whipple

During 1970s and 1980s, the Indian team selection displayed very little regional bias. It was quite common to see a particular state having high representation and at the same time, many states being completely unrepresented. There was a time when the India's eleven had five players from Karnataka—G.R. Vishwanath, E.A.S, Prasanna, B.S. Chandrashekar, Brijesh Patel, and Syed Kirmani. Bombay (Mumbai) also dominated the cricketing scene with talented players like Sunil Gavaskar, Dilip Vengsarkar, Sandeep Patil, and Ravi Shastri playing in the same era. There were no talks of parochialism or favouritism because the best players were selected to represent the country.

Unfortunately 1990s changed all that. The structure of the Indian selection committee changed.

It was decided that the selection committee would have five representatives, each representing a zone. This new structure led to the quota system because in most cases the zonal representatives focused on having at least one player from their respective zones.

The impact would have been less if cricketers from different zones had the same levels of skill and competence. Unfortunately the reality was quite different. Without sounding parochial the reality was that west, north, and south zones had more cricketers as compared to east or central zones.

This created two kinds of problems. There was too much competition among players from west, north, and south zones. So invariably a few talented cricketers were left out in the lurch. There have been numerous cases where excellent players from these zones could not make it into the Indian Test team because 'the quota was filled.'

The other problem is exactly the opposite. There have been instances of mediocre players from east and central zone being selected purely because the 'quota had to be filled'. I have the highest regard for many cricketers from east and central zones but there is no denying the fact that there is less competition in these zones. Though there is no official rule about the quota system, it is a well-known fact that zonal bias comes into play while the team is selected.

Yash Birla Group is an Indian industrial conglomerate owned by the famous Birla family. It currently has fourteen companies in diverse businesses such as auto-components, engineering, power solutions, textiles, infrastructure, property development etc. and its chairman is Yashovardhan Birla.

In 1990, when Yashovardhan was just 23, his parents Ashok Vardhanand, Sunanda Birla, and his sister Sujata were killed in a plane crash. Since Yash was quite young to manage Ashok Birla's huge empire, his relatives pitched in and helped him manage some of the businesses. However, this did not solve the problems affecting the growth of the Birla Empire.

In 2005, Yash Birla met P.V.R. Murthy and asked him to join his group. Murthy joined as the director, Finance and began the process of re-organizing the Yash Birla group of companies. He infused fresh blood by bringing in fresh people at various levels in the organization. Yash realized that some of his relatives who were helping him manage his businesses were not competent enough to be in leadership positions. This resulted in those industries turning sick. He realized that the only solution to bring back the group on track was to sack some of his relatives and sell off the sick companies.

Yash Birla gave full powers to Murthy for implementing the organizational changes. Since Murthy was a finance professional, he was able to quickly judge the financial factors that were affecting the growth of the organization. He implemented changes in the financial policy and borrowings of the company and divided the group companies into verticals. He hired Ernst & Young to evaluate the company's performance and give recommendations. These actions helped him turnaround the performance of many companies in his group.

Today, the Yash Birla Group has a diverse portfolio ranging from lifestyle products, power solutions, to information technology. It has a turnover of around ₹30 billion and employs around 3,300 people. Yash Birla continues to be the chairman of the group and his right hand man, Murthy is the group director for finance, legal, HR, strategy, and corporate communications.

Whenever the Indian cricket team has been hit by favouritism or regional bias, it has invariably fielded a weak team. This has two adverse effects—firstly, the team does not consist of its best players; and secondly, it adds extra pressure on the good players because they have to make up for their mediocre coplayers. There have been numerous instances when the captains themselves had no faith on certain players. This makes it tough for the player too because one billion Indians would be eagerly waiting for him to fail. When a player selected by nepotism, favouritism, or parochialism fails to deliver the goods, one billion 'experts' in India would be itching to say 'I told you so!'

The effect of favouritism is worse in the corporate world. Apart from the above mentioned disadvantages of having a weak team and adding extra pressure on good performers, there is one more major drawback—attrition!

Nothing hurts a professional more than seeing his manager showing favouritism. In majority of the cases, even if a person sees a regional bias or favouritism in the team, he does not complain. He is scared to fight against his own management. He would rather leave the company than stay in an environment that smacks of favouritism.

India, because of its cultural diversity, probably suffers from this syndrome much more than other countries. India has 29 states and most of them have their own language, culture, and tradition. This has given rise to parochial feelings. It is quite common to see a manager recruit people from his state or show favouritism at the time of promotions and salary hikes. This leads to frustration among his other team members.

Yash Birla took the bold step of removing those non-performers who had reached to the top purely on the basis of caste and region. By bringing in Murthy, he instilled professionalism at the top and meritocracy and performance was rewarded. This has now been emulated in many other companies too. When a founder or CEO retires, it is quite common to see him being replaced by an 'outside' professional rather than his own son or daughter. This is a step in the right direction towards bringing professionalism into the organization.

LEADING THE STARS

(CLIVE LLOYD, SAURAV GANGULY—NARAYAN MURTHY, INFOSYS)

'The task of leadership is not to put greatness into people, but to elicit it, for the greatness is there already.'

—John Buchan

People believe that it is tough to lead a bunch of non-performers but a cakewalk to lead a group of stars. Nothing can be farther away from truth. Many of the big stars come with inflated egos and each star thinks he is a leader in his own right. It is never easy to handle a team of high achievers where each one wants to pull the team in his direction and think that he is the king.

During the 1980s, when Clive Lloyd's West Indies team was bulldozing all the teams and he was being hailed as one of the best captains of the world, it is believed that one of his team members quipped, 'we are such a strong side that leadership hardly matters. Even my mother can lead this team!'

However, reality is completely different. Clive Lloyd had to use all his experience and people management skills to bring his stars together and make it one cohesive unit. He had to contend with people from different cultures and countries of West Indies. It was no easy task to lead seasoned players like Gordon Greenidge, Alvin Kallicharan, Desmond Haynes, Vivian Richards, and the volatile fast bowling pack: Andy Roberts, Michael Holding, Joel Garner, and Colin Croft.

In the Indian context, it is worth mentioning the captaincy of Saurav Ganguly, whom Geoffrey Boycott calls the 'Prince of Calcutta'. During his captaincy, he had to manage some of the greatest cricketers that India had ever produced, including the 'Fab Four'—Sachin Tendulkar, Rahul Dravid, VVS Laxman, and Anil Kumble. The additional difficulty that any Indian captain faces is the cultural differences among the players. India with its 29 states is like a mini continent with 29 countries—each with its own culture, language, food, and behaviour.

Saurav Ganguly was the most successful Indian captain having won 21 of the 49 test matches that he led. The most heartening factor of Saurav Ganguly's captaincy was that he actually enjoyed his role. He did not allow the extra burden of captaincy affect his batting. If anything, it improved once he took over the captaincy of the star studded Indian team. Contrast this with the other cricketing greats like Sachin Tendulkar or Ian Botham—both players whose performance dipped due to captaincy and were too happy to give it away.

N.R. Narayan Murthy, the current additional director and executive chairman of Infosys Limited started his career as chief systems programmer at IIM Ahmedabad. Later, he joined Patni Computer Systems, Pune. In July 1981, he left Patni and started Infosys with a paltry capital of $250!

Narayan Murthy took six of his former colleagues with him to Infosys—Nandan Nilekani, Kris Gopalakrishnan, S.D. Shibulal, K Dinesh, Ashok Arora, and N.S. Raghavan.

Narayan Murthy faced the usual problems that anyone heading a startup company would face. Apart from those challenges, he had to lead a company whose management team consisted of six of his former colleagues from Patni. Murthy was quick to realize that he was leading a team of highly competent professionals. Infosys was not a company comprising of senior leaders who were related to each other. Unlike some of the other family owned businesses, he brought in a culture of professionalism and transparency into the organization. He did a fantastic job and converted Infosys from a small startup company in the 1980s to one of the biggest software companies in the world. He served as the CEO for 21 years and as of 2012, the company had a revenue of approximately $7.39 billion, with more than 1,57,000 employees spread across 30 countries.

Narayan Murthy was the CEO of Infosys from its inception till 2002. During his tenure, he made the company rank among the top three IT companies in the world. He was rated as Asia's 'Businessman of the Year' in 2003. In December 2005, he was voted as the 7th most admired CEO/chairman in the world in a global study conducted by Burson-Marsteller with the Economist Intelligence Unit. He also received the Ernst & Young World Entrepreneur of the Year award in 2003 and Padma Vibhushan five years later.

Sourav Ganguly and Narayan Murthy clearly showed excellent leadership skills in leading a team of stalwarts and achieving their vision. During their tenure, they knit the team into a strong cohesive unit. India always had many talented cricketers but what was lacking was self-belief and confidence. There were numerous instances where Indians lost matches that they could have won. Teams like Australia and England were experts at playing mind games, especially against the Indians. Ganguly instilled self-belief and a never-say-die spirit among his teammates. Indians began to make eye contact with the Australians and did not hesitate to sledge back. The team members began to believe in themselves. They began to win or draw matches that seemed to be heading towards an Indian defeat. Suddenly India became one of the most powerful cricketing nations in the world—a team that could no longer be dismissed as 'a bunch of softies'.

Murthy, along with Premji did the same to the Indian IT industry. Till 1980s, USA and a few European countries were associated with high technology industries. India was regarded as a poor third world country. However, with the advent of Infosys and Wipro, India became one of the most favoured destinations for software development. These two IT giants can be credited with putting India on the global IT map. India was no longer a nation of snake charmers and fakirs sleeping on a bed of nails, it was an international IT giant. Seeing the kind of software developed by these two companies, practically every major multinational company headed towards India.

The other commendable feature of Ganguly's and Murthy's leadership skills was the fact that their departure had little impact on their respective teams' fortunes. Their successors have been able to fill their shoes quite admirably.

Sourav Ganguly was one of the most successful captains of India. In 2006, he was replaced by Rahul Dravid, who maintained the winning streak for his country. Under his leadership, India won a Test series against West Indies on their home soil, something that had not happened since 1971. During Dravid's captaincy, India tied the earlier record of most consecutive ODI wins. Incidentally, the earlier record was set by his predecessor Ganguly! India also had a dream run of winning 17 ODI matches while batting second—Ganguly was the captain for 2 matches and Dravid for the remaining 15. In 2007, Dravid was replaced by Anil Kumble. The Indian team maintained its fighting spirit, something that it had developed during Ganguly's leadership. One of the best evidences of this was the victory against Australia at Perth, just a few days after the 'Monkeygate' episode where Kumble's team was pushed to the wall. After Kumble's brief stint, Dhoni became the Indian captain. Under his leadership, India won the Twenty20 World Cup in 2007 and the ODI World Cup in 2011.

The case of Infosys was also quite similar.

Narayan Murthy was the CEO of Infosys since its inception till 2002. Despite Infosys being one of the top IT companies in the country, Murthy felt it was time to move on and bring in a new CEO. He had no qualms about handing over the complete operations to Nandan Nilekani, who in 2002, became the CEO of Infosys and Narayan Murthy became the chairman of the board. Many people predicted that Murthy's exit would see a decline in the company's fortunes. However, Murthy and Nilekani proved them wrong. Murthy clearly knew how to change gears while moving from the role of a CEO to that of a chairman. During his 21-year tenure as the CEO, he was completely 'hands-on' but the moment he became the chairman, he stopped involving himself in day-to-day operations of the company. Nilekani's tenure at the top saw Infosys grow in strength and remain among the top three IT companies in India.

In 2006, Narayan Murthy became the non-executive chairman of the board and chief mentor. A year later, Nandan Nilekani made way for Kris Gopalakrishnan. Murthy's role was more strategic in nature and he focused on mentoring the organization. In August 2011, he retired from the company and took the title of chairman emeritus. By then, the industry had realized the robustness of Infosys and even its biggest critic did not predict a disaster for the company. Kris Gopalakrishnan matched Nandan Nilekani and further consolidated Infosys' position in the global IT market. Like Nandan Nilekani he too was awarded the Padma Bhushan. During those years, Infosys had seen many different CEOs. However, it had no impact on its position, growth, revenue, customer satisfaction, employee motivation, and attrition. A great deal of credit should go to Narayan Murthy who was instrumental in building Infosys on a strong foundation.

Whether you are leading a cricket team or a team of corporate professionals, the situation is the same. Like in cricket, in the corporate world too, most of the big stars come with a baggage. The competent members in your team may even be thinking that they are far superior than you. There might be young rising stars aspiring for your role. You might also have former leaders in your team and these are the most difficult to handle. Firstly, they can feel they did not deserve to be demoted to a lower role. Secondly since in all probability you would have replaced one of them, they would be nursing a grudge against you!

In such situations, it is imperative that the leader should initially focus on winning the confidence of his team. His team members should feel comfortable working with him rather than perceive him as a threat or a competitor. Some of the ways of winning their trust and confidence could be:

- Evolve your vision and mission along with them so that you have their buy-in
- Involve them while taking important decisions
- Be a good listener and empathize with their concerns
- Constantly assure them that you are there to help them achieve their goals
- Show them the bigger picture and how they fit into it

Coach to Win

(John Wright, Gary Kirsten — Larry Bossidy, Allied Signal)

'The coach's job is to get the best players and get them to play together.'

—Bernie Ebbers

John Wright, former New Zealand batsman, was the coach of the Indian cricket team from 2000 to 2005. When his name was announced, there were many sceptics in India because we never had a foreign coach till then. There were doubts about his ability to succeed—could he handle the stars in the Indian side, the cultural differences, and the language issues?

While a majority of them wrote him off even before he landed on the Indian soil, a few were willing to wait and watch. Wright proved all sceptics wrong and turned out to be one of the best cricket coaches India ever had. The Indian team had a dream run during his tenure.

John Wright was extremely successful as the Indian coach because he had a very simple philosophy: 'It is the players who are more important than the coach because it is finally the players who win the game.' To quote him from another interview, 'the one thing I wouldn't do is overestimate the importance of the role of a coach. Because I think there's a lot written about this and that. It's the players that win you the games, that's it. As a coach you can do some things, but when you sum it all up, matches are won because D.W. Smith got 124 or S.L. Patel took 6 for 38, and they, the players, did it.'

Wright was fully aware of the role of a coach and therefore drew clear boundaries between the roles of a captain and a coach. He always felt that as a coach, he should give his inputs and ideas but it was finally upto the captain to take the final decision. There were a few occasions when he and Ganguly didn't agree upon certain things, including team selection. But he would finally allow Ganguly to take a call because he was well aware that the 'buck stops with the captain'. If India lost a match, people would question the captain and not the coach. Since the captain's head was on the chopping block, he had every right to take the final decision.

Wright perfectly understood the importance of striking a good rapport with the captain and the senior members of the team. Again, to quote him, 'In the end it's about working particularly with your captain and your senior players, to say that, "Well, look this is probably the way to go if you guys want to be a part of a winning team." You have got to be able to sell it to them. Not only sell it, sometimes you have to convince them and sometimes you just instruct. But in the end they have got to take ownership. If you can't sell it, you can end up frustrated and you are probably not a right fit with that group.'

Wright knew that unlike the New Zealand team which had no big names, the Indian team had many stars. He was conscious of the iconic status of cricketing greats like Sachin Tendulkar, Anil Kumble, Rahul Dravid, VVS Laxman, and Saurav Ganguly. However, Wright's style of functioning ensured that he had no problems working with them. Saurav Ganguly was the skipper of the Indian team and Wright built an excellent rapport with him right from the first day. He also struck a good relationship with other members of the Indian team.

The other big advantage that John Wright had was that he was not a big name in cricket. With due respect to him and his batting abilities, he was not a star like Lara,Tendulkar, or Bradman. And this worked to his advantage. Since he was not a big star from New Zealand, he was more grounded and humble than any star cricketer-turned coach.He was also quick to recognize the talents of players like Tendulkar, Kumble, Dravid, Laxman, and Ganguly, and knew that these boys didn't really need coaching on basic techniques. He felt his main job would be to iron out any technical flaws that they might have developed over the years and to mould them together as a strong team.

Wright studied the behaviour of many of his team members and felt that though they were a talented lot, they lacked the self-belief and the desire to win—something always seen in abundance in the Australian side. He had seen Indians lose many close matches that they could have won. He had seen his team snatch defeat from the jaws of victory! He was also concerned about their ability to handle high pressure situations. These observations helped Wright prioritize his tasks. He knew that he needed to focus on the soft skills of these talented cricketers so that they would be able to handle 'crunch time' and 'pressure cooker situations' better. Most importantly, he knew he had to instil self-belief and confidence to win tight games.

Wright was successful in implementing his ideas and one of the best examples was the 2001 home series against the Australians. Australia had scored 445 runs and India, in reply, collapsed for just 171 runs. When India came in to bat the second time, Wright instilled the self-belief and conviction that they could still make a match out of it and probably try and win it. With inspirational words from Wright, Laxman played the innings of his life to score a brilliant 281, ably supported by Rahul Dravid who scored 180. India scored a mammoth 657 runs in the second innings. In reply, the mighty Australians could muster only 212 runs and lost the match by 171 runs!

Some of the other memorable series include the 1–1 Test series against Australia in 2003–2004, winning a series against arch-rivals Pakistan, and reaching the finals of the 2003 World Cup.

Gary Kirsten, former South African opener took over as Indian cricket team's coach in March 2008. Till then, India had mixed fortunes with foreign coaches. The team had done very well under John Wight as the coach; it also had a very turbulent relationship with Australian Greg Chappell as its coach. Gary Kirsten became the coach at a time when the sceptics were wondering if it was wise to again have another foreign coach.

When Gary Kirsten took over as the Indian coach, he was well aware of the friction that his predecessor Greg Chappell had with the Indian team. Kirsten was a shrewd coach and ensured that he didn't commit the same mistakes as Chappell. Though he had travelled with the Indian team to Australia, his first full series was against his own native team, South Africa. This proved to be a blessing—he was able to contribute very well because India was playing his home country and the series drew 1–1. India then defeated the mighty Australians 2–0 in a home series. Anil Kumble announced his retirement and MS Dhoni took over as the captain of the Indian Test team. This had no impact on Kirsten and his relationship with the Indian players. Under him, India defeated Sri Lanka in 2009 to become the No.1 Test side in the world. India also won the Compaq Cup, defeating Sri Lanka in the finals by 46 runs.

Gary Kirsten was one of South Africa's best players of spin and pace, so he was able to easily identify the chinks in the armour of the Indian batsmen. Being a strict disciplinarian himself during his playing days, he was able to instill the same level of discipline among the team members. Unlike some of the coaches who had played very little at the highest level, Kirsten had represented South Africa in both forms of cricket for a long time. He had an awesome record in tests scoring 7,289 runs in 101 Test matches at an average of 45.27. In ODIs, he was equally good, having scored 6,798 runs in 185 matches at an average of 40.95. Having played the game for so many years at the highest level, he was a 'hands-on' coach rather than a 'text book' one. Within months after he joined the Indian team, one could see the transformation among the players, whether it was batting technique, fielding, or self-confidence.

The icing on the cake came on 2nd April 2011 when India won the 2011 World Cup defeating Sri Lanka by 6 wickets at the Wankhede Stadium, Mumbai. Gary Kirsten had already expressed his desire to return to South Africa instead of applying for an extension of his contract. He received the best parting gift from victorious Indian team when its members carried him on their shoulders and ran across the Wankhede Stadium. Dhoni aptly described him as, 'the best thing to happen to Indian cricket.'

Larry Bossidy worked for 34 years at General Electric (GE) and rose to the post of vice chairman. In 1991, he left GE and joined Allied Signal as its chairman and CEO. Allied Signal was a manufacturer of aerospace and automotive parts. When Bossidy took over as its CEO, it was undergoing stagnated earnings. The company consisted of many business units that had been acquired and each operated as a different entity with very little synergy.

Luckily for Allied Signal, its new CEO was a completely 'hands-on' person who could roll up his sleeves and talk to the junior-most employee on the shopfloor. He was a tough person with a high bar of excellence but at the same time, an excellent coach who could speak the shopfloor language.

Bossidy was aware that though his company had many excellent people, no one in the past had bothered to speak to them and taken their views and suggestions. He decided that this was the most important issue that had to be addressed immediately. Within the first couple of months after his joining, he visited most of the sites where Allied Signal had operations and spoke to thousands of employees.

Bossidy knew that the only way he could succeed was by getting full support from his employees. For this, he had to talk to them and explain the problem. He had to coach them on how to be more focused towards achieving their business goals. He decided to focus on three primary goals—meeting the numbers, reduction in cycle time, and ensuring growth. He spoke passionately about this in all his communication meetings. He also used the same three goals while reviewing the performance of his managers.

Unlike many CEOs who would bang and pound the table when the numbers were not met, Bossidy was willing to patiently listen to his managers when they did not meet any of the three goals. This made the employees comfortable to speak the truth during his review meetings. The other difference that Bossidy made was—he was always willing to coach and mentor the underperformers.

Bossidy recognized that one of the main reasons why Allied Signal was internally focused was because of its organizational structure. He removed layers of hierarchy and centralized many functions. At the same time, he empowered the junior employees so that they could take quick decisions.

During his nine years as the CEO of Allied Signal, he transformed it into one of the most respected companies in the world. He served as the chairman and CEO from 1991 to 1999. In 1999, he played a major role in the merger of Allied Signal with Honeywell. After the merger, he was made the chairman and CEO of Honeywell.

Collaboration at the Top

(Greg Chappell, Saurav Ganguly—Harry Stonecipher, Phil Condit, Boeing)

'When two elephants fight, it is the grass that gets trampled.'

—African proverb

In the earlier chapter, we have seen John Wright and Gary Kirsten having successful stints as Indian coaches. There were two prime reasons for their success—firstly, they knew the importance of building a good rapport with the captain and the team; and secondly, they knew that as coaches, they should work in the background and allow the captain to take the final decision because the accountability of the team's performance rests with the captain.

There are many examples of the damage that occurs because of ego clashes. The best illustration of this can be seen by the spate of unpleasant incidents that occurred during Greg Chappell's tenure as the Indian coach.

Greg Chappell was the second of three brothers to play Test cricket for Australia. Younger brother of another Australian captain, Ian Chappell, Greg quickly emerged from the shadows of his illustrious brother to carve a niche for himself. He was an excellent batsman who coupled elegant stroke play with a sound technique and defense. He was considered a 'batting all-rounder' because he bowled medium pace and was also an excellent fielder.

At the time of his retirement, he held the world record for the most number of catches.

Greg Chappell started his Test career with a century on his debut and also scored a century in his last Test match in January 1984, making 182 in his final innings. Thus, he became the first batsman in the history of cricket to score centuries in his first and last Test innings.

Chappell captained Australia between 1975 and 1977, and then joined the breakaway World Series Cricket, before returning to the Australian captaincy in 1979—a position he held until his retirement. Chappell was appointed captain of the Australian side during the home series against West Indies in 1975. In his first Test as a captain, he began with a century in each innings to win the first Test against West Indies in Brisbane. This is a unique record in Test cricket. He led Australia to a crushing 5–1 win over the mighty West Indies.

In 87 test matches, he scored 7,110 runs at an awesome average of 53.86 runs, studded with 24 centuries. He proved to be a handy ODI player too, scoring 2,331 runs at an average of 40.18 runs in 74 ODIs. He was hailed as one of the greatest Australian cricketers.

In May 2005, Chappell was appointed coach of the Indian cricket team. He signed a two-year contract, until the 2007 World Cup to be played in West Indies. When his appointment was announced, everyone felt that this was the best thing to have happened to Indian cricket. During the past few decades, the choice of some of the Indian coaches had been highly questionable. On many occasions, it was felt that the best person did not get the job. However, this time around, there were no questions asked, no murmurs in the cricketing circles. With a cricketing record as enviable as that of Chappell's, there was no doubt in people's mind that the selection was purely on merit.

However, the next two years were the most tumultuous years for Indian cricket. Though Sourav Ganguly, the then Indian captain, had played a major role in the appointment of Greg Chappell as the Indian coach, the relationship between the two soured. Chappell's first overseas tour as the coach of the Indian cricket team was to Zimbabwe during September 2005. Ganguly hit a century in the first Test. However, after the match, he announced that Chappell had asked him to step down as the captain on the eve of the match. This news generated a lot of negative publicity and the media was quick to write the allegations and the counter allegations between the Indian captain and the coach. Ganguly was soon dropped on the grounds of poor form but many suggested that his omission was influenced by his row with the coach.

Chappell had a difficult relationship with many other Indian players too such as Virender Sehwag, Zaheer Khan, and Harbhajan Singh. They were not happy with his unorthodox coaching methods and his outspokenness. There were numerous occasions when Chappell made his displeasure public. The discussions in the dressing room were no longer kept confidential and the cricketers and the coach leaked many private conversations to the ever hungry media.

India had won the World Cup in 1983 which was almost three decades back. It was expected that Chappell, with his rich experience of Australian cricket would play an important role in bringing home the coveted trophy. Since Australia had won the World Cup on a few earlier occasions, it was felt that only an Australian coach could ensure India's success at the limited format of the game.

Unfortunately, the frequent tinkering with the batting line-up had left many gaps in the Indian team. One of the examples was Sachin Tendulkar's batting slot. Though the Little Master was one of the best openers in the ODIs, Chappell felt that he should play lower down to bolster the Indian middle order. This not only weakened the Indian opening slot but also curbed Tendulkar's aggressiveness. By the time Tendulkar walked in to bat, the power-plays and field restrictions would be over so he could not play his natural flamboyant style. He had to change his natural aggressive game and become a 'nudger' and 'pusher'. The boundaries were replaced with ones and twos

It did not surprise anyone when India had a disastrous World Cup in West Indies. India made a very early exit and the blame-game started. Chappell resigned from his position in April 2007, and even before the Indian cricket fans could realize what had happened, he had boarded the first flight home.

In the corporate world, this analogy can be extended to the relationship among senior management team members. One of the best examples of this occurred at Boeing. The leadership styles of its former CEO Philip Condit and former president Harry Stonecipher is worth studying.

Phil Condit joined Boeing in 1965 as an aerodynamics engineer, and held various posts and was associated with different functions during his three decade tenure. When Boeing acquired McDonnell Douglas in 1997, he became the CEO of the merged entity. Since he had worked for more than 30 years in a single organization, Condit valued qualities like legacy and loyalty in his employees. He operated in a consensus mode, preferring to go by the majority. He had grown up on the Boeing values of people management.

Unfortunately for him, during Boeing's acquisition of McDonnell Douglas, Harry Stonecipher, till then the head of McDonnell Douglas, was made the chairman. Unlike Condit, Stonecipher had worked for various companies so he neither came with any legacy baggage nor had he grown up on Boeing's style of operation. He had begun his career at General Motors and subsequently worked for General Electric for 27 years. During his stint at General Electric, he imbibed Jack Welsh's quest for performance and strong focus on business results. He brought to Boeing the same degree of ruthlessness. He did not hesitate to fire the under performers, something rare in Boeing during those days.

In September 1994, he became the CEO of McDonnell Douglas and continued to remain in that post till the company's merger with Boeing in 1997. He remained on the board serving as its president. Boeing went through a difficult phase during the 1990s and the contrasting leadership styles of Phil Condit and Harry Stonecipher didn't make it any easier. It was always 'consensus' and 'decentralized decision making' versus 'centralized decision making'; it was 'people first' versus 'bottom line'.

The tumultuous relationship between the top two leaders continued till 2003 when Phil Condit was forced to resign over the fallout from the freezing of a defence contract with US Air Force. This was in violation of Boeing's ethics.

Following Condit's resignation, Stonecipher was asked to take over as the CEO of Boeing. He introduced many rules to ensure that there was no breach of ethics in future. It was an irony that he too fell victim to Boeing's code of conduct, when he developed a consensual relationship with a Boeing executive. Harry Stonecipher tendered his resignation in March 2005.

Though it is always good to strive for sound interpersonal relationships between colleagues, in a real-life scenario there are bound to be cases of poor rapport within the team. The impact is probably less if it happens at the junior level, but can be very serious if it occurs at the top level. This is true for cricket and any organization.

These examples show the importance of relationships between a coach and a captain. Greg Chappell and Gary Kirsten were one of finest batsmen for their respective countries but as coaches, they were a study in contrast. Chappell had a poor rapport with the Indian team that led to the dismal performance of many players and consequently the team's performance suffered. Its early exit in 2007 World Cup under Chappell and its winning the championship in 2011 under Kirsten sums up the impact that a coach has on its team.

What happened at Boeing was quite similar. The two most important people for the company were Philip Condit and Harry Stonecipher. If the CEO and the chairman had worked together,it could have done wonders to the great airline company. Unfortunately, both came from different backgrounds, had different ideologies and styles. When two people at the top work in conflicting directions, the company gets pulled in the direction of the stronger one. However, this may not be the right path for the company's employees, customers, and shareholders. The infighting at the top affected Boeing's performance. It saw a dip in its growth and profits and for the first time it lost its No.1 position to its arch rival, Airbus.

3

ETHICS AND VALUES

'You are fired for unethical practices! My IS department says you have 15 fake email addresses, 18 fake accounts in various social networking sites, and 7 fake photographs on a video website impersonating famous rock stars!'
PINK SLIP

INTEGRITY VS. WINNING

(G.R. VISHWANATH, AUSTRALIAN CRICKET BOARD — 'THE HP WAY', MARK HURD)

'Live so that when your children think of fairness and integrity, they think of you.'

— H. Jackson Brown Jr

In today's competitive world, everyone wants to win. This starts right from childhood when parents ask their children to excel in school. It continues as the child grows up till he is in college. The pressure to perform well in academics is extremely high and persists even after the person gets a job. He is constantly told by his managers to excel in his work. At the beginning of each year high goals are set for professionals and at the end of the year they are evaluated against them. The next year the bar of excellence is raised a notch higher so the expectations increase. Sadly, the focus is primarily on meeting the deliverables with respect to desired quality and timelines. Very little attention is paid to the methods adopted to achieve the goals. There are very few instances of people being penalized for adopting unfair methods.

The same is true for cricket as well. At the end of every match or series, people remember the batsmen who scored centuries or bowlers who had 5 wicket hauls. People seldom discuss the behaviour of the players. We have seen many cricketers who have been dropped due to poor performance. How many instances can we recall of a star cricketer being dropped due to poor attitude or behaviour? What has made it worse is the fact that at the end of each series, the media publishes statistics of each player with respect to number of runs scored, number of centuries hit, number of wickets taken, etc. There are no statistics with respect to attitude and behaviour.

In 1980, India played against England at the Wankhede Stadium, Mumbai. It was a very prestigious match between the two teams since it was played to commemorate the Golden Jubilee of Board of Control for Cricket in India (BCCI). It was known as the 'Golden Jubilee' Test match.

India batted first and scored 242 runs. England started off disastrously losing 5 wickets for just 58 runs. This brought Ian Botham and Bob Taylor to the crease. During the course of their partnership, Bob Taylor was wrongly judged 'out', caught by the wicket keeper. Indian skipper G.R. Vishwanath, standing at first slip felt that Bob Taylor had not nicked the ball. He ran to the umpire and asked him to reverse his decision. Unfortunately for India, Bob Taylor played a fantastic knock and along with the cricketing legend Ian Botham, he added 171 runs for the 6th wicket. Botham scored a brilliant century and took 13 wickets which helped England win by ten wickets.

Had Vishwanath not recalled Bob Taylor, the result might have been different. However, the Indian skipper had no regrets about losing the match to a better team. 'As a captain, I did what was right at the stage without thinking about the final result. It was clear that he (Taylor) was not out and that was the only thing that mattered,' Vishwanath said. This great incident of sportsmanship was a testament to the sort of individual that Vishwanath was.

Just before the World Cup in February 2003, Shane Warne, the star of the Australian team and arguably the best leg spinner in the world, failed a drug test. He tested positive for a banned diuretic and the Australian Cricket Board (ACB) slapped him with a one year ban. The substance that he had taken was a banned drug because it masked the presence of other drugs.

While the media was ready to write off the Australian team even before the first ball of the 2003 World Cup had been bowled, their captain Ricky Ponting was unruffled and went about his task with great poise and aplomb. Australia won the World Cup in style. It is important to note that the ACB had no hesitation in showing the door to Warne, despite him being the most important member of their team.

There are many occasions when our critical resources violate the company's norms but we tend to treat them with kid-gloves for the fear of jeopardizing the company's deliverables. However, we should realize that ethics and compliance come first, irrespective of the person's competence.

Hewlett Packard (HP) is one of the top American IT companies. Major product lines include personal computing devices, enterprise and industry standard servers, related storage devices, networking products, software, and a diverse range of printers and other imaging products. HP also has strong services and consulting businesses around its products and partner products and was founded by Bill Hewlett and Dave Packard in a garage in Palo Alto, California, USA.

In 1957, Hewlett and Packard decided to have the company's first off-site meeting. This was a two day meeting that was held in Sonoma Mission Inn, near San Francisco. The participants were the senior managers of the organization.

The duo had already prepared a draft set of corporate guidelines and objectives. One of the main reasons for this meeting was to present it to the senior managers and explain how to manage the organization. Hewlett and Packard wanted everyone to be aware of the company's objectives, what they planned to do, and more importantly, how they planned to achieve this. This has come to be known as 'The HP Way'.

Initially, there were six objectives. Over the next few years, these were modified and the second version consisting of the following seven objectives was released in 1966:

1. Profits
2. Customers
3. Field of interest
4. Growth
5. Employees
6. Organization
7. Citizenship

In Bill's words, 'The HP Way' is 'a core ideology which includes a deep respect for the individual, a dedication to affordable quality and reliability, a commitment to community responsibility, and a view that the company exists to make technical contributions for the advancement and welfare of humanity.' One of the main tenets of 'The HP Way' was to conduct business with uncompromising integrity.

Mark Hurd was the CEO, president, and chairman of Hewlett Packard. In 2005, he succeeded Robert Wayman who was the interim CEO after the exit of former CEO, Carly Fiorina. The following year he became the chairman after the departure of Pat Dunn.

Hurd had spent 25 years at NCR Corporation and played various roles in the organization. His last two years at NCR was as its CEO and president. During his tenure at NCR, he had displayed excellent leadership skills and improved its operating efficiency and product lines. He was known for his aggressive leadership style which included tight cost reduction measures, reduction in workforce, etc. Since HP was itself going through a very difficult phase, Hurd was considered as the best candidate to turn around the company.

Hurd did not disappoint people who had chosen him for

the top post. He implemented lots of cost cutting measures in the organization. Around 15,000 workers were laid off. The headcount in IT department was reduced by more than 50%. HP had 85 data centres which was reduced to 6. Hurd also cut salaries by 5% and reduced many benefits. After the acquisition of EDS, he adjusted the salaries of EDS employees to match that of their HP counterparts.

All these measures helped HP achieve significant increase in revenues and profitability. The stock rose by 130%. Hurd was considered as one of the 'Top Gun CEOs' by Brendon Wood International and hailed as one of the best CEOs of the century.

Unfortunately, all this was to change soon. In August 2010, Hurd had to resign from HP following the discovery of expense account irregularities. When Hurd stepped down from his top position, he honestly admitted that he did not live up to the standards and principles of trust and integrity that is expected at HP.

Let us once again look at all the case studies.

In the 1980 'Golden Jubilee' Test match, India was in a very strong position. When Bob Taylor came to the crease, his team was trailing by 184 runs and half the side was back in the pavilion. He and Ian Botham were the last recognized pair at the crease. One more wicket at this stage and the floodgates would have opened. Taylor was given out by the umpire.

Who knows what would have happened had Vishwanath not recalled Taylor back!

India was in a very strong position to press for victory. However, Vishwanath, a player known for his exemplary behaviour both on and off the field, chose integrity over victory.

At the beginning of the 2003 World Cup, Australia Cricket Board faced the biggest dilemma when its star leg spinner Shane Warne tested positive to a banned drug. ACB knew that its fortunes depended on Shane Warne's availability. The Board could have devised many creative ways to retain Warne in the World Cup squad, however, it didn't. It dropped Warne from the team even if it meant that the defending champions may not be able to retain the World Cup. For ACB, integrity was more important than victory. However, its players came up with stellar performances and won the championship.

In the HP example, Hurd joined the company in 2005 and by the end of his five year tenure, the company's fortunes had changed signiicantly. He took HP to No.1 position in the sale of desktop computers and laptops. HP also considerably increased its market share in inkjet and laser printers and was one of the top IT companies in the world. However, when Hurd's conduct was found to be not in line with 'The HP Way', he was shown the door. The board was well aware of his capability, incredible performance, and the manner in which he had turned around HP's revenues, profitability, and image. If the HP Board wanted, it could have retained Hurd by administering him with a small penalty. This way, they could have still had their star performer CEO at the top. However, the company chose integrity over success and preferred to let go Hurd though it knew that it would greatly affect the company's fortunes. It has shown the corporate world that you need not break rules to be a market leader.

Ethisphere Institute honours firms that promote ethical business standards and practices by going beyond legal minimums, introducing innovative ideas that benefit the public. In May 2010, HP was named one of the world's most ethical companies by this institute. It was second year in a row when HP had made it to the list. Ethisphere reviewed, researched, and analysed thousands of nominations in more than 100 countries and 35 industries to create the 2010 list. HP was one of only 100 companies to earn this distinction and it was also the only computer hardware vendor to be recognized. In 2010, the company ranked No. 4 in the Ponemon Institute's annual study of the most trusted companies for privacy. HP has also won nine straight annual 'Most Respected Company in China' awards from the *Economic Observer* and Peking University.

In a world where people think that winning is everything, these people and organizations chose to be different. For them, the means was more important than the final result.

Fairness is the Name of the Game
(Douglas Jardine — Enron Corporation)

'Fairness is what justice really is.'

—Potter Stewart

The English cricket team, led by Douglas Jardine, visited Australia in 1932–1933. The team's biggest challenge was to control Australia's legendary batsman Donald Bradman, who was already hailed as one the best and most prolific run getters in cricket.

Jardine decided that the only way to control Bradman and other Australian batsmen was to resort to effective but unfair tactics. He instructed his fast bowlers Harold Larwood and Bill Voce to pitch the cricket ball short on the leg stump so that it rises towards the body of the batsman. He hoped that this would make the batsmen jump and hop, and while trying to take an evasive action, they might edge it to the close-in fielders. This plan was hatched even before Jardine left the shores of England.

The first Test between England and Australia was played at Sydney. Jardine asked all his fielders to stand in the quadrant of the field behind square leg. As planned, the two bowlers kept bowling short pitched balls on the leg stump. Those were the days when the batsmen neither wore helmets nor used any other protective gears like chest guard or arm guard. Fearing that the ball might injure them, the poor Australian batsmen had to take evasive action. They would jab at the ball without even looking at it. This resulted in the batsmen spooning simple catches to the close-in fielders and Australia lost the match by 10 wickets. Harold Larwood captured 10 wickets. This tactic of intimidating bowling was infamously known as bodyline bowling.

The Australians managed to square the series, thanks to a brilliant century by their star batsman Donald Bradman. However, Jardine continued to employ bodyline tactics and his team won the next Test at Adelaide Oval. Many Australians were badly injured and they lost the match. England managed to win the next two Tests since most Australian cricketers were injured. Though England won the series 4–1, they did not win any friends in Australia. In fact, at one point in time, the relationship between the two cricketing teams soured so much that it threatened to snowball into a major diplomatic controversy between the two nations. Even in England, there were many traditionalists who did not approve of Jardine's bodyline tactics. They felt that cricket was a 'gentleman's game' and the spirit of the game was above 'winning at all costs'. Needless to say Jardine is a captain whom every Englishman would like to forget, and bodyline series was the biggest stain in the cricketing history.

Enron Corporation was one of the most admired American companies, with businesses in the areas of energy, electricity, natural gas, communications, and pulp & paper. This Texas based company had revenue of $101 billion and employed approximately 22,000 people. It was rated as America's Most Innovative Company for six consecutive years from 1995 to 2001.

However, it filed for bankruptcy protection in the southern district of New York in late 2001!

How did this happen?

What made one of America's most innovative and admired companies file for bankruptcy?

Enron was originally involved in transmitting and distributing electricity and natural gas throughout the US. It was on *Fortune*'s 100 Best Companies to Work for in America list in 2000. Held in high esteem and known for its excellent people management practices, its pension plans made it one of the most sought after companies to work for.

However, very few were aware of what was happening behind the scenes. It was later revealed that many of Enron's recorded assets and profits were inflated or even fraudulent and non-existent. Debts and losses were put as 'offshore' since those were not included in the firm's financial statements.Enron had created offshore entities which were used for planning and avoiding taxes. It also helped the company to raise its profitability and made Enron look more profitable than it actually was. The company became a darling at the stock market, climbing new heights. But the reality was, the company was actually bleeding money.

Some of the employees were aware of what was happening inside the company so they began to sell their shares. Unfortunately, the investors had no clue about it.

In 2000, as the scandal unfolded, the value of its shares dropped from over $90 to just a few cents. Enron had always been considered a blue chip company so this was an unprecedented and disastrous event in the financial world. It was announced that much of its debts and the losses were not reported in its financial statements.

At the end of 2001, it was revealed that its reported financial condition was achieved through creative accounting fraud, known as the 'Enron scandal'. It made the company a symbol of corporate fraud and bad accounting practices. The scandal also unearthed the accounting practices of many corporations throughout the US, and resulted in the creation of the Sarbanes–Oxley Act of 2002. Since Arthur Andersen was the accounting firm for Enron, it led to a severe damage in the former's reputation and ultimately resulted in its dissolution. In 2001, Enron filed for bankruptcy, which was one of the biggest in the American history.

The bodyline incident is considered as the biggest black mark in the history of cricket. It tainted the reputation of England as a cricketing nation. Though more than seven decades have passed since the incident took place, it is still recalled as the worst phase in the history of cricket. The Enron event is a much recent one, but like the bodyline episode it too had a major worldwide impact. The Enron incident shook the corporate world just as the bodyline incident shook the cricketing world. The bodyline series resulted in the cricketing authorities making many changes to the rules of the game. Similarly, the Enron episode also resulted in the creation of new laws to ensure that such incidents don't happen in future.

In both the cases, there was a strong urge to 'win at all costs'. England knew that they would be facing a very strong Australian team and that too on their home soil. Enron was under pressure to maintain high revenues and profits. Both took the easy option—they broke the rules of the game to achieve their goals. Even today, the names Douglas Jardine and Enron evoke strong negative feelings.

Honesty is the Best Policy

(Stephen Fleming, MS Dhoni, Sachin Tendulkar, Ricky Ponting — 'Tata Code of Conduct', Tata Group)

'There is no pillow so soft as a clear conscience.'

— French Proverb

The examples in the previous chapter are very simple and straightforward because they clearly differentiate between right and wrong. Both the bodyline and Enron episodes are clear examples of violation of rules. However, not all incidents are so obvious. There are many examples where you may have to choose between 'what is technically legal and correct' and 'what is in the right spirit'.

In 2006, Sri Lanka played against New Zealand at Christchurch. Kumar Sangakkara, in a rescue act with Muralitharan, played a brilliant innings. When Sangakkara reached his century, Muralitharan, the non-striker, walked up to him to congratulate him. New Zealand wicket keeper Brendon McCullum took advantage of his opponent's negligence, and whipped off the bails. Since Muralitharan was outside his crease, the run out appeal was within the rules of the game and he was ruled out. Though New Zealand had played within the rules of cricket, it was against the spirit of the game. It was a great shock to the cricketing world.

The Sri Lankan team was bitter and shocked by McCullum's

act. Mahela Jayawardene said, 'we play in that kind of spirit. We wouldn't have done it, full stop'.

McCullum was unrepentant as he later said, 'as far as I'm concerned it was an opportunity to take a wicket. I'd do the same thing again.'

New Zealand skipper Stephen Fleming had the authority to annul the appeal and call back Muralitharan but he did not. Fleming maintained that he was 'more than comfortable' with the manner of the dismissal.

New Zealand was not punished for their behaviour since they were well within the rules of the game. Ironically, in the same year, New Zealand won the ICC Fair Play Award!

It is also ironical that the same New Zealanders still talk bitterly about the underarm delivery bowled many years back by Australia's Trevor Chappell. Australian captain Greg Chappell had instructed his younger brother Trevor to bowl an underarm delivery to avoid a last-ball defeat in an ODI against New Zealand. This incident was not a violation of the rules but against the spirit of the game.

During India's tour to England in 2011, the 2nd Test match was played at Trent Bridge. Eoin Morgan and Ian Bell were involved in a huge partnership. The last ball before tea break was hit by Morgan and the batsmen took 3 runs. It appeared as if Bell was going for the fourth run so the Indian fielder whipped off the bails and the batsman was declared out.

Since it was the last ball before tea break, the teams went into the pavilion immediately. During the tea break, the English coach Andy Flower and captain Andrew Strauss went to the Indian team's dressing room. They explained to the Indian coach Duncan Fletcher and Indian captain MS Dhoni that Bell was not attempting the fourth run and on the contrary, returning to the pavilion for tea. The Indian players had a team meeting and they saw the replays and concluded that Bell was probably not attempting the fourth run. They asked the umpires to reverse the decision and recall Bell.

When the Indian team came to field, the entire stadium initially booed the Indian team but the moment they realized what had happened, the spectators stood up and gave a standing ovation to the Indian team for upholding the spirit of the game. After the day's play, Bell was interviewed on TV. He was extremely happy with India's sportive gesture. He told that he had been very naive to have walked across when the ball was 'still in play' and not yet a 'dead ball'. He said that he was ready to accept the umpire's decision because as per the rules of the game, he was out. Though the Indians lost the match, they received accolades from thousands of English fans for playing the game in the right spirit.

There are two contrasting examples described here. In the first example, New Zealand chose to tread the path of 'following the rules but not the spirit of the game'. No one can question the umpire's decision but both Fleming and McCullum's stocks crashed in the eyes of the cricketing fraternity. In the second case, which was quite similar to the first one, the Indian captain showed a fine example of sportsman spirit. He acted as a role model for others.

The above examples are about teams that faced a moral dilemma. Let us take two more examples where the batsmen faced similar situations

During the 2011 World Cup, India played against West Indies at Chennai. Sachin Tendulkar edged a delivery from the West Indian fast bowler Ravi Rampaul. The umpire, Steve Davis ruled him 'not out' but Tendulkar just turned back and headed towards the pavilion. This was not the first time when Sachin Tendulkar had walked back to the pavillion without waiting for the umpire's decision. He had done it in the past and will continue to do so in the future. He showed that the gentleman's game is still alive and kicking. This gesture had the entire West Indian team applauding the Little Master.

This was in sharp contrast to what had happened on the previous day. In a game against Pakistan, Australia's Ricky Ponting edged the ball to wicket keeper Kamran Akmal. Ponting's edge was not spotted by umpire Marius Erasmus, so he did not declare him out. Even as Ponting stood his ground, the Pakistan fielders immediately referred the decision for a review. Ponting's batting partner Brad Haddin pushed two Pakistan fielders as they appealed to the umpire. The third umpire had no hesitation in ruling Ponting out. He was jeered by the packed cricket stadium as he made his way back to the dressing room.

What was even more brazen was Ponting's post-match confession, 'there were no doubts about the nick. I knew I had hit it'.

There are many similar instances in the corporate world too where we face such dilemmas. Ironically, when the rules are tough and rigid, it becomes simple to follow them because then it is easy to distinguish between right and wrong. Moral dilemma comes into play when things are not pure black and white but have shades of grey.

In the Indian corporate world, the first name that comes to our minds in terms of ethics and code of conduct is the Tata Group. The name Tata has been respected in India for 140 years for its strong values and business ethics.

Tata companies have always believed in returning wealth to the society they serve. Two-thirds of the equity of Tata Sons, the Tata promoter company, is held by philanthropic trusts that have created national institutions for science and technology, medical research, social studies, and performing arts. The trusts also provide aid and assistance to non-government organizations working in the areas of education, healthcare, and livelihoods. Tata companies also extend social welfare activities to communities around their industrial units. This pioneering spirit has been showcased by companies such as TCS, India's first software company, and Tata Motors.

The Tata Code of Conduct is a comprehensive document that serves as an ethical road map for Tata employees and companies, and provides the guidelines by which the group conducts its businesses. It consists of 25 clauses. These clauses cover different areas such as—working as per nation's interest, financial reporting, competition, equal opportunity employer, gifts & donations, interfacing with government agencies, political non-alignment, health, safety, environment, product quality, corporate citizenship, interactions within Tata companies, public representation, third party representation, use of Tata brand, group policies, shareholders, ethical conduct, regulatory compliance, concurrent employment, conflict of interest, handling of confidential information, protecting company's assets, citizenship, integrity of data, and reporting.

There have been numerous instances where the Tata companies have refused to take the bait and preferred to lose an important order or a prestigious project if the company had to compromise on its integrity and ethics. This has made Tatas the most respectable household name in the Indian industry.

Tatas had pioneered the aviation industry in India by setting up Tata Airlines in 1930s. Later, the Indian Government took over the company and the nationalised airline company became Air India. Ratan Tata always had a strong desire to re-enter the aviation industry. He wanted to setup a domestic airlines company in collaboration with Singapore Airlines. He had multiple discussions with the Indian Government. Frequent changes at the top meant that he had to meet three Prime Ministers of the country. He also had discussions with the Civil Aviation ministers and their officials.

During his interaction with the government officials, Ratan

Tata realized that in order to get the required approvals, he would have to compromise on Tata's code of conduct. It was reported in the press that he was expected to pay a bribe of ₹15 crore but he refused to compromise on the group's integrity. For fellow industrialists, this might have appeared as stupid decision because ₹15 crore was a very paltry amount for the Tatas. But for him, it was not the magnitude of the amount but a question of ethics and values. It is believed that Ratan Tata said, 'I did not want to go to the bed knowing well that I set up an airline by paying ₹15 crore'.

Good Corporate Citizen
(Steve Waugh — Jamnalal Bajaj, Bajaj Group)

'Never doubt that a small group of thoughtful, committed citizens can change the world. Indeed it is the only thing that ever has.'

— Margaret Mead

There are numerous instances where touring sides, especially from Australia, New Zealand, and England, struggle to cope up with the challenges of playing in the Indian subcontinent. It is very common to hear overseas players complain about the heat, dust, humidity, and food during their tour to India. These complaints reach a higher pitch if the overseas team loses any of the matches. Any illness is attributed to the spicy food and stomach upsets. One of the reasons why these teams struggle is because majority of them do not make an attempt to appreciate and adapt to the local environment, culture, and cuisine. Indians too face challenges of cold weather, wet conditions, and unfamiliar cuisine when they travel outside the subcontinent.

Former Australian captain Steve Waugh had a very different approach to this. He did not believe in complaining about the local environment, climate, and food because he knew that these things were beyond his control. He also knew that even if he complained to the highest authority, they would not be able to change any of this. His motto was to embrace the local favour and make it a part of your professional challenge. Rather than fight these changes, he accepted them with open arms. Steve Waugh was not a person who would bring tins of baked beans from Australia. Neither would he go around hunting for continental cuisine. He would always make it a point to imbibe the local culture. He would not hesitate to mingle with the local people in each of the cities that he visited. He would try different cuisines and not restrict himself to the food that he was familiar with. He also keenly explored life beyond cricket, even if it meant travelling through the dusty bylanes of a city. One such visit, during his Kolkata trip, led him to Udayan.

During one of Steve Waugh's visits to Kolkata, he had an opportunity to meet Mother Teresa and her Missionaries of Charity. Her work greatly inspired him and he realized that he could contribute in many areas other than cricket. In 1998, Waugh visited Udayan through the Calcutta Foundation. He was touched by the plight of hundreds of children who were affected by leprosy. His sincerity, hard work, and commitment ensured the timely completion of many initiatives, one of them being a dormitory for girls. He has been actively involved with Udayan for more than a decade now. Through his contributions and dedication, he has been able to change the lives of hundreds of underprivileged children. He continues to actively support Udayan through the Steve Waugh Foundation.

To quote his own words, 'India gave me this life-changing moment when I met Mother Teresa in Kolkata. While touring India during one of our games, I happened to visit the Missionaries of Charity and Mother whose work greatly inspired me. So meeting Mother Teresa was a catalyst. I got associated with Udayan where, I think, Reverend James Stevens has done an incredible job.'

Bajaj is one of the most famous names in the Indian corporate world. A few decades back, its name was synonymous with the most famous scooter manufactured and sold in India. The founder of Bajaj industries was Jamnalal Bajaj, an Indian industrialist, philanthropist, and freedom fighter.

Jamnalal Bajaj founded the Bajaj Group in 1926. The group has 24 companies. The flagship company is Bajaj Auto and other famous companies in the Bajaj Group are Mukand Ltd, Bajaj Electricals, and Bajaj Hindustan Ltd. Currently, one of his grandsons, Rahul Bajaj runs the prestigious Bajaj Auto.

Jamnalal Bajaj was born into a poor family and led a difficult childhood. He was the third son of Kaniram and Birdibai. He spent his initial years in a village near Sikar. Under the guidance of Seth Bachhraj, Jamnalal got involved in the family business of his grandfather. During this period, he acquired the skills of a tradesman which involved keeping accounts of buying and selling commodities. In 1926, he founded what would become the Bajaj group of industries.

Jamnalal Bajaj was not just an ordinary business entrepreneur. He was involved in many aspects that had a great impact on the Indian society. He was a close associate and follower of Mahatma Gandhi. It is believed that Gandhi too was very fond of him and looked upon him as his son.

Jamnalal's association with Gandhi began after the latter's return from South Africa. He was greatly impressed by Gandhi's path of 'ahimsa' or non-violence. He was convinced that India could achieve freedom only through non-violence. Jamnalal was also interested in Gandhi's initiatives like preferment of local industries, promotion of Hindi, and removal of untouchability.

Mahatma Gandhi firmly believed that India could eradicate poverty and become self-reliant only by manufacturing and consuming home-made goods. He asked people to boycott foreign goods since that neither generated jobs nor income for Indians. He promoted the usage of Khadi clothes which were made by village industries. Jamnalal Bajaj too took whole hearted interest in promoting Khadi and toured the entire country to promote it.

In 1925, he was chosen as the treasurer of the All India Spinners Association.

Since India is a land of many languages and culture, there was no unity among the Indians. The British cleverly exploited this major weakness. Gandhi was aware that Hindi was the most widely spoken language of the country and it was the only language that could unite all Indians. Jamnalal helped Gandhi pursue this dream of spreading Hindi. He was instrumental in publishing Hindi magazines and books and initiated the Gandhi Hindi Pustak Bhandar, a bookshop in Bombay. He also started a publishing house, the Sasta Sahitya Mandal. He was elected the president of the All India Hindi Sahitya Sammelan, a Literary Convention that promoted Hindi as the single language to unite all Indians. Subsequently, Jamnalal founded the Dakshin Bharat Hindi Prachar Sabha along with C. Rajagopalachari. This was done to spread Hindi across the southern states of India.

Along with Gandhi, Jamnalal fought against untouchability. He battled for admission of Harijans into the temples in his home town. When faced with stiff opposition from orthodox Hindu priests, he started his own temple. The Laxmi Narayan temple started by him in Wardha was open to all castes. He encouraged people to mix freely with the Harijans. Since Harijans were not allowed to use public wells, he built many new wells for them. In 1938, in recognition of his efforts, he was elected as the chief of the Jaipur Rajya Praja Mandal.

In honour of his social work, Jamnalal Bajaj Award has been instituted by the Bajaj Foundation. One of the top Management Institutes in the country, Jamnalal Bajaj Institute of Management Studies, bears the name of this legendary figure. Also JB Nagar, a locality in Mumbai, has been named after him.

Steve Waugh was one of the greatest captains and batsmen of Australia. Like Bajaj, he too played an important role in the activities that went beyond his profession. He did not restrict his life to cricket. He played a significant role in helping the underprivileged children of Kolkata. On the cricket field, he was known for his mental toughness and steely determination. He could disintegrate anyone with his mind games and sledging. But beneath this tough exterior, he had a heart of gold. There are millions of Indians who admire him for his cricketing successes. For hundreds of poor children in Udayan, he is their God.

Jamnalal Bajaj too was a man of many hues. He was a very famous industrialist and along with the Tatas and Birlas, formed the Indian trinity of industrialists. Though he was responsible for making Bajaj a household name in India, he was more than just a brilliant industrialist. Apart from an intelligent industrial brain, he had the Indian society in his heart and worked tirelessly for its upliftment. His philanthropic activities made him one of the most revered industrialists in India.

Graceful in Defeat

(Shahid Afridi, Kumar Sangakkara — Carly Fiorina, HP)

'Success is never final, failure is never fatal. It's courage that counts.'

— John Wooden

No one likes to fail and more importantly, no one likes to be associated with failures and failed people. As the well-known adage goes: Success has many fathers but failure is an orphan. In sports, everyone likes to be associated with world champions and Olympic gold medallists. The winners become the darling of crazy fans and media. The losers are treated like outcasts and untouchables.

It takes a lot of courage for the losing sportsmen to acknowledge their inadequacies and attribute their failures to their own performance rather than blame the opposition or the environment. It is very important that the losing team, especially the captain, remains graceful in defeat.

In some of the Asian countries like India, Pakistan, and Sri Lanka, cricket is a religion and the cricketers are treated as Gods. Passions run very high during all cricket matches, especially those involving these neighbouring countries. During the 2011 World Cup, India played and won against both its neighbours, Pakistan as well as Sri Lanka. During the tournament, there were contrasting behaviours by the two losing cricket captains.

India first defeated Pakistan in Mohali during the world cup semi-finals. Shahid Afridi, the skipper of the losing team made many disparaging remarks about India and Indians. What made a sad reading was the fact that his remarks were not just restricted to the eleven players of the Indian cricket team but also directed towards 1.27 billion Indians. His outburst in a subsequent interview was on communal lines. Rather than accept the fact that his team was outplayed by India, he talked about Indians, Pakistanis, and Muslims!

Shahid Afridi told the media that Indians were not large-hearted and could never be like Muslims and Pakistanis. He did not realize that India itself has a very high population of Muslims and thus his words made little sense. He didn't even spare the Indian media and allegedly told that Indian media was very negative in its approach and Pakistan media was hundred times better. Not surprisingly, even the Indian Muslims didn't approve of his outbursts.

The entire country was disappointed with Afridi's remarks. It was a well-known fact that Afridi had flown in his close family members and friends to Mohali to watch the semi-finals between the two nations. The local Punjabis felt completely let down by his stinging remarks because they had played excellent hosts to his family and ensured that they had an enjoyable free stay at Mohali. Instead of thanking his hosts for their love and affection, he made disparaging remarks about their country and people.

Contrast this immature prattle of Afridi with Kumar Sangakkara's behaviour which was as graceful as his silken-touch batting. Sri Lanka lost the 2011 World Cup finals against India in Mumbai. During the post-match presentation, a dejected but gracious Sangakkara was all praise for the Indian team's performance. He quipped, 'looks like you need to make something like 350 runs to put them under pressure.'

Sangakkara commended a few Indian cricketers including the winning captain MS Dhoni. He said that Indian batting was unbelievable; best in ODI cricket. He also said that MS Dhoni was a very intelligent and smart captain. He applauded Gautam Gambhir as one of the best left-hand players he had seen, and his partnership with Virat Kohli and MS Dhoni made the difference between the two sides.

The corporate world too is full of such stories. There are numerous instances where the fired CEO refuses to acknowledge his shortcomings and ends up making a messy exit. We also have a few cases where the CEOs themselves feel that they have failed in their job and step down gracefully.

Carly Fiorina served as the CEO of HP from 1999 to 2005. She initiated merger talks with Compaq in order to increase HP's market share in the field of computers. She faced stiff opposition from employees and stock holders and the biggest opposition came from Walter Hewlett, the eldest son of HP's co-founder Bill Hewlett. However, Carly chose to ignore all the opposition and went ahead with the merger. Unfortunately, the merger didn't perform as per her expectations. HP's stock had lost half of its value and the company was also facing stiff competition from Dell. People blamed Carly's lack of operational skills and her failure to set a proper focus. However, she was not convinced about her poor judgement. It needed a lot of courage to have initiated the merger between HP and Compaq, and even more courage to accept the blame of its failure. Carly had the courage to go ahead with the merger despite stiff opposition, but probably lacked the courage to own up her mistakes.

In one of the earlier chapters, I mentioned 'The HP Way' and how it made HP one of the most respected and admired companies in the world. However, this took a major beating during Carly Fiorina's tenure as the CEO. She focused on increasing the market share, earnings, and share price, but was not bothered about the traditional HP principles like respect, trust, and concern for people. Her obsession with numbers put

HP's values and ethics at constant risk. Carly's obsession in setting abnormally high sales targets resulted in sales executives engaging in 'channel stuffing'. Customers were offered huge discounts and other incentives to ensure that they purchase more than they originally planned. This had great short-term benefits because the monthly and quarterly targets were met. However, on the flip side, the long-term demand suffered since the customers were burdened with a large supply of HP's products. Carly also changed the company's reward and recognition systems. This again had negative consequences, undermining HP's collaborative culture that encouraged teamwork.

Carly Fiorina was struggling to meet her numbers on many occasions, and each time she found scapegoats for her failures. It is alleged that on one occasion, when she discovered that three of her executives had not met their targets, she fired them in a teleconference call held at five o'clock in the morning!

Her obsession with high sales targets didn't start at HP. Earlier at Lucent, Carly set similar high sales targets that resulted in her sales managers using a variety of tactics to boost sales. They indulged in 'channel stuffing' and loosening credit terms. Many deals happened with dot-com companies which went bankrupt without repaying the loans. Such sales practices were a major cause of Lucent's financial problems.

What differentiates a great leader from an ordinary one is the courage to own up mistakes. Every leader is forced to take numerous risks for the success of the company and each risk is fraught with danger. As a leader, if you are lucky, you can pull it off. However, on more than one occasion, you are bound to fail and the media, shareholders, and the board will be sharpening their knives. The best way to counter such attacks is to stand up and acknowledge the mistakes that led to your failure; something that Carly and Afridi probably failed to do.

4

EXECUTION

'Go and get five photocopies of these extremely important documents immediately!'
EXTREMELY IMPORTANT DOCUMENTS
Sure!
'Why is it taking so long?'
?
EXTREMELY HEAVY DUTY
SHREDDER
Garbage

Tracking and Governance
(South African Cricket Team—Iridium)

'He who controls the present, controls the past. He who controls the past, controls the future.'

—George Orwell

South Africa has one of the best cricket teams in the world but unfortunately they've never won the World Cup. There were at least two instances where their exit from the tournament was due to poor execution. The first instance was during the match against Australia in the semi-finals of the 1999 World Cup, and the second instance was against Sri Lanka in one of the qualifying rounds of the 2003 World Cup.

South Africa played against Australia in the 1999 World Cup semi-finals at Edgbaston, Birmingham, England. Australia batted first and scored 213 runs in their allotted 50 overs. At the end of their 49 overs, South Africa was at 205 runs for the loss of 9 wickets. They needed nine runs off the last over, with one wicket remaining. Lance Klusener and Allan Donald were at the crease.

Luckily for the South Africans, the strong hitting Lance Klusener was taking strike at the beginning of the 50th over. The first two balls from the Australian fast bowler Damien Fleming were promptly despatched to the boundary by Klusener. Suddenly, the target was reduced from 9 runs in 6 balls to just 1 run in 4 balls. The South Africans had all the opportunity to just tap the ball gently and amble across for a single—and they had 4 balls to do that!

Klusener hit the 3rd ball straight to Darren Lehmann. There was no run in that shot but Alan Donald, the non-striker, ran for a quick single. He managed to survive because Lehmann's throw didn't hit the stumps. Despite this close call, the South African committed hara-kiri of the next ball. The 4th ball was straight hit to Mark Waugh, one of the best fielders in the Australian side. There was no run in it, and the South Africans still had 2 more balls to attempt the single. No one knows what was going on in the minds of Klusener and Donald.It is quite likely that they were either not tracking the number of balls left or the number of runs required. Despite the ball going straight to Mark Waugh, they decided to run for a quick single. Waugh threw the ball to Fleming who in turn threw it to Gilchrist, who broke the stumps. When the South African innings folded, there were still 2 balls remaining to be bowled!

The South Africans were tied at the same score as the Australians. Since the Australians had finished higher than the South Africans in the Super Six round, the former qualified for the finals. The Australians went on to win the finals and the World Cup Trophy, and the South Africans returned home empty handed and devastated by the result.

If the South Africans had over-estimated the target in the 1999 World Cup, then it was quite the opposite during their last match of World Cup 2003.

During the qualifying round, hosts South Africa played against Sri Lanka in Kingsmead, Durban. Batting first, the Sri Lankans scored 268 for the loss of 9 wickets. The match was interrupted due to rain and this resulted in the target getting revised to 230 runs to be scored in 45 overs.

At the time of rain interruption, two of South Africa's greatest 'finishers'—Lance Klusener and Mark Boucher were batting.

When the game resumed, the South African team gave a slip of paper to the batsmen. This contained a table showing the number of runs required after each ball to equal the Sri Lankan total based on Duckworth Lewis (D/L) method. Unfortunately, the two batsmen at the crease got confused. They assumed that the table showed the number of runs required to win and not tie!

Because of this, on the last ball of the innings, they decided not to risk a single because they felt they were ahead as per D/L method whereas in reality, they were tied to the Sri Lankan score! This resulted in South Africa losing the opportunity to qualify for the Super Sixes. It was extremely disappointing for the South African spectators because their home team, despite being one of the best in the world, had been eliminated in the preliminary round.

In 1985, Bary Bertiger, an engineer from Motorola went on a holiday with his wife to Bahamas. His wife complained that she couldn't reach her friends and clients using her mobile phone due to the non-availability of cellular network. Bary Bertiger and two more engineers felt that the only solution to this problem was to develop low earth-orbiting satellites that would allow communication from any remote corner of the globe. This was the origin of the 'Iridium' concept.

Though Bary's superiors rejected this idea due to the high costs involved, Bob Galvin, the CEO of Motorola approved the Iridium project. He felt that with this product, Motorola could show its technological prowess to the entire world. In 1991, Motorola established Iridium Limited Liability Corporation as a separate entity. Motorola, with an investment of $400 million had a 25% stake in the company. Though the Iridium project was a technology marvel with 66 low earth-orbiting satellites, it had many challenges ahead.

Since Iridium phones were quite bulky and expensive, it was always looked at as a supplement rather than an alternative to cellular phones. When the Iridium project was first conceived, the cellular phone technology was in its infancy and had a low coverage base. Because of this, it was estimated that Iridium would start with a subscriber base of around 5,00,000.

Unfortunately the Iridium project suffered many delays and by then cellular technology had advanced so much that it was able to install cellular base stations even in remote areas. The potential subscriber base of Iridium had eroded by more than 75%. However, the project team at Iridium was neither tracking the project delays nor the erosion in potential subscriber base.

Iridium also suffered from manufacturing problems. One of its suppliers, Kyocera was having software problems and this delayed the delivery of the phones in the market. However, no one at Iridium seemed to be tracking this delay. They decided to go ahead with the product launch during which neither the service providers were ready nor the handsets geared up for mass production.

It was not just the project execution delays that went unnoticed. The Iridium phone suffered from major design flaws too. It depended on line-of-sight communication between the phone's antenna and the satellite; hence, subscribers could not use it in cars, inside buildings, and areas that had tall edifices. The size of the handset was also huge, especially compared to the sleek cellular phones that were bombarding the consumer market.

The product was officially launched on 1st November 1998, by the American Vice President Al Gore. At the time of its launch, the cost of a handset was $3,000 and the cost of a call was $3–$8 per minute! This made the Iridium phones prohibitively expensive. Due to high costs and poor design, the company had just 10,000 customers in April 1999, forcing its high-profile CEO Edward Staiano to resign. By June, the company fired 15% of its staff, and two months later, it filed for Chapter 11 bankruptcy. The Iridium share price which had started at $20 per share during its

IPO, and had risen once to $72 had now sunk to $3. By November 1999, NASDAQ had delisted Iridium shares in the share market.

Some of these problems could have been avoided if the senior management was closely monitoring the project with respect to schedule and product performance. Unfortunately, this did not happen due to insufficient governance. Iridium board had 28 directors, and 27 of them were either Iridium employees or Iridium's partners. This resulted in the lack of objective and 'outside-in' view. Most of the directors were inward looking which led to inadequate corporate oversight.

South Africa was involved in two tied matches in the World Cup, and in both these games they were in a strong position to win the match. But due to poor execution and tracking of their end goals, they could not force a victory. It was heart breaking for South African fans to watch their team commit such hara-kiri, not once but on two occasions.

Like the South African side, Iridium project too had all the recipes for success. In both the cases, core competency was never an issue. The teams had the required skills to execute a winning story. Unfortunately, both floundered during the execution phase. South Africa made a hash of the run chase because they didn't seem to be tracking the number of runs required for victory. Similarly, Iridium was neither tracking the changes in the global cellular market like better coverage lower costs, etc., nor was it tracking internal issues such as poor product design, high product cost, etc. There was no one in the organization who could declare that the product was becoming financially unviable and this resulted in the loss of billions of dollars to the company. A proper governance model could probably have saved Iridium from bankruptcy.

Goals to Actions

(VVS Laxman, Rahul Dravid — Boeing 747)

'The test of character is having the ability to meet challenges.'

—Walter Annenberg

Australia, under the captaincy of Steve Waugh, toured India in 2001. The second Test match of the series was played at the famous Eden Gardens, Kolkata. Australia batted first and scored a mammoth 445 runs. In reply, India crumbled for just 171 runs. Since India was trailing by 274 runs, Steve Waugh asked India to 'follow-on'.

In the second innings, India was off to a decent start, but nowhere close to match the Australian total. India lost its first opener Ramesh at the score of 52 and by the time the score reached 97, even its second opener Das was back in the pavilion. Disaster struck when Sachin Tendulkar got out for a paltry 10 runs, and India was at 115 for the loss of 3 wickets. When Indian skipper Saurav Ganguly got out for 48, the writing was on the wall. India at 232 for the loss of 4 wickets seemed to be dead and buried.

In walked VVS Laxman to join Rahul Dravid who was batting at the other end. Both Laxman and Dravid knew that they had a herculean task ahead of them. The team still trailed by 42 runs with the last 'recognized pair' at the crease.

The situation was daunting enough for any batsman to throw in the towel and call it quits. The normal reaction of the batsmen would be to defend each and every ball. The problem with such an approach is that the score board does not keep ticking and it just takes one good ball to get the batsman out. When that happens, the opposition has a small target to chase. Dravid and Laxman were aware that there was plenty of time still left in the match so it was pointless to just try and block every ball. Hence, they both decided to play their natural game. The good balls were defended and the bad ones were promptly despatched to the boundary.

The two batsmen decided to take session by session. Instead of getting over-awed by the seemingly hopeless situation, they decided to break their tasks into many small milestones and tried to achieve them. Their first milestone was to wipe off the deficit of 274 runs which they did effortlessly. Next was to build a sizeable lead so that their bowlers could have a defendable target. Dravid and Laxman slowly built up a huge partnership which was worth 376 runs for the 5th wicket. When Laxman departed after scoring 281 runs, India's total looked a healthy 608 runs. India was already leading by 334 runs and its lead had risen to 355 runs by the time Rahul Dravid departed after scoring 180 runs. The Indian innings finally ended at 657 runs and Australia needed 384 runs for victory. Some fine piece of bowling by Harbhajan Singh and Sachin Tendulkar saw Australians collapse for just 212 runs, losing the match by 171 runs!

This match is considered one of India's finest victories of the century specifically for two reasons. First, it was against the mighty Australians on an Eden Gardens wicket which is known to assist bowlers. Second, because Indians managed to win from a seemingly impossible situation.

The partnership of 376 runs for the 5th wicket between Dravid and Laxman is rated as the best partnership for any wicket—not in terms of the number of runs but in terms of the quality of batting. VVS Laxman's innings of 281 runs is rated by many cricketing pundits as the best innings by any Indian batsman in a Test cricket.

An equally overwhelming situation was faced by Boeing during 1960s when they had to design and manufacture the Boeing 747, popularly known as the 'jumbo jet'.

In the area of commercial jet aircrafts, Boeing had the hugely successful Boeing 707 which competed with Douglas' DC-8. However, air travel had begun to increase in most countries across Europe and the US. This led to frequent congestion of airports because the small aircrafts were not sufficient to carry the huge number of passengers. Juan Trippe, the president of Pan Am, one of Boeing's most important customers, felt a strong need to have an aircraft which was twice the size and capacity of Boeing 707. He explained that this was the only way to handle airport congestion problem.

With this requirement in mind, Boeing conceived a plan to design Boeing 747 which would be two and a half times the size of Boeing 707 aircraft. The entire airline industry was shocked because this seemed to be a near impossible task. There were many even within Boeing who felt that this ambition was doomed for failure. The only person who seemed to have the conviction and confidence was William Allen, the president of Boeing.

Boeing faced huge challenges at every step. To start with, it did not even have a manufacturing plant which was large enough to assemble the new model. They decided to build a new plant to cater to the new model. The company evaluated 50 locations before finalizing on a site adjoining a military base at Paine Field, Washington. The 780 acre site was 30 miles north of Seattle. At that point of time, it was one of the biggest buildings by volume.

The next major challenge was to get a level ground. For this, more than 4 million cubic yards of earth had to be moved. Malcolm Stamper, the head of the company's turbine division, was asked to oversee the construction of the new factory.

The lead time for construction of the plant was very high and William Allen knew that the design of the prototype would get delayed if the tasks were handled in a sequential manner. He decided to go ahead with the prototype design and manufacture even before the factory had a roof above it!

Initially, the design had a full length double deck fuselage with rows of 8 seats on the lower deck and rows of 7 seats on the upper deck. Both the decks were to have two aisles. This design had to be modified due to concerns of over evacuation speed and cargo carrying capacity. The modified design had a wider single deck design. The cockpit was, therefore, placed on a shortened upper deck so that a freight-loading door could be included in the nose cone.

Since it had to meet stringent safety requirements, the design had to take care of structural redundancy, hydraulic system redundancy, etc. In order to handle the huge size and weight of 747, it was decided to try a new engine. The high bypass turbo fan engine was installed because it could deliver double the power of the earlier turbojets but at just one-third of the original fuel consumption. The 'Fault Tree Analysis' methodology was used to understand the effects of the failure of a particular component on the rest of the system.

The challenges of Boeing didn't stop here. During the 'test flights' they faced problem with the engines due to rapid throttle movements and distortion of turbine casings. Because of these engine problems, many aircrafts in the manufacturing plant were stranded. This, in turn, delayed the aircraft deliveries by several months.

The enormous cost in building the new plant and designing the Boeing 747 resulted in the organization having to borrow from the banks. As the project deliveries kept getting repeatedly delayed, it had to request for additional funding. Even members of the management team had grown restless. William Allen, the president, kept egging on. His perseverance and conviction finally succeeded and the 747 turned out to be one the most successful models not only for Boeing but for the entire avionics industry. It earned the nickname 'Queen of the Skies' and achieved iconic status in no time.

The ability to overcome difficult challenges successfully was the key to success of the Dravid–Laxman partnership and the Boeing 747 launch. In both cases, the situation looked hopelessly impossible in the beginning but turned around in the end.

In most cricket matches, the team which 'follows on' invariably collapses in the 2nd innings. This happens because the team crumbles under psychological pressure. However, this did not happen in the Kolkata test. So what did Dravid and Laxman do differently?

Firstly, they weren't overawed by the situation because they had the conviction and self-belief that they could overcome the challenge.

Secondly, they broke down their goal into small achievable tasks. Their first task was to steady the Indian innings which they did by not losing their wickets. Next, they had to wipe out the huge deficit. Once this was achieved, they went about building a lead which was good enough for their bowlers to defend.

In the case of Boeing, it decided to design and manufacture a type of aircraft which no one had dared to. There was enough of cynicism within and outside the organization but Boeing executed its plan in an immaculate manner that led to its success. The employees faced many challenges on the design, manufacturing, and financial front but they were equal to the challenge. They broke down the Boeing 747 Program into small achievable tasks and went about accomplishing them. The company showed that proper project execution could help overcome even the most difficult challenges.

KEEP IT SIMPLE, STUPID! [KISS]

(VIRENDER SEHWAG—GOOGLE)

'In character, in manner, in style, in all things, the supreme excellence is simplicity.'

—H.W. Longfellow

Virender Sehwag, popularly known as Viru or 'Nawab of Najafgarh', is one of India's leading batsmen. He is also one of the most destructive batsmen in the world.

Sehwag had a very ordinary ODI debut against Pakistan in 1999. His first success came only in his 4th ODI match against Australia in Bangalore where he scored 58 runs off 54 balls and took three wickets. This earned him his first Man of the Match award.

During the triseries in 2001, involving Sri Lanka and New Zealand, Sehwag was promoted to the opening slot because Sachin Tendulkar, the regular Indian opener, was injured. Sehwag seized this opportunity with both hands and scored his first ODI century off just 69 balls. At that point in time, this was the 3rd fastest century by an Indian.

Sehwag's philosophy was very simple—'smack the ball out of the ground'. This led to a perception that Sehwag's aggressive batting style was more suited for ODIs than Test matches because the field restrictions in ODIs allowed him to loft the ball over the in-fielders. Hence, despite his century in Sri Lanka, he was not selected for the Test team.

He finally made his debut against South Africa in late 2001 where he scored a century on his Test debut in the 1st Test at Bloemfontein. Inspite of scoring a century on debut against one of the best bowling attacks in the world, and that too on a fast paced wicket, many cynics felt that Sehwag's century was just a flash in the pan. However, his performance over the years has proved his detractors wrong.

Sehwag has always played with a very unorthodox technique and a carefree attitude. The cricket coaches express shock at his footwork, or lack of it. His adventurous mind-set and lofting the ball in the air has brought about his dismissal on numerous occasions. However, he has also had a very high degree of success. Unlike many players who pour over their videos, studying their faults, and try ironing them out, Sehwag has a very simple approach to the game. He plays each ball with a very simple attitude—'if it's a bad ball then it needs to be hit'.

There was a time when Sehwag, like many other players, went through a lean period. His big scores had dried up and the critics were baying for his blood. There were comments about his inability to score on the leg-side. The opposition bowlers too declared that they could control Sehwag by bowling inswingers directed towards the middle and leg stump. His poor footwork made matters worse, especially on seaming tracks.

When any cricketer loses form, he spends the next few weeks studying his batting techniques. If he is an Indian cricketer then it makes matters worse because he has to listen to the advice of 1.2 billion Indians! There have been many instances where players have lost their natural abilities due to excessive analysis—commonly known as 'analysis-paralysis'. Luckily Sehwag was not in this mould. Despite advices from his coach and others, he refused to drastically change his natural game. The only change he brought into his game was to improve his ability to score on the leg side. The runs and the big centuries returned.

One of his early big scores came against Australia at Melbourne Cricket Ground in 2003 when he scored 195 runs. In 2004, he became the first Indian to score a triple century in Test cricket when he scored 309 against Pakistan in the 1st Test in Multan. This was Sehwag's sixth century in 21 Tests. He broke his own record when he scored 319 runs against South Africa in March 2008 at Chennai.

Sehwag broke the record for the fastest century in ODI by an Indian when he scored 100 runs off just 60 balls against New Zealand in 2009.

Though the sceptics predicted that Sehwag's fast-paced risky style would result in him making quick but brief scores, the reality was completely different! His last 11 centuries have been over 150 runs, surpassing even Sir Donald Bradman's record of 7 consecutive centuries with scores beyond 150 runs.

He and Tendulkar are the only Indians who have scored 200 plus runs on six occasions. He is the only Indian batsman to have scored a triple century and that too on two occasions. He is one of the four batsmen in the world to score two triple centuries.

In 2009, Sehwag was honoured the 'Wisden Leading Cricketer in the World' award for his performance in 2008, and the next year, he became the first person in the world to retain the award. He was also awarded Arjuna Award in 2002 and Padma Shree in 2010.

Google Inc. is an American multinational company which is a leader in the areas of Internet searches, Internet based advertising, and other related Internet services and products. The company was founded by Larry Page and Sergey Brin while they were studying at Standford University. The company was incorporated in September 1998.

Google was not the first Internet search engine. Major companies like Yahoo and Microsoft were already in the arena. However, what differentiated Google from its competitors was its simplicity. It had an extremely user-friendly and intuitive interface without any unnecessary buttons and links. Its competitors had too much of information and data on the home page which scared the common user. Google's plain white uncluttered home page made even the most Internet-illiterate user feel comfortable.

Very few people know that the home page design was by accident. In 1998, Google's founders Sergey Brin and Larry Page did most of the coding for their search engine. The company did not have a Webmaster and Brin did not prefer HTML. Because of this, he designed a very 'basic homepage' which just served the purpose of initiating a search.

Google has one of the simplest home pages on the Internet. It has just 30 words, a six-letter coloured logo 'Google', and a simple but big search-box. During the initial days, Google users got confused by its simplicity. The white spaces on the page made users feel that it was not fully loaded and would therefore wait for the rest of the page to load!

Though the search engine seems to appear very simple for the end-user, the actual technology that powers it is very complex. In a fraction of a second, it can solve the most complex equations and display millions of results.

Google's simplicity was not restricted just to its user-friendly interface. Though the requirement of the search engine was to hunt and display millions of files in a fraction of a second, Google used a very simple hardware to achieve this. Their first search engine was built with just 30 PCs running on Linux operating system. Linux was chosen because it was reliable, easy to customize, simple to use, and more importantly, it was free!

Google focused on building extremely innovative and powerful algorithms to achieve great speeds while keeping the hardware very simple and inexpensive. They developed some of the finest data indexing and retrieval algorithms in the industry. The system architecture was so modular and scalable that even today, though the number of machines has gone up by thousands, the basic architecture has remained almost unchanged.

Marissa Mayer, former director of consumer web products at Google, compared Google with a Swiss Army knife which is 'closed'—something that is simple and can be slipped in your pocket but has lots of useful tools built within. She remarked that their competitors were like an 'open' Swiss Army knife that could be intimidating and occasionally harmful.

Google also optimized on the number of results that are displayed per page. They tried experimenting with three options—10, 20, and 30 results per page. They discovered that putting 30 results per page was more time consuming and because of this there were one-fifth fewer searches. Based on this finding, they reduced the number of results per page which helped them achieve 0.5 million results in less than 0.2 seconds. Google knew that if the speed was high then people would search more, and if people searched more, their search engine would be the most sought after in the industry. This, in turn, would result in higher revenues.

Today, Google has become synonymous with 'search' and it is quite common to see people using it as a verb: 'Can you please google this information?'

Innovation can be quite a paradox because on one hand, people want more features, functions, power, and speed and on the other hand, they want a very simple user interface. It is always a big challenge to strike the right balance between the two. Many of the products fail because in an attempt to add more features, simplicity is sacrificed. The products become so complicated and cumbersome that the users get intimidated and stay away from it. The success lies in those products that might be difficult to create but be simplest to use.

In an industry where there is a constant tussle between adding more features and making the product simple, Google came up as the clear winner. Their simple homepage combined with extremely high speed made Google the darling of Internet users and soon it became the world leader in online search engines.

Benchmark the Best
(Virender Sehwag, VVS Laxman — Toyota, Dell Inc., McDonald's)

'People never improve unless they look to some standard or example higher and better than themselves.'

— Tyron Edwards

Virender Sehwag, one of the most destructive batsmen in the world has modelled his game on Sachin Tendulkar's. As a young boy, he would often watch his idol, Tendulkar bat on TV and later, try and imitate his batting style while playing in the fields of Najafgarh. Unlike some of the celebrity actors and sportsmen who don't like to disclose the names of the people whom they admire and imitate, Sehwag has no such qualms. He has told on numerous occasions that 'Sachin Tendulkar is my role model and the only reason why I am playing cricket.'

Sehwag rates Sachin Tendulkar's double hundred as one of the finest innings he has ever seen and unabashedly said, 'I can watch it in a theatre a hundred times. I already have a CD which I will copy on my laptop's hard disk and watch it any time I want.'

Both Tendulkar and Sehwag are short in stature and have very similar batting styles. On many occasions, when they are batting together, it is difficult to differentiate between the two. The 'master' and the 'pupil' have shared many great partnerships together. Though Sehwag started off as a fan of Tendulkar, he has carved a niche for himself. His awesome batting record has made him a legend in his own right.

VVS Laxman has been one of India's most stylish middle order batsmen. Laxman grew up playing cricket in Hyderabad, the city of former Indian captain Mohammed Azharuddin. Right from his early days, Laxman looked upon Azharuddin as his role model. Azharuddin was a sweet-timer of the ball and was extremely wristy. His supple wrists allowed him to play against the spin and hit the ball to any part of the ground. Laxman too developed the same skills as his idol. He too became one of the best timers of the ball and his wrist-work was absolutely brilliant. He was one of the few batsmen in the world who could flick a ball outside the off stump to the midwicket boundary for a four. Laxman has also confessed that his footwork resembled David Gower's. David Gower, former England batsman, was also one of the greatest timers of the cricket ball and a delight to watch.

One of the most common concepts in corporate world is 'benchmarking'. This is quite similar to the above examples. However, it is important to note that you need to analyse the situation before you adopt another company as your benchmark. If the circumstances are different then blindly aping another company is a sure shot recipe for disaster.

After the Second World War, the Japanese automobile industry faced a major crisis in terms of sales, revenue, and profitability. Majority of the Japanese automobile companies tried to benchmark their style of operations with their American counterparts. However, they realized that they could not adopt the American way because of many reasons. Firstly, the American car manufacturers produced in 'lots' which was not suitable for the Japanese market since it was comparatively small. Secondly, since the Japanese customers were very cost conscious, the pressure to maintain low manufacturing costs was extremely important.

In order to reduce the manufacturing cycle-time and costs, Toyota adopted the 'Just-In-Time' (JIT) concept which was aimed at reducing the inventory levels in the shopfloor, cutting manufacturing cycle-time, eliminating wastes, and enhancing product quality.

As a part of JIT implementation, Toyota set up the following practices:

1. Changed the equipment layout on the shopfloor to reduce transporting the raw materials back and forth between machines.
2. Introduced the concept of 'Kanban'—a technique where the raw material is brought into the shopfloor just in time for their introduction into the assembly. In the traditional 'Kanban' system, cards are used to signal the need to take action. The action could even be procuring raw materials from the supplier.
3. Toyota worked very closely with its suppliers to optimize the supply chain management of the organization. This helped in having very low inventory levels in its stores and shopfloor.
4. It introduced the concept of SMED (Single Minute Exchange of Die) to reduce setup time required while moving from one product to another on the shopfloor. The traditional way of re-tooling used to take several days whereas the SMED reduced it around 30 minutes!

All these continual improvements helped Toyota achieve reduced cycle time for manufacturing, less inventory, better cash flow, enhanced product quality, and higher levels of customer satisfaction.

Buoyed by the success of Toyota, there were lots of companies that benchmarked and successfully adopted the JIT philosophy. Dell was one of the pioneers in the IT industry that adopted this strategy with great success.

Michael Dell introduced the concept of 'Built-To-Order' in the computer industry. Instead of the traditional method of building computers and then trying to sell them, Dell did exactly the opposite! Only after a person placed an order for a Dell computer on the Internet does the company swing into action. The company does not possess the components needed to execute an order until that order is placed, but it is still capable of executing the order within the best possible lead time.

Once an order is placed, Dell receives the components from the suppliers. The components are assembled and tested at one of Dell's manufacturing sites and then the computers are shipped to the customer. Dell has an excellent relationship with their suppliers so their supply chain management process has been highly successful. This ensures that the supplier is able to deliver just in time to the shopfloor resulting in almost a zero dead inventory in the shopfloor.

As in the case of Toyota, the layout of assembly equipments on Dell's manufacturing line are organized in a manner that ensures seamless assembly process. The supplier loads the components in his truck and drives his vehicle right up to the Dell shopfloor. The parked vehicle resembles a 'mini stores' and is almost an extension of Dell's manufacturing line!

Dell too achieved a great deal of success using the JIT concept. Though Dell had the 'first mover advantage' in introducing the 'Built-to-Order' system, its competitors benchmarked Dell and introduced similar systems and processes!

It is important to note that even if you are a pioneer in introducing a new product or a system, the 'first mover advantage' that you gain will be short-lived. Your competitors will swiftly benchmark you and imbibe your processes. The only way to stay ahead of competition is to keep innovating new products, techniques, and processes.

McDonald's Corporation is the world's largest chain of

hamburger fast food restaurants. It is headquartered in the US and has operations in more than 100 countries. It has also deployed the JIT concept successfully.

During the initial days, McDonalds would cook a batch of hamburgers and keep them under heat lamps. Because of this, the customers invariably didn't get freshly cooked hamburgers. This resulted in low sales and the company had to throw away the unsold hamburgers.

McDonald's realized that the only way to boost sales and customer satisfaction was by giving the customers hot and fresh hamburgers. It decided to adopt the 'Just-In-Time' concept for their kitchen. This meant that the hamburgers were no longer pre-cooked and stored. Once a customer placed an order at the counter, the backend team in the kitchen swung into action and executed the order. Though this had the advantage of low wastage, it had an inherent disadvantage of the customer having to wait till his order was processed. This meant that the cooking and assembly cycle time had to be as short as possible. To improve the cooking cycle time, McDonald's decided to install some highly sophisticated burger making equipments. McDonald's also trained its staff to execute customers' orders in a swift manner. Since hamburger is considered as 'fast food', the customer at McDonald's would be much more conscious of the 'waiting time' than a customer at a traditional restaurant.

Like Toyota and Dell, McDonald's also achieved great success in terms of high customer satisfaction, low inventory costs, and less wastage. Since the customers were served with freshly prepared hamburgers, it was quite natural that they welcomed this. Low inventories had one more advantage for McDonald's. Unlike Toyota and Dell where the raw materials are non-perishable items such as mechanical and electronic components, in McDonald's the raw material consist of perishable ingredients like meat, vegetables, and cheese. Since McDonald's was able to drastically reduce its inventory levels, it could eliminate wastage of unused raw materials.

These examples show how we can succeed if we have role models or if we benchmark ourselves with the best in business. Virender Sehwag became one of the best stroke players in the world like his idol Sachin Tendulkar. VVS Laxman's artistry and sweet-timing was a delight to watch and could be matched only to his role models—his fellow Hyderabadi Mohammed Azharuddin and former England player David Gower.

There are two important points to note about benchmarking and having role models in the corporate world. Firstly, you need not restrict your benchmarking to companies that make similar products. For example, Toyota made JIT very popular in the automobile manufacturing industry but the companies that emulated this concept with a great degree of success were from completely different industries such as computers (Dell) and food (McDonald's).

Secondly, you can have more than one role model for your organization. Let us consider this. Toyota is known for its innovative manufacturing practices, Unilever is renowned for HR practices,Tatas are famous for their fair play, Singapore Airlines has one of the best customer services in the airline industry, and when it comes to branding you can't beat Coca Cola. If you want to benchmark yourself with the best then you can treat Toyota, Unilever, Singapore Airlines, and Coke as role models for your manufacturing, HR, customer service, and advertising functions and bond them together with a sound foundation of ethics that you have learnt from the Tatas!

Consistency in Performance
(Donald Bradman — Microsoft)

'If you don't see yourself as a winner, then you cannot perform as a winner.'

—ZigZiglar

Sir Donald Bradman has been acknowledged as one of the greatest batsmen in the world. He made his debut in 1928 and retired in 1948. Despite losing more than five years due to the World War, he established lots of world records. Some of his records are still intact and seem likely to remain so in the years to come.

Few know that his cricketing journey started in the most modest manner. During his childhood, he used to practise with the help of a cricket stump and a golf ball. He had modified the game so that he could play alone. Behind his home, he had a water tank which was mounted on a curved brick stand. He would hit the curved brick stand, using the cricket stump and the golf ball. When the ball would rebound, he would again hit it back. His game was similar to modern day squash.

Bradman hit his first century at the age of 12. Though he had a very ordinary debut against England, he scored a century in his second Test match. There was no looking back after this. Most of his matches were against England since they were the major cricket playing nation apart from Australia. Such was his consistency with the bat that England devised bodyline tactics primarily to contain Bradman.

Bradman played his final Test at The Oval against England. His batting average was an astounding 101.39 and he received a standing ovation from all the spectators who had come to witness 'The Don' for the last time. Unfortunately, he got out for a second-ball duck and his Test average dropped down marginally to 99.94. England batted poorly so they lost the match by an innings and because of this, Australia did not bat the second time. Since Bradman did not bat again, his Test career ended with an average just below 100. Bradman later confessed that his eyes were moist with emotions and he could not see the ball properly! Had he scored just four runs in his last innings, he would have averaged 100 runs per innings!

What differentiated Bradman from other batsmen was his sheer consistency and appetite for big scores.

Bradman's excellent record has resulted in the word 'Bradmanesque' being coined to denote consistency and high performance. His consistency can be seen from the fact that he scored a century or a double century in more than 50% of his innings. He had a tally of 12 double centuries and 2 triple centuries during his cricketing career.

In the 52 tests that he played, he scored 6,996 runs studded with 29 centuries and 13 half centuries. He averaged more than 100 in seven calendar years. His high level of consistency made former Australian captain Bill Woodfullsay, 'Bradman is worth three batsmen to Australia!'

In 1979, the Australian government awarded him the 'Companion of the Order of Australia' which was the country's second highest civilian honour. He became the first living Australian to have a museum dedicated to him. In 2008, the Royal Australian Mint issued $5 gold coins with his image. In 2009, he was inducted into the ICC Cricket Hall of Fame.

In the corporate world too, what distinguishes a great company from a good company is consistency whcih has to be maintained in all respects—share value, revenues, profits, customer satisfaction, innovation, and product quality. One of the biggest names in the IT Industry that is known for delivering great performance consistently is Microsoft Corporation.

Microsoft is an American multinational corporation headquartered in Redmond, USA. It develops and supports a wide range of products and services primarily in the area of computer software. It was established in 1975 by Bill Gates and Paul Allen, and became a household name during 1980s with its MS-DOS operating systems. It has continued to rule the IT world through its products like Microsoft Windows, Microsoft Office, and other popular applications.

During 1980s, along with Microsoft there were many other great computer companies like Digital Equipment Corporation, Wang Laboratories, Compaq, etc. Unfortunately some of these companies cease to exist today. Either they have closed down or have been bought over by competitors. However, Microsoft is still going strong. In the year 2013, it had a revenue of $77.85 billion and a net income of $21.86 billion. Its total assets were worth $142.43 billion.

What did Microsoft do that others failed to do? It consistently produced great products. Let us look at two of Microsoft's greatest products—Microsoft Office and Microsoft Windows.

Microsoft Office is an office suite of desktop applications for Microsoft Windows and Mac OS X operating systems. It was first developed in August 1989, and over the years it has grown with increasing number of features and user-friendly applications.

The first version of Microsoft Office for Windows was commercially available from October 1990 and consisted of Word, Excel, and PowerPoint applications. This was followed with Microsoft Office 1.5 and later 1.6. Microsoft Access was added to the package and was released as Microsoft Office Professional.

The Microsoft Office 3.0 was released in August 1992 and it became the first version of Office to be available on CD-ROM. In 1994, Microsoft Office 4.0 was released followed by Microsoft Office 4.2 for Windows NT. Microsoft Office 4.3 was released as the 16-bit version while Microsoft Office 95 was released in August 1995 to cater to 32-bit requirements.

Microsoft Office 97 had lots of new features and introduced command bars. It also had natural Language Systems and the ability to check grammar. It was also the first version to include Office Assistant. Microsoft Office 2000 had adaptive menu and introduced a new security feature using digital signatures.

Microsoft Office XP was a major release which introduced the Safe Mode feature. Microsoft Office 2003 was released in 2003 with two new applications—Microsoft InfoPath and OneNote. In 2007, Microsoft Office 2007 was released with a new graphical user interface known as Fluent User Interface. The latest to be released in 2010 has been Microsoft Office 2010.

Along with the periodic releases of Microsoft Office versions, the company has also been periodically upgrading its operating system.

It released Windows 1.0 in November 1985. It made many improvements to the user interface and memory management and released Windows 2.0 in October 1987. Windows 3.0 was released in 1990 and was quickly followed by Windows 3.1 in 1992. Both had better multi-tasking abilities because of virtual memory and loadable virtual device drivers.

Windows 95 was a major release because this 1995 version had a new user interface, and the ability to automatically detect and configure installed hardware. The company released Windows 98 in June 1998 and Windows 2000 in February 2000. In September 2000, the Windows Millennium Edition was released.The NT family was first released in 1993. In August

2001, Microsoft combined its consumer and business operating systems and released Windows XP. Windows Server 2003 was released in 2003, followed by Windows Vista in 2006. This was followed by Windows Server 2008 in 2008 and Windows 7 in October 2009.

Microsoft Corporation has not only developed great products such as Microsoft Office and Windows but also continuously enhanced them during the past two decades.

Life was never a bed of roses for 'The Don' of Australian cricket. During one of his visits to England he suffered from a major illness which almost proved fatal. He also had to face bodyline tactics during one of the Ashes series against England. When he was at his career's peak, he had to take a break from the game because of Second World War. When he resumed cricket after the war, he was on the wrong side of 30s. Despite all these challenges he managed to set every possible world record.

Microsoft too has faced tough challenges since its inception in 1970s. Its MS-DOS and Windows had to compete against Apple's Mac-OS. Its Internet browser, Internet Explorer faced stiff competition from Netscape Navigator. MS Word and Excel faced competition from Word Perfect and Quattro Pro respectively. Each time when it appeared that Microsoft would end up playing second fiddle to its competitor, it would enhance its products and emerge as a winner.

The ability to sustain high performance for long periods of time is a sign of truly great individuals or organizations. This was a quality that Don Bradman and Microsoft excelled at. Don Bradman is hailed as one of the best cricketers in the world. His batting average is always considered as statistically the greatest achievement by any sportsman. Microsoft too has been an epitome of consistency since its inception. There are very few software companies that have been as successful as Microsoft since past three decades.

There is a very well-known proverb—'The biggest enemy of great is good.'.

What differentiates the great from the good? Consistency differentiates the two.

Performance is Reality
(Kapil Dev—Agilent Technologies)

'It is an immutable law in business that words are words, explanations are explanations, promises are promises but only performance is reality.'

—Harold S. Geneen

KapilDev was one of India's greatest all-rounders and also the first Indian captain to win the World Cup. He made his debut in 1978 during India's tour to Pakistan. Nicknamed 'Haryana Hurricane', he was one of the fastest bowlers India had ever produced. During his initial days, he took most of his wickets with prodigious outswingers and later developed a very useful inswinging Yorker as well. He was also one of the most aggressive batsmen in the Indian team and believed in the famous adage: 'Attack is the best form of defense'. His ability to play aggressively even when the chips were down helped his team on more than one occasion.

He is the only player in the history of cricket to have taken more than 400 wickets and score more than 5,000 runs in Tests, making him one of the greatest all-rounders the game has ever produced. In 131 test matches, he took 434 wickets and scored 5,248 runs. In 225 ODIs, he took 253 wickets and scored 3,783 runs. He broke Richard Hadlee's world record of 431 wickets and held this record till Courtney Walsh bettered it. Kapil Dev was inducted into the ICC Cricket Hall of Fame in March 2010.

Though Kapil Dev had an excellent strike rate during his best cricketing years, he could not sustain it towards the end of his career. In 1992, he took his 400th Test wcket in his 115th Test match at Perth but needed another 15 tests to take the next 34 wickets. During his last 17 Tests, he had just a single 5 wicket haul. He went wicketless on 11 occasions, got one wicket in an innings 10 times, and captured 2 wickets in an innings on seven occasions.

It was a sad sight to watch India's greatest all-rounder and prime strike bowler struggling to take wickets. Despite his lack of form, the Indian selectors persisted with him. It was a common belief that the Indian selectors retained him since he was approaching Richard Hadlee's record of 431 wickets. The golden moment finally came during the 3rd Test against Sri Lanka at Motera Stadium, Ahmedabad. HashanTillekaratne jabbed at a Kapil Dev delivery and the ball was snapped by Sanjay Manjrekar at forward short-leg. This dismissal was the record breaking dismissal for Kapil Dev as he went past Richard Hadlee's haul to become the highest wicket taker in the world.

Kapil Dev's prolonged career created a problem for the Indian team. Though Javagal Srinath, playing for Karnataka, was making waves in domestic cricket, he was unable to break into the Indian team. During those days, India normally played with just two pace bowlers. Since Kapil was the first choice, there would be stiff competition for the second pace bowler's slot. The two pace bowlers in the Indian team were Kapil Dev and Manoj Prabhakar. There were many in the cricketing circles who felt that Kapil's presence was adversely affecting the balance of the team.

Though Javagal Srinath had entered the Karnataka team in 1989, he could make his debut only in 1992 at Brisbane. Since this was a match played on a seamer friendly pitch, India decided to go in with three seamers and Srinath was the third one. There were enough whispers that the Indian selectors were not picking the team based on current form but allowing a player to extend his career based on his past credentials.

In 1999, Hewlett Packard decided to create an independent company by spinning off the divisions that were not connected with computers, storage, and imaging. These divisions were grouped into a separate company—Agilent Technologies. This new company consisted of test and measurement instruments, semiconductors, chemical analysis, and medical businesses. It was headquartered in Santa Clara, California, USA, with Ned Barnholt as its president and CEO.

Ned Barnholt received his MS in electrical engineering from Stanford University in 1966 and joined HP at its Palo Alto headquarters. He was a strong believer in 'The HP Way'—a style of management that focused on the trust of employees, respect for employees, and management integrity. He had also observed the way the company's founders Bill Hewlett and Dave Packard were running the company. When Barnholt became the CEO of Agilent, he practiced the same principles as that of the founders of HP.

The initial public stock offering in 1999 raised $2.1 billion and this IPO was probably the largest in the history of Silicon Valley. Unfortunately, the company could not sustain the initial expectations and euphoria. During the 2000 global recession, 50% of orders for Agilent products were cancelled. The company introduced many cost-cutting measures but it was still losing hundreds of millions of dollars.

Barnholt was averse to cutting jobs so when the situation became worse, in 2001, he responded by selling off Agilent's healthcare services division to Holland's Philips Electronics NV. This move transferred around 5000 employees and their jobs out of Agilent.

The situation did not improve so he initiated 10% pay-cuts to all employees, including himself. Despite this, the company was still bleeding. Since he had handled the situation with a great deal of sensitivity towards the employees, the motivational levels within the company remained high. When Bill Sullivan took over as the CEO of Agilent in 2005, the company was still struggling in its semiconductor business

The semiconductor business of Agilent was not as profitable as the rest of its businesses. Added to this, the semiconductor industry itself was going through turbulent times. Most of them, including Agilent, suffered at the stock market. Despite so many problems, selling off the semiconductor business had been unthinkable for many of the company's top leaders.

However, Bill Sullivan was quite different from his predecessor. He was convinced that the only way to stop Agilent from bleeding was to sell off its semiconductor business. In August 2005, Agilent Technologies sold off its ailing business to Kohlberg Kravis Roberts & Co. and Silver Lake Partners

The sale of the semiconductor business changed the fortunes of Agilent Technologies. It was no longer saddled with an unprofitable business. It also used the money obtained for its research and development. Since the semiconductor companies were going through turbulent times, Wall Street had given them a lower price/earning ratio. Since Agilent Technologies had semiconductors as one of its main businesses, it too was given a low price/earning ratio. Once Agilent sold off its semiconductors division, Wall Street gave it a higher price/earning ratio. This in turn saw a sharp rise in Agilent's share prices.

This case study of Agilent Technologies is quite similar to that of Indian selectors. In both cases, the situation was unproductive but was allowed to drag. However, there was one major difference. In the cricketing example, the Indian selectors chose to live with the problem. Despite the great all-rounder struggling in the twilight of his illustrious career, they persisted with him till he broke the world record. However, in the Agilent example, luckily there was a change at the top and the new CEO, Bill Sullivan took the tough call of hiving off the company's unprofitable semiconductor business. This move brought his company on the path to profitability.

What we have seen in these examples is quite common in our everyday life. We have many instances of employees being rewarded based on their past rather than current performances. There are numerous instances where a high performer's contribution drops significantly but the senior management continues to retain him. There are different reasons for this. In some cases, the senior management feels that the employee is indispensible despite a drop in performance. In certain cases, the senior management feels indebted to the employee's past performance and feels guilty to replace him.

It is quite common to see people get confused between competence and performance. A person's competence indicates the potential that he has to perform. However, it is not necessary that high potential will always get converted to top performance. In one of my earlier organizations, as a part of senior management, each one of us had to present the performance ratings of our team members. The objective of this meeting was to normalize the performance ratings across all departments of the organization. During these meetings, I would often notice mediocre performers being highly rated. When I would question the manager, the typical justification for recommending a high rating would be, 'he has extremely good domain knowledge' or 'she is a very competent and knowledgeable person'. It was quite obvious that this manager was confused between competence and performance.

A good leader should realize that great performance from a team member is not a ticket for eternal survival. Reward a star performer when he delivers great performance. However, if the same star employee's performance drops, try to find out the reasons and see if you can help him regain his past sterling performance. If it does not improve despite efforts from both sides then you should be ready to take the hard call. A good leader should be able to 'separate the grain from chaff' as seen in the example of Agilent Technologies.

Fun@Work

(W.G. Grace, Derek Randall—Southwest Airlines)

'Happiness is an attitude. We either make ourselves miserable or happy and strong. The amount of work is the same.'

—Francesca Reigler

Cricket is one of those rare sports where a lot of good humoured bantering goes on. One of the reasons for this could be the slow pace of the game compared to fast paced ones like rugby, football, or basketball where there is no time to indulge in fun.

Unfortunately, over the years, there have been many instances where the players have crossed the limits and used intimidatory tactics. In cricketing parlance, this is known as sledging. In the earlier days when cricket was still a gentleman's game, it was pure fun but unfortunately as the game progressed and became more competitive, sledging became a tool to weaken the opponent's concentration, thereby causing him to make mistakes or underperform.

Sledging can be effective because the batsman stands within the hearing range of the bowler and close fielders. The insults may be directly addressed to the batsman or could feature in conversations among fielders. These insults are designed to be overheard by the batsman. It is not just the bowlers or fielders who are the culprits—there are many instances of the batsmen also indulging in sledging.

Former English batsman, Dr W.G. Grace was one of England's best batsmen. He was also known to be a cricketer who valued his wicket a lot and hated to get out. There are many humorous anecdotes that denote his love for batting. On one occasion, when he was clean bowled, he quietly replaced the dislodged bail and told the umpire, 'the wind is very strong today.' The umpire couldn't help smiling and replied, 'yes, please mind your hat on your way to the pavilion!'

There was another instance where he was repeatedly given not out. The bowler to suffer on all those occasions was Charles Kortright. Finally, Kotright knocked two of Grace's stumps. As a dejected Grace walked back towards the pavilion, the bowler told him in a mock shock, 'Doctor! Surely you are not going? There is still one stump which is standing!'

In most of these cases, the bowlers knew Dr W.G. Grace's love for batting and his witty replies so it was all in good humour. There are many instances where bringing humour into the game has diffused a hostile situation. England played Australia in the Centenary Test in 1977 at Melbourne. England was chasing a marathon score of 463 to win. Derek Randall, who played first class cricket for Nottinghamshire, was the English batsman at the crease. As he stroked his way to a valiant 174, he was subject to continuous sledging by Dennis Lillee, the star Australian fast bowler. Lillee, in one of the most hostile spells of fast bowling, bombarded Randall with a mix of sledging and bouncers. On one occasion, during the course of his innings, Derek Randall evaded a Lillee bouncer which almost knocked him out. Randall doffed his cap and pointing to his head, told Lillee, 'there is nothing much out there!' Even Lillee, who had been bowling a hostile spell, couldn't help but smile at Randall. What could have been a potentially nasty situation was cleverly averted by Randall, known for his fantastic sense of humour.

Derek Randall was well-known for his antics and great sense

of humour. The English dressing room always wore a different look when he was around.

Unfortunately, in the past few years, there have been many instances when sledging has crossed the line and become an abuse. There have been numerous occasions where bowlers have made personal attacks on the batsman's personal life and family members. The Australians were very strong in sledging and their former captain Steve Waugh referred to it as 'mental disintegration'. They believed that the best way to get a good batsman out was to distract him with continuous sledging. The bowlers and the close-in fielders were the main culprits.

Southwest Airlines is one of the largest airlines in the US. It is based in Dallas, Texas. It was started on March 15th 1967 by Rollin King and Herb Kelleher. As of June 2010, it operated more than 3,400 flights a day, utilizing a fleet of 552 aircrafts.

Herb Kelleher, the founder of Southwest Airlines, studied California-based Pacific Southwest Airlines extensively and used many of the airline's ideas to form the corporate culture at Southwest Airlines. He decided that the best way to attract passengers would be to do things differently. He wanted his passengers to think of the flight journey as something that they should look forward to and not as a 'necessary evil to traverse long distances. He introduced the concept of 'fun at work' on all Southwest Airline flights.

The Airlines employed humour in all aspects of its operations, starting right from its catchy advertisements such as 'Just Plane Smart' and 'Somebody else up there loves you'!

Herb Kelleher treated all his employees as a part of one big family. He knew that not everyone would be comfortable with his concept of 'fun at work'. Hence, he made the recruitment process extremely stringent. Apart from technical / functional area skills, candidates were checked on attributes like optimism, team spirit, communication, and cheerfulness. This test was administered for all positions and functions. The new recruits were sent to its unique training centre at Dallas, Texas. Here, they got trained on all aspects pertaining to Southwest's culture and principles.

The original flight attendants that worked for Southwest Airlines were chosen by a committee of individuals that included the same person who had selected hostesses for Hugh Hefner's Playboy jet. The selection resulted in a group of female flight attendants that looked like long-legged dancers and cheerleaders. The Airlines asked them to dress in hot pants and go-go boots. The cabin crew and flight attendants were also taught to bring humour into their announcements. There is a website dedicated to the jokes told by the flight attendants. Here is a sample of what you can expect on a Southwest Airlines flight:

'We'll be dimming the lights in the cabin. Pushing the light-bulb button will turn your reading lights on. However, pushing the flight-attendant button will not turn your flight attendant on.'

Announcement by a pilot: 'We've reached our cruising altitude now, and I'm turning off the seat belt sign. I'm switching to autopilot too so I can come back there and visit all of you for the rest of the flight.'

Announcement after a bumpy landing: "That was quite a bump and I know what ya'll are thinking. I'm here to tell you it wasn't the airline's fault, it wasn't the pilot's fault, it wasn't the flight attendants' fault...it was the asphalt!'

On September 11, 2001, after the attack on the World Trade Center in the US, most of the airlines had grounded their planes. A Southwest plane was directed to land at an airport that Southwest did not serve, and the passengers and crew were put up in a hotel. When Southwest management called the hotel to inquire about the passengers and the crew, they were told that no one was there—the pilot had taken everyone from that plane out to the movies!

Southwest Airlines was a company that always believed in

keeping its crew and customers smiling and happy. It comes as no surprise that *Fortune* had ranked Southwest Airlines among the top five of the 'Best Companies to Work For' in America. It ranked first in 1997 and 1998, second in 1999, and fourth in 2000. During 2007, for the eighth year in a row, *Business Ethics* magazine listed Southwest Airlines in its '100 Best Corporate Citizens'.

It is very important to have 'fun at work' in our professional workplace. Gone are the days when humour and fun was frowned upon. These days the atmosphere in most companies is informal. One of the reasons for this change in culture could be the advent of IT companies. VeriFone, an IT company, was one of the pioneers in introducing fun events every Friday evenings, known as TGIF (Thank God It's Friday).

During the manufacturing era, the company's prime assets were the machines and equipments—no longer so. Today, for any IT Company, its people are its biggest assets. As Narayan Murthy, former CEO of Infosys, once remarked, 'our assets walk out of the door each evening. We have to make sure that they come back the next morning.' The best way to ensure this is to give them an environment where they can have fun@work.

As we can see from the anecdotes related to Derek Randall's innings during the Centenary Test and Southwest's handling ofthe 9/11 incident, a hostile situation can be diffused through 'fun at work'. If Derek Randall could bring a smile on Dennis Lillee's lips, so could the pilot of Southwest Airlines to his passengers. In our daily grind, we are so busy with our deliverables, meetings, teleconferences, video conferences, etc., that we forget to pause and enjoy life. If we could add a little fun to our workplace then wouldn't it be a much better place to work at.

5

INNOVATION AND CHANGE

'Along with birth certificate we create Gmail, Facebook, Twitter, and YouTube accounts for new born babies.'

Off the Beaten Track

(Martin Crowe—Hotmail)

'Innovation is the specific instrument of entrepreneurship. The act that endows resources with a new capacity to create wealth.'

—Peter Drucker

Martin Crowe was not only a great batsman but also one of the shrewdest captains New Zealand has ever produced. Under his captaincy in the 1990s, he introduced many innovative techniques in cricket which took his opposition completely by surprise. During Test matches, the opening batsmen has to normally 'see off the new ball'. The primary job is to defend good balls, nudge for ones and twos, and an occasional bad ball is hammered to the boundary. By the time the numbers four, five, and six come in to bat, the ball would be old and will no longer assist the fast bowlers. This is when these middle-order batsmen would quicken the scoring with aggressive shots all around the park.

ODIs having evolved from Test matches followed a smilar pattern during 1970s and 1980s. Within a few years, the ODIs became very predictable—the batsmen would play cautiously during the initial 30 overs and accelerate in the last 20 overs.

Martin Crowe changed this pattern during the 1992 World Cup.

John Wright, the regular opening batsman for New Zealand,

opened the batting during the initial matches against Australia and Zimbabwe. His subsequent injury led to the selection of Mark Greatbatch. Though Greatbatch was a middle order batsman, Crowe asked him to open the innings, a decision that seemed quite strange to the cricket pundits. Crowe asked him to take advantage of the field restrictions during the initial overs.

Greatbatch completely transformed the role of an opening batsman in ODI cricket. Since only two players were allowed outside the 'circle', he lofted the ball to all parts of the ground. The fact that New Zealand grounds were small further helped his cause. The opposition bowlers were totally taken by surprise by his unconventional game. They were clueless on how to tackle a rampaging Greatbatch who aggregated 313 runs at a healthy average of 44.71 runs. Based on Greatbatch's style of aggressive hitting, a new term 'pinch hitter' was introduced in the lexicon of cricket.

Martin Crowe not only pioneered unconventional style in batting, he also introduced innovative methods when his team came out to bowl. Traditionally, in the ODIs, the first 10–15 overs were bowled by fast bowlers. The spinners were introduced only during the 'middle overs', once the ball was old and devoid of its shine. Since specialist opening batsmen are quite adept against fast bowling, they could not only defend their wickets but also score briskly. The game had become quite predictable for players and spectators. Crowe surprised everyone by starting the innings with Dipak Patel who was a spinner. This strategy worked very well against the Australians. The Australian openers, traditionally very good players of fast bowling, struggled against the gentle spin of Dipak Patel. Crowe used the same strategy successfully in the remaining matches.

These two innovations helped New Zealand reach semi-finals of the 1992 World Cup, and it took the brilliance of Pakistan's Inzamam-ul-Haq to stop their progress.

We have discussed about 'role models' and 'benchmarking with winners' in earlier chapters. The same happened in this case too. The opposition had watched New Zealand's success with the pinch hitting of Greatbatch and opening the bowling with a spinner, Dipak Patel. Soon, most teams began to copy this strategy, with good results. The innovations of Martin Crowe are still emulated, 20 years later.

Hotmail is a fine example of how to innovate existing practices. Till a few decades back, written correspondence was only through 'letters', and people wrote letters on paper and delivered it to the nearest post office. The post office would deliver it to the appropriate person for a small fee—in the form of 'postage stamps'. This form of communication was slow since a letter within India would take at least 3–4 days to reach the destination, and an international mail could take upto 4 weeks!

In 1970s, the concept of email revolutionalized the entire way of corresponding with people. People could send mails and the recipient could receive it withn a few seconds. A mail written and sent from India could reach USA in a matter of seconds compared to the earlier cycle time of around 4 weeks. However, there was one major problem with the email form of communication. Setting up an email network was quite expensive since it involved the purchase of high speed computer networks, storage devices, high speed broadband communication links, and licenses for the email software. This meant that only big organizations could afford emails. Small organizations had to still rely on the old form of communication: 'letters'. This was true for 'personal mails' too since no one could afford to have huge computer networks and data communication links for personal use.

All this changed in 1996 when Sabeer Bhatia and Jack Smith developed Hotmail, one of the first free webmail services. It was launched on 4th July (American Independence Day) to symbolize freedom from Internet Service Provider based email and was initially funded by venture capital company Draper Fisher Jurvetson.

Hotmail had the following features:

1. It was absolutely free and anyone could register and setup an email account
2. It could be accessed from anywhere in the world since it was powered by Internet
3. It had free storage space for the users

Hotmail became extremely popular all over the world because of these advantages. It completely revolutionized the way people communicated. By December 1997, it had around 8.5 million users and by February 1999, it was the world's largest webmail service with more than 30 million users.

Hotmail did to mails what Martin Crowe did to ODI cricket—both introduced innovations that revolutionalised the existing structure. Both quickened the pace of the game to such an extent that the legacy structure became unrecognizable. Earlier, a total of 250 in a ODI would be a match winning target but in today's fast pace game, even a score of 320 looks chaseable. The fast paced nature of ODIs has rubbed off on the traditional Test cricket too. In 1970s and 1980s, most of the teams would score around 220–230 runs in a day but these days it is quite common to see teams score 350+ runs in a day. The expectations of the spectators have also increased. Everyone wants to watch high scoring matches, scored at a brisk pace.

Similarly, during the early days of mail correspondence, people would be happy if their letter reached the destination country within a fortnight. These days, if we send an email from India to the US and don't get a response within a few minutes, we go to the sent folder and check if we have mailed it to the right recipient. There has been a drastic change in our expectations!

These examples show how innovation can change both—the

complexion of the game and the expectations of the people. It also shows that innovation can bring out winners—one of New Zealand's finest performances came in the 1992 World Cup, and similarly Hotmail became the world's largest webmail service provider in the late 1990s and Microsoft purchased it for a staggering $400 million!

Nothing is Permanent Except Change
(Twenty20 — Facebook)

'You can't suppress creativity, you can't suppress innovation.'

—James Daly

Test matches are the traditional form of cricket. These are played for five days and each team gets to play two innings. There are hardly any restrictions for the batsmen and the bowlers. Over the years, Test matches began to lose their popularity, primarily because of three reasons. Firstly, the game was slow because the batsmen had all the time in the world to score runs. Secondly, people were no longer willing to watch a match spread over five days. Thirdly, there were numerous occasions where the match would end in a 'draw' (no result), thus the crowd would feel let down when there was no result even after waiting for five days.

'Limited Overs Cricket' was introduced to address some of these shortcomings. These are also known as One Day Internationals (ODIs) since the game does not exceed a day. The first ODI played in 1971 between England and Australia in Melbourne was actually an unplanned event. During the 3rd Test match between teams, the first three days of the match was washed out due to rain. So the cricket officials decided to play a 'limited overs cricket' consisting of 40 overs per team. During the initial days, the ODIs consisted of 40, 50, or 60 overs per team. Nowadays, it is only 50 overs per side.

With the advent of Kerry Packer's 'World Series Cricket'(WSC) in the late 1970s, the ODI itself underwent many changes. Matches were played under flood-lights in the day–night games. Players wore coloured uniforms instead of the 'traditional white'. Red balls and white sight screens were replaced by white balls and black sight screens.

During 1980s and 1990s, the general perception was that ODI cricket was here to stay. No one had dreamt that the game would again get transformed within the next few years.

However, as years rolled by, people felt that the 50-over game was getting dull and predictable. Though pinch hitters made the game interesting during the initial 15 overs and the last 5 overs, the game became very predictable and slow between the 15th and the 45th over. Moreover, the spectators began to dwindle because people could come to the stadium only after college or office hours. Even the day–night format couldn't help much since the matches would start at around 2 pm.

This led to the idea of a shorter format of the game. The initial concept was discussed by the England and Wales Cricket Board in 1998 but it was not until 2003 when the first Twenty20 match was played. This was initially introduced for inter-county competitions. This format consists of two teams playing 20 overs each. Twenty20 cricket had two major advantages over the ODIs. Firstly, the entire game lasted just 40 overs compared to 100 overs in ODI, so the game became much shorter and quicker. Secondly, most of the Twenty20 games started in the evening, so students and working professionals could conveniently spare time to watch it.

The first Twenty20 match was played in 2003 between the English county teams. The game slowly grew in popularity and when Middlesex played Surrey in 2004 at Lord's, a capacity crowd of 26,500 came to watch the match. This was one of the largest attendances for a county match.

The introduction of music bands, cheerleaders, and other such marketing promotions began to pull the younger generation back to the stadium. The boost in the game's popularity also attracted many sponsors and by the time IPL tournament started in India, players were earning millions of dollars every season. It had become comparable with some of the European football tournaments where players signed multi-million dollar contracts.

These are clear instances where the rules of the game keep changing. Test cricket gave birth to the ODIs and the ODIs themselves underwent changes that led to the Twenty20 format of the game.

This is true in the corporate world too. The traditional way of postal communication gave way to emails and soon these were enhanced by web-based free emails like Hotmail, Yahoo! mail, and Gmail. If you thought that these remained the most popular ways of communication, then think again. Social networking sites revolutionalized the way the world communicated. Facebook, Orkut, Twitter, YouTube etc., are the latest fad, and in many cases, these have replaced email as a form of communication. The biggest advantage of these social networking sites is—any message that is posted can be instantly viewed by millions of people at the same time. Many people can join a chat by posting their comments on each other's pages. At the same time, these websites also provide the ption of sending 'personal messages' in the form of private emails.

Facebook is a social networking site that was launched in 2004. It was founded by Mark Zuckerberg and his fellow college computer science students Eduardo Saverin, Dustin Moskovitz, Andrew McCollum, and Chris Hughes.

During October 2003, Mark Zuckerberg, as a sophomore at Havard University, developed Facemash which was the predecessor to Facebook. It is widely believed that he accessed Harvard's computer network and copied the houses' dormitory images. He uploaded these photos on his website and asked users to compare the photos and declare who was hot and who was not. This became a huge success as it attracted 450 visitors and 22,000 views within its first four hours.

Initially, Facemash was restricted to Harvard students but later it expanded to other colleges in the Boston area. Slowly, it expanded to universities across USA. Unfortunately, this site was shut down by the Harvard administration because they felt it was a breach of security and violated copyright and privacy.

However, Zuckerberg continued to work on his pet project. He developed a new website which had one image per page along with a comment section. In February 2004, he launched 'The facebook'. He was joined by his fellow classmates—Eduardo Saverin took care of the business aspects, Dustin Moskovtz did the programming, Andrew McCollum was the graphic artist, and Chris Hughes helped in promoting the website.

Facebook gained in popularity and expanded to other universities in the US. It also moved its operations to Palo Alto, California, which was the technology hub of USA. By 2006, it provided access to everyone who was above 13 years and had a valid email address. Users not only used it as a means of exchanging messages but also created common interest user groups to share and exchange ideas and information. The comments section on Facebook was one of the key reasons for its popularity. Any comment posted could be viewed instantly and replied by millions of other users.

Today Facebook has more than a billion users and is one of the most popular social networking sites in the world. Its speed and innovativeness has completely changed the concept of social networking.

The evolution of cricket and Internet communication has proved that nothing is permanent except change. Who would have thought forty years back that Test cricket would undergo a major transformation leading to the formation of ODI? Similarly, who would have imagined ten years back that ODI itself would undergo a metamorphosis and result in the Twenty20 cricket?

No one had ever imagined that the conventional way of postal communication could be replaced by emails. Similarly, who would have imagined ten years back that the email form of communication itself would be challenged by social networking sites? Currently Facebook and other social networking sites are very popular among Gen-Y, but it won't be long before these are replaced by more innovative and faster modes of communication.

These instances teach us that though there are thousands of innovations happening every year in all walks of life, these innovations are not permanent. Sustaining an innovation is tougher than creating a new one.

Challenge the Status Quo
(Arjuna Ranatunga—Louis Gerstner, Sam Palmisano, IBM)

'Don't be afraid to challenge the pros, even in their own backyard.'
—Colin Powell

The first three World Cup tournaments in 1975, 1979, and 1983 were played in England. The 1st World Cup finals was played between West Indies and Australia, in which West Indies won by 17 runs. In the 2nd World Cup finals, West Indies defeated England by 92 runs. India won the 3rd edition of the championship, beating West Indies by 43 runs. In 1987, for the first time, this championship moved out of England and was played in the Indian subcontinent. Australia narrowly beat England by 7 runs and became the World Champions. The 1992, World Cup was co-hosted by Australia and New Zealand, in which Pakistan won by defeating England by 22 runs. The common factor among all the five finals was the fact that the team batting first won the match as well as the championship.

In 1996, the tournament was once again co-hosted in the Indian subcontinent. The qualifying rounds were played in India, Sri Lanka, and Pakistan. Sri Lanka and Australia played the finals on 17th March at the Gadaffi Stadium, Lahore. When the two captains walked out for the 'toss', expert commentators and former cricketers were of the opinion that the captain who wins the toss will elect to bat since the teams batting first had been victorious in the previous five World Cup matches.

Arjuna Ranatunga won the toss and did something unthinkable! He elected to field! While most commentators felt that chasing a mammoth score in a 'high pressure' final would be tough, Ranatunga did not feel so. He also didn't bother about the past records that the expert commentators kept mentioning. He felt his team's strength was in its batting and the ability to chase high scores.

Riding on Mark Taylor's 74 runs off 83 balls, Australia scored 241 runs for the loss of 7 wickets. When the Sri Lankans came out to bat, they were initially in a spot. However, a brilliant partnership between Aravinda de Silva (107 runs off 124 balls) and Gurusinha (65 runs off 95 balls) saw Sri Lanka romp home by 7 wickets. Arjuna Ranatunga's decision to field first, coupled by de Silva's classy century, saw Sri Lanka win the World Cup for the first time. Ranatunga also defied the odds of a host / co-host country winning the championship.

Though it is always good to look at historical data and past trends, we should recognize the current scenario and our strengths. Ranatunga knew that his team's batting strength and the dew factor for a team bowling second far outweighed the past statistics. He was well aware that if his team lost the finals, daggers would be pointing at him. However, he was willing to challenge the past and that helped him register an emphatic win over the mighty Australians.

IBM, one of the greatest IT companies in the world, had to undergo a very lean phase during the late 1980s and early 1990s. When Louis Gerstner took over as its CEO in 1993, the biggest challenge he faced was making IBM come out of its legacy practices. During the initial days, it was a huge struggle for Gerstner because he was confronted with many old time IBMers who were clinging to the old ways with a 'we always did it this way' attitude.

Gerstner went against the IBM culture and introduced many drastic changes. Though some of the businesses were bleeding with accumulated losses in excess of $16 billion, the earlier CEOs were not willing to challenge IBM's style of providing lifetime employment to its employees. Gerstner was willing to take a tough stance which resulted in a cumulative layoff of over 1,00,000 employees. He realized that the computer giant could be made profitable by making it 'lean and mean'.

The second major change that Gerstner introduced was in the field of OS/2 development. The company had invested tens of millions of dollars in developing the OS/2 operating system. Though it was technically a superior product, it never became a commercial success like Microsoft's Windows. Gerstner's predecessor, John Akers was well aware of OS/2's problems but being a hardcore IBM employee, he was unwilling to challenge the feasibility of OS/2's development. However, Gerstner was an 'outsider' and had no emotional bonding towards IBM's products. This enabled him to take the tough decision of halting new development of OS/2 operating system in 1994. This was an emotional decision for many old time IBMers since many person-years of effort had been invested into the product but for Gerstner, it was just one more business decision.

Gerstner was highly valued at IBM not only during his tenure as its chief but even after his retirement. Upon his departure from IBM in 2002, Gerstner received a 10 year consultancy contract worth $2 million annually, plus expenses and full use of IBM facilities and services, such as office, cars, aircraft, and financial planning. He was only required to work one month out of the year. Gerstner was named a Knight Commander of the British Empire (KBE) on the recommendation of former United Kingdom Prime Minister, Tony Blair. The award was for his services to UK's education and his contribution to the Internet.

When Gerstner retired in 2002, Sam Palmisano took over as

the CEO of IBM. Like his predecessor, Palmisano was also willing to challenge the legacy practices and continued the good work that Gerstner had started.

Palmisano introduced the concept of 'on-demand computing' in which the customers were allowed to rent computing power from IBM rather than purchasing them. This was a big success because the clients were able to save millions of dollars by avoiding purchase of computer hardware.

Though IBM was one of the pioneers in the field of Personal Computers, it slowly became an unprofitable business during late 1990s and early 2000s. This was primarily due to stiff competition from Dell, HP, Lenovo, Compaq, etc. Moreover, PC was no longer a 'high-tech' product but a 'commodity' since any computer manufacturer could buy the mother board, hard disk, monitor, etc. and assemble it in his backyard. It had become a high volume but low margin business, something that no longer suited a giant like IBM. Palmisano had no hesitation in selling off the PC division to Chinese computer manufacturer Lenovo. He also sold off the disk drive business to Hitachi.

IBM's fortunes changed due to the efforts of its CEOs Louis Gerstner and Sam Palmisano. They challenged the legacy and became the change agents. For both of them, the current market scenario and the organization's inherent strengths were more important than what had worked earlier for IBM.

Haven't we too been in the shoes of Louis Gerstner where we have joined a company which is still struggling to find its feet? Haven't we encountered problems similar to the ones that he encountered in an ailing IBM? When we join a new company, we have absolutely no emotional bonding of the past and that helps us think objectively. For the first few months, we are able to bring the 'outside-in perspective'—something that might be sorely lacking in the struggling company. Being fresh into the company, we want to implement many changes, including the ones that have worked for us in our earlier organizations.

Unfortunately, the biggest hurdle that we face is neither from the shareholders nor the customers. The opposition is within the organization, from the existing employees. The more years they have spent in the organization, the more 'baggage' they tend to carry. Each time you suggest a fresh idea, you have to be ready for a 'why should we change because we have always done it this way and we were successful in the past' kind of a reply.

In one of the earlier chapters, we saw how an organization that rests on its past laurels struggles. The only way to overcome this is to do what Arjuna Ranatunga did in 1996 World Cup final or what Loius Gerstner and Sam Palmisano did for IBM—which was to challenge the legacy. There is no guarantee that what worked well in the past will work for you in the future too.

Re-invent Your Game

(Rahul Dravid—Apple)

'When things are bad, it's the best time to reinvent yourself.'

—George Lopez

Rahul Dravid played his test match debut in 1996 at Lord's, England where he scored a brilliant 95. After this, there was no looking back for him. He became one of the world's most technically sound batsmen who could handle both pace and spin with equal aplomb. In fact he is one of the few Indian batsmen who averaged above 50 at both at home and foreign soil. He is also one of those rare Indian batsmen who did not struggle on the fast paced, seaming, and bouncy Australian and English wickets.

Dravid's biggest strength was his ability to play a sheet anchor role and block one end. He was successful on the seaming tracks of England because of his ability to leave the outswingers that pitched and mowed away. This attribute earned him the nickname of 'The Wall'. In Test cricket, your ability to leave an outswinger is as important as your ability to defend a short pitched ball. Dravid, with a high degree of concentration, had mastered the waiting game. He could patiently wait for hours and frustrate the bowlers before smacking a bad ball towards the boundary.

Unfortunately for Dravid, all these attributes, which were strengths in a Test match, proved to be handicap while playing the limited version of the game. Since each team bats only for

50 overs in the ODIs, the batsmen have to play fast, aggressive cricket. You have to be either a powerful hitter like Chris Gayle or Vivian Richards or someone who can nudge and push into the gaps for quick singles like Steve Waugh or Javed Miandad. Sadly, Dravid was neither and this resulted in a mediocre strike rate. He made his ODI debut in 1996 but struggled during the initial years. He continued to play proper cricketing shots and very rarely lofted the ball over the 30-yard circle. His aesthetically good looking ondrives invariably found a fielder. Though Dravid was a classy batsman, he struggled to convert his sound technique into big scores. He was dropped from the Indian ODI team in 1998.

Dravid realized that he had to change his game if he had to become a permanent member in the Indian ODI side. He practised hard at the nets and made many changes to his technique. He developed the ability to play with soft hands which allowed him to scamper for a quick single before the ball reached the fielder. He also improved his ability to find gaps and run quickly between the wickets.

Within twelve months, Dravid had transformed his game and was back with a bang. During the 1999 World Cup at England, he scored the highest—461 runs. For a person who was considered a 'no-hope' in the ODI format of the game, Rahul Dravid was involved in two of the largest partnerships in ODIs—first was a 318 run partnership with Saurav Ganguly and the second was a 331 run partnership with Sachin Tendulkar.

This was not the only instance where Dravid reinvented his game. During the 2003 World Cup, he showed what a great team man he was when he agreed to don the wicket keeper's gloves, though he had kept wickets only during his college days. His willingness to play as a wicket keeper-batsman provided great flexibility to the Indian captain because he could now accommodate an extra batsman or a bowler, depending on the situation. Dravid had played different roles for his team—he had opened the batting, batted in the middle order at number three, four, and five, and also kept wickets.

Though Rahul Dravid is known as one of the greatest Test batsmen in the world, he has an equally awesome ODI record. In 344 ODI matches, he has scored 10,889 runs at an average of 39.16 runs. He has won Man of the Match on 14 occasions and captained the team to a 17 match winning streak!

He won the Arjuna Award in 1998, Ceat Cricketer of the World Cup in 1999, Wisden Cricketer of the Year in 2000, Padma Shri in 2004, and Padma Bhushan in 2013.

If Rahul Dravid is one of the best examples of a cricketer who kept reinventing himself as per the situation, Apple Inc. in the corporate world has done the same.

Apple Inc. is an American multinational company that designs and manufactures personal computers, computer software, and consumer electronic products. It was founded in 1976 by Steve Jobs, Steve Wozniak, and Ronald Wayne. It has its headquarters in Cupertino, California.

Most of the personal computers during late 1970s and early 1980s had a very non-intuitive user interface. The DOS prompt and commands made the PC quite intimidating to a person who was not 'computer literate'. Apple changed all that by developing Macintosh in 1984 which had one of the best user interfaces in the world.

Apple Macintosh, combined with the LaserWriter and PageMaker, revolutionalized the desktop publishing industry. The intuitive user interface made it a darling among thousands of Mac users around the world. Unfortunately for Apple, its competition wasted no time in developing similar user friendly GUIs. Microsoft developed Windows and priced it much lower. Apple also made a few strategic errors such as keeping its OS proprietary and pricing its products much higher than the competitors.

During late 1980s and early 1990s, Apple tried to introduce a few more products like digital cameras, portable CD players, etc. but met with limited success. It also struggled with its Apple II Series because it was found to be very expensive. It finally stopped making this product in 1993.

The first signs of a turnaround came in 1998, when Apple launched iMac, which was a computer with a completely new design. This was a tremendous success and the company sold 8,00,000 units within the first five months of its launch.

The turning point for Apple came in 2001 when it once again reinvented itself and entered the consumer electronics market in a big way. It introduced the iPod portable digital audio player which took the world by storm. People who were used to Sony's cassette based Walkmans suddenly saw a hard disk based audio product that could store more than 1,000 songs! Within six years of its launch, Apple sold more than 100 million iPods. Apple's price per share grew more than ten-fold—from $6 to around $80.

While delivering his keynote speech at the MacWorld Expo in 2007, Steve Jobs announced that his company's name would change from Apple Computers to Apple Inc. since it was focusing beyond computers. Soon, it entered the mobile communication business by launching iPhone. The company also launched App Store to sell third party applications for iPhone and iPod Touch. By then, it shares were selling at around $100 per share. Despite being a very late entrant in the field of mobile communication, Apple was among the top 3 mobile handset suppliers in the world.

In January 2010, Apple came up with yet another innovative product, the iPad. It had the same popular touch based operating system that was used in iPhone. Since most of iPhone's applications were compatible with iPad, it allowed the company to have a very short design cycle time and introduce the product ahead of some of its competitors. iPad too was a roaring success and the first week saw a sale of 5,00,000 units!

When Rahul Dravid went through a lean phase and was axed from the Indian ODI team, he did not get demotivated and lose his focus. Instead, he took it as a challenge and improvised to suit the shorter format of the game. He went on to become one of the highest scorers in the world in ODIs too!

Apple too made an excellent debut with its innovative user-friendly computers. It took on the likes of IBM, DEC, Microsoft, etc. Unfortunately, it made a few strategic mistakes which resulted in losing its market share to PCs and Windows. 1980s was considered as the era of Apple and Microsoft. During the next decade, Microsoft became one of the biggest and most profitable IT companies in the world but Apple was clearly struggling. People began to write off Apple as a 'has been' but Steve Jobs was not ready to give up. Like Rahul Dravid, Apple too constantly reinvented itself. Between 2001 and 2010, it launched innovative products like iPod, iPad, and iPhone. In 2010, it helped the organization achieve a market cap that was higher than its rival Microsoft.

Winning Globally

(Ashok Mankad, Graeme Hick—Kellogg's, McDonald's)

'Adapt or perish, now as ever, is nature's inexorable imperative.'

— H.G. Wells

What differentiates Australia from other cricketing nations? It is their ability to win consistently in all forms of the game and on all sorts of surfaces.

Indian cricket has been on the ascendency ever since we won the 1983 World Cup in England. We have beaten practically every cricketing side in the world during the past three decades. Unfortunately a majority of these victories have been in India. Most Indian pitches are devoid of grass that prevents high bounce and speed. The kind of soil used to prepare the turf also results in low bounce, making the pitch 'batsmen-friendly'. It is quite common to see teams score 500+ runs in domestic matches such as Ranji trophy and Duleep trophy tournaments. Even today, an Indian batsman hardly gets exposed to balls that bounce above the waist. When he tours Australia and South Africa, he struggles on the bouncier tracks like Perth, Brisbane, Durban, and Johannesburg.

The same holds true with respect to Indian batsmen's susceptibility against swing. Indian climate and pitches do not assist swing bowling. Thus a majority of the Indian batsmen are not used to playing good swing bowling. The new ball hardly swings beyond ten overs so if the batsmen negotiate the initial overs then they are safe. However, the situation is completely different in England where even a 50 over-ball swings prodigiously. Because of this, the Indian batsmen invariably struggle under English conditions at Lord's, Manchester, Leeds, etc.

This is probably why Ashok Mankad, son of the legendary Vinoo Mankad, had an excellent record in domestic cricket (12,980 runs at an average of 50.9 runs) but a modest record in Test matches (991 runs at an average of 25.41 runs).

This problem of struggling in alien conditions is common among non-Asian nations too. England and New Zealand's batsmen have always played well in their home conditions where the ball swings and seams but they struggle on 'slow turners' of the Indian subcontinent. England's Graeme Hick is an example of this phenomenon—he scored 41,112 runs at an average of 52.23 runs in domestic cricket but averaged just 31.32 runs in Test cricket.

The adaptability problem is not restricted to the batsmen alone. The case of Indian spinners is no different. They are used to bowling on the 'dust bowls' in India which assist a great degree of turn. In India, it is quite common to see the ball turning right from the second day of a Test match. However the conditions are quite different when they travel abroad. Apart from a rare pitch that assists spin like Sydney or Port of Spain, majority of the pitches abroad offer very little turn. The Indian spinners struggle while bowling on faster pitches that don't assist spin.

The case of English pace bowlers is quite similar. Since most of them are not 'lightning quick', they depend on favourable weather and pitch conditions. This is why majority of their bowlers look like world beaters under helpful home conditions but the same bowlers look mediocre while bowling in India, Pakistan, and Sri Lanka because the pitches and climate do not assist them.

This is what makes Australian cricket worth admiring. They not only have an excellent track record at home but have also won lots of matches in India, Sri Lanka, England, South Africa, and West Indies. Their batsmen are quick to adapt to low bounce in India and high swing in England. Similarly, their pace bowlers know how to extract bounce on slow Sri Lankan pitches while their spinners spin the ball prodigiously even on South African pitches. They probably have one of the best track records among touring sides.

The other important feature of Australian cricket has been their adaptability to different formats of the game. It is probably because they were one of the first nations in the world to realize the importance of 'horses for courses' theory. They decided to have different players for Tests and ODIs. While their Test team had specialist batsmen and bowlers, their ODI squad consisted of many all-rounders and aggressive players. This helped them achieve the same degree of success in both Tests and ODIs.

England has traditionally done well in Test cricket but struggled to win any major ODI championship. Sri Lanka has been exactly the opposite—they have an awesome ODI record, including the famous 1996 World Cup victory, but their Test record has been relatively mediocre.

However, Australia has been right at the top in both forms of the game. They have won the World Cup on four occasions—1987, 1999, 2003, and 2007. They have also been among the top three Test cricketing nations in the world since the past three decades. They were the number one cricketing side from late 1990s till late 2000s in both forms of the game. Where others failed Australia succeeded probably because of two reasons—they knew how to adapt to the foreign conditions better and they strongly believed and implemented the 'horses for courses' theory.

Kellogg's Company is an example of how one of the biggest multinational companies struggled initially in India because it did not adapt to Indian culture. It is one of the largest producers of cereal related food products with famous brands like Corn Flakes, Rice Krispies, Frosted Mini-Wheats, etc. It has manufacturing units in 18 countries and its products are marketed in more than 180 countries.

During the early 1990s, the market for cereal food was getting saturated in the US and some of the European countries. At the same time, India was undergoing 'liberalization' of its economy and the government was simplifying its rules for foreign multinationals to establish their base—right from computers to automobiles to food industry. The saturation of western market coupled with India's liberalization made Kellogg's target India. In 1995, they decided to enter the Indian market with their flagship product, Corn Flakes. The marketing pundits felt that if Kellogg's could capture even 10% of India's population of 900 million, then they would be feeding 90 million Indians with Corn Flakes every morning!

Despite great expectations, both from within the company and outside, the product failed. It could hardly achieve 20% of its sales target. Kellogg's tried many different branding techniques but they struggled to make a headway.

There were three primary causes for Kelloggs' failure:

1. Worldwide people ate Corn Flakes with cold milk and Kellogg's assumed that the same would be true for India too. This proved to be wrong because traditionally, Indians prefer hot items during breakfast. When the Indians poured hot milk over Corn Flakes, it turned soggy. This product had been designed to be used with cold milk so it was not suitable for the Indian environment.
2. Since Indian population is primarily middle-class, Corn Flakes proved to be an expensive proposition.
3. Kellogg's probably was slow in recognizing who its real competitors were. In India, people were not used to having a cereal-based breakfast. In South India, it is primarily

Idli, Vada, and Dosa. In North India the staple breakfast is Paranthas. Kelloggs had to compete with these food items. It was difficult to convince a South Indian, who traditionally ate Dosa with a steaming cup of filter coffee, to suddenly switch over to Corn Flakes with cold milk.

Kellogg's realized that it had to do a few things quickly to rectify the situation. Firstly, it had to modify its product so that it would not become soggy when hot milk is poured over it. Secondly, it had to create a market and sell the concept—it had to educate people about this kind of breakfast. Once Kelloggs got its act together, it was able to turn around the situation, and make the Indian venture into a profitable one.

McDonald's is a study in contrast. They did an excellent study of Indians and their food habits including religious beliefs.

One of their main products worldwide is the 'Big Mac' which is a burger made of beef but they were well aware that this would not become their flagship product in a country where cows are considered sacred. They were also aware that the most popular meat dishes in India were chicken and mutton. Their homework also showed that Indians loved spicy food. Equipped with this preliminary knowledge, they decided to launch 'Maharaja Mac' which was made of grilled chicken patties topped with onions, tomatoes, cheese, and spicy mayonnaise. The other dish that they introduced specifically for the Indian market was 'Chicken McCurry Pan' which consists of a rectangular shaped crust topped with chicken, bell peppers, cheese, tomato curry sauce, and spices.

Since India has a very high vegetarian population, McDonald's was quick to realize that it had to introduce sufficient vegetarian dishes to attract a major part of the nation's population. It introduced two vegetarian burgers 'McAlooTikki Burger' and 'McVeggie Burger'. Both contained patties made of vegetables like potatoes, peas, carrots, beans, bell peppers, etc. topped with tomato slices, onions, and seasoning. Since Chinese food is very popular in India, McDonald's also introduced 'Crispy Chinese' consisting of vegetarian patty topped with Szechuan sauce and lettuce. The popularity of paneer in most parts of India drove them to launch the 'Paneer Salsa Wrap'.

McDonald's was sensitive to the religious beliefs of Indians so it ensured that the vegetarian and non-vegetarian meals were prepared in separate parts of the restaurant. Even the cooks preparing vegetarian food wore green aprons.

McDonald's, like the Australian cricket team practiced the 'horses for courses' theory very well; so it is not surprising that they had a successful launch in the Indian market—a market which is culturally quite different from the American and European ones that they were accustomed to. If a company is making products only for its domestic market then it just needs to focus on the product's quality and cost. However, if it wants to become a global leader and succeed beyond its home markets, it should not only be sensitive to alien conditions but also be quick in adapting them.

6

KNOW YOUR MARKET

Year 1950
TOMATOES
ONIONS
CARROTS
POTATOES
PUMPKIN
Year 2013
MOBILEPHONES
DVDs
TABLETS
SMARTPHONES
LAPTOPS
HIGH TECH

Protectionism Doesn't Work
(Indian Cricket — Hindustan Motors)

'I have been up against tough competition all my life. I wouldn't know how to get along without it.'

— Walt Disney

What differentiates a great team from a good team is the ability to win in hostile conditions. The Indian cricket team has always performed well on its home soil but struggled to win on fast bouncy tracks of places like Australia and South Africa. One of the main reasons for this is the inability of Indian batsmen to handle short-pitched bowling.

In each and every cricketing nation, the tracks are prepared to suit the home team and India is no different. Most of the pitches in India are known as 'dust bowls' with very little grass on the surface. Due to this the ball rarely bounces above the waist. The Indian batsmen are very comfortable in playing under such conditions. However, in 2004, the home team was extremely shocked on the eve of the 3rd Test against Australia. The Nagpur pitch had a green top and resembled the pitch of Brisbane or Perth of Australia!

The Australians were naturally delighted because it resembled their home pitches. Being experts in playing mind games, the Australian players began to say that this match was theirs, and India had very little hopes of even salvaging a draw!

The Indians on their part made matters worse for themselves.

Instead of practising for the game which was bound to help fast bowlers, they wasted a lot of time in repeatedly inspecting the green pitch and complaining about it. There seemed to be more discussions about the green top, the groundsman who had laid it, the Vidharba Cricket Association, etc—no one seemed to be discussing strategies to combat the rampaging Aussies on a green top!

India had mentally lost the match even before the first ball was bowled. Indian skipper withdrew, complaining of illness. There were allegations that he didn't want to face the Australian pace battery on such a surface. The Indian team, without its captain, sank faster than the Titanic. The Australians batted first and scored 398 runs. The Indians, who were demoralized by the look of the green grass, collapsed for just 185 runs. In the second innings, Australians scored 329 runs and in reply, India once again meekly succumbed for just 200 runs. Australia won the match within four days by 342 runs!

This Test match proved two things. Firstly, over the years, India had failed to develop the required competence to bat on a grassy surface. Secondly, when suddenly faced with a situation where the local conditions didn't favour them, the Indian team did not focus on winning the game in a seemingly hostile environment. The team members and officials seemed to be discussing the green surface, the amount of grass that should be retained, etc. No one in the team said, 'Right, here we have a wicket that will definitely favour the visiting team. What should we do to combat their pace attack on such a wicket? What should we do differently?'

Hindustan Motors was India's leading automobile company and the flagship company of the C.K. Birla Group. Established in 1942 by B.M. Birla in a small assembly plant in Gujarat, it was later moved to West Bengal in 1948. The rise and fall of Hindustan Motors is a good case study of a company which was unable to adapt itself when the business environment changed.

The company's initial models were based on Morris Oxford III, designed by Morris Motor Company at Cowley, Oxford, United Kingdom. The company's leading brand 'Ambassador' became the most popular car in India. Its good suspension made customers feel that it was the most suitable car for the Indian road conditions. Its size gave the look of a 'family car'. It soon achieved iconic status because it became the most preferred car by India's government officials, politicians, including the Prime Minister of the country.

From 1950s to 1980s, the Indian Government did not allow foreign car manufacturers to enter the Indian market. Due to these restrictions Hindustan Motors and Premier Automobiles had a monopoly in the Indian automobile market and were the leading car brands.

1980s and 1990s changed all of that. The government opened its doors for foreign players and this resulted in many multinational companies like Suzuki, Honda, Toyota, Ford, General Motors, Hyundai, etc. setting up in India. Hindustan Motors, with three decades of favourable environment backing, had become very complacent. It was unable to create an entry barrier for the new entrants. It was also unable to compete with them on features, quality, service, and cost—the main attributes that a customer looks for.

Hindustan Motors hired consultants McKinsey & Co. to turn around its business. It implemented McKinsey & Co.'s recommendations of restructuring the organization. It setup a plant in Indore to assemble engines and gearboxes. Subsequently, it tied up with Mahindra & Mahindra for developing petrol engines. It sold its earthmoving equipment division to reduce its debts. It also made changes in its distribution system to make it more customer-friendly. It launched Contessa to compete in the luxury car segment. Unfortunately most of these changes were 'too little, too late'.

Hindustan Motors lost its major market share due to numerous factors—complacency due to lack of global competition till 1980s, obsolete technology, poor product quality, lack of focus on distribution, and customer service. Added to these, it also suffered from labour problems at its production facility.

The company also depended heavily on sales of taxis and government vehicles. Unfortunately, with the entry of Maruti Suzuki, it lost its stranglehold in both these sectors. Hindustan Motors also didn't come up with any new models apart from Ambassador and Contessa.

The case of the Indian cricket team at Nagpur is very similar to the Hindustan Motors situation in the 1980s. In both cases, they performed very well under favourable local conditions, but struggled when the local conditions didn't favour them.

What could have been done differently?

In case of the Indian cricket team, there were two possible approaches—one was short-term and the other was long-term. The short-term solution should have been to quickly regroup, select the best team suited for playing under such conditions, and in the brief time that they had at the nets, practice the art of playing short-pitched bowling. The long-term strategy would have been to proactively develop fast tracks in India so that the Indian batsmen could be accustomed to playing on hard and bouncy surfaces right from their entry into domestic cricket.

Hindustan Motors could also have taken a similar two-pronged approach. Their short-term strategy could have been to ramp up the quality of their customer service, and their long-term strategy should have been to proactively improve the quality of their products and services. Had they been manufacturing inexpensive fuel efficient cars backed by good customer service then it would have raised the entry barrier for new foreign entrants into the Indian automobile market. Unfortunately, similar to the Indian cricket team, Hindustan Motors was happy with being kings in their own backyard, and never imagined that one day the situation might turn hostile and lead them to be defeated at the hands of global giants who had better paraphernalia to exploit the prevailing local conditions.

Whether it is a cricket team or an organization, the ability to perform equally well under hostile conditions is the hallmark of greatness.

Value for Money

(West Indies, India—Southwest Airlines, Maruti Suzuki)

'Price is what you pay. Value is what you get.'

—Warren Buffet

An important aspect that we have not discussed so far is the cost of the product. You might have the best product in the world, but if itscost is not in line with the customer's expectations then the product will bomb in the market.

Since time immemorial, West Indies and the Indian subcontinent have been known to draw huge crowds for cricket matches. In the Caribbean matches, the spectators flock in large numbers and bring with them different kinds of musical instruments. You can hear West Indian calypso songs being played during such matches. The atmosphere in the cricket stadium is that of a carnival.

The 1987 and 1996 World Cup tournaments were conducted in the Indian subcontinent. As anticipated, huge crowds flocked the stadia in India, Pakistan, Sri Lanka, and Bangladesh. West Indies decided to host the World Cup tournament in 2007. Since West Indians are also extremely passionate about cricket, ICC was confident of huge crowds at Bridgetown, Georgetown, Port of Spain, Kingston, Antigua, and other centres.

Unfortunately, West Indies Cricket Board priced the tickets very high which made it unaffordable to the common man. As in case of India, the spectators in West Indies primarily consist of middle-class people and the high cost of tickets meant that they preferred to stay away from the stadium. For a country where it was common to witness packed stadia, it was shocking to see half empty stands during the World Cup matches. The situation was far worse in matches that did not involve the home team.

A few years later, we saw a repition of this in 2011 when England toured India. England and India played five ODI matches at Hyderabad, Mohali, New Delhi, Mumbai, and Kolkata. Cricket is a religion in India and draws the highest number of spectators in the world. If BCCI had expected to see full houses, they were in for a rude shock. The first game at Hyderabad was played in front of many empty stands. People were quick to attribute this to the Telengana issue that was hounding the city since the past one year. However, the next two matches at Mohali and New Delhi fared no better. The spectators stayed away from these venues too.

The 4th match was played at the famous Wankhede Stadium in Mumbai. Mumbai is known as the Mecca for Indian cricket, and hence everyone expected a full house especially since India had won the thrilling finals of the 2011 World Cup against Sri Lanka at the same venue a few months ago. Sadly, the stadium was half empty as India won its fourth match in a row. The 5th match was played at Eden Gardens, Kolkata. Eden Gardens, with a capacity of 1,00,000, is the second largest stadium in the world, next only to Melbourne Cricket Ground. Most of the past matches have been played to the full gallery and this was expected to be no different. Unfortunately, this game too saw a poor crowd turnout.

Normally crowds keep away if the home team is playing poorly. However, this was not the case because India was on a winning spree and completed a 5–0 'whitewash'. The reason for low turnout was analysed and attributed to the high cost of tickets and too much cricket.

The problem of high cost of tickets resulting in poor turnouts has affected other nations too. Each country has tried to come up with innovative solutions to attract crowds. In certain countries, the entry for Test matches has been made free. In a few countries, school children are exempted from entry tickets—this has been done to make the game more popular with the youth.

In one of the earlier chapters we have seen the concept of 'fun@ work' at Southwest Airlines as one of the reasons for the airlines' popularity. The other important reason for the tremendous success of this American airliner was its low cost.

Southwest Airlines was able to reduce the fares to less than half of its competitors. It could achieve this by doing the following:

1. It operated with only one kind of aircraft—Boeing 737s. Because of this, it spent less on staff training, aircraft maintenance, and spares inventory. The pilots had to undergo training only on one aircraft so it kept their training budget low. Having only 737s, they had to stock critical spares of only one type of aircraft.
2. Once their aircraft landed, they were able to turn around and depart to the next destination in less than half an hour. This was achieved by having its staff play multiple roles, Pilots, cabin crew, gate attendants—everyone played a role in ensuring that the idle time between landing and the next take off was minimum. Due to this, the number of flights operated per aircraft per day at Southwest Airlines was much higher than its competitors. This ensured that its overhead costs got amortised over more flights and in turn, this resulted in lower operating costs per flight.
3. Most of its flights were operated point to point—this ensured that each Southwest Airlines plane had more flights per day compared to its competitors.
4. Southwest has also been a no frills airlines to keep its cost under control. It does not serve meals to its passengers. There

are also no electronic gadgets for inflight entertainment of the passengers.

All these measures have made Southwest Airlines one of the largest airlines in the US in terms of domestic air passengers. As per 2011 figures, it operated 3,400 flights per day. The Southwest model has become very popular and an inspiration for many low-cost airlines all over the world.

The two major car manufacturers in India during 1950s– 1970s were Hindustan Motors and Premier Automobiles. Their flagship products were Ambassador and Premier Padmini respectively. Though both these cars were neither fuel efficient nor used the latest technology, they could jointly garner a market share of more than 90%, primarily because of the government's restrictions on foreign automobile manufacturers' entry into the Indian market. For a common man, Ambassador and Premier Padmini cars were not affordable due to high costs. This led to a very slow growth of the automotive market till late 1970s.

As the oil prices shot up during late 1970s, the Indian government felt the need to have fuel efficient cars at affordable prices. It decided to create an automobile company which would be a joint venture between the Indian government and a foreign automobile manufacturer. Toyota, Nissan, Honda, and Suzuki were invited for initial discussions and finally Suzuki was selected. This led to the formation of Maruti Udyog Limited in 1981.

Japanese automobile manufacturers were famous for low-cost, fuel-efficient cars and Suzuki was no different. It brought the latest technology to its Indian venture. Japanese companies were also known for good shopfloor practices like JIT, Kaizen, etc. and Suzuki introduced the same concepts in Maruti Suzuki. The company also developed a very strong vendor network in India. Ancillary units in and around Gurgoan were setup to make automotive parts for Maruti Suzuki. This not only helped the company to lower its raw material cost (through indigenisation) but also helped it achieve fast turnaround time between the design and manufacture of these components.

All these helped Maruti Suzuki become India's largest passenger car company. The company initially introduced 'Maruti 800' which was the cheapest and most fuel-efficient car in India. It became the darling of the masses and the symbol of the common man. It soon introduced 'Maruti Omni' which was also a major hit among the consumers. The success of Maruti 800 saw the company introduce its classier version—the 1000cc Maruti Zen. These models from the Maruti Suzuki stable took the country by a storm and left their competitors far behind. It was not just the low price, people preferred these cars because they had more features than many of their competitors.

Today, the company has a wide range of products starting from entry level products such as Alto to hatchback models like Eeco, Estilo, Ritz, A-Star, Swift, Wagon-R, and premium products like Dzire, Ertiga, and SX4. The Maruti 800 model alone has sold more than a million cars so far.

These examples help us understand the importance of price and value of a product. When we enter any shop and examine the product, our fingers invariably go on the price tag. Price is measureable and hence tangible and easy to understand. This is why most of the discussions in any corporate meetings—be it finance, manufacturing, or sales—are centred on the price of the product. What is invariably missed out is the focus on its value. Value is difficult to understand and measure because it's intangible and subjective. It is also not an absolute number but relative to the other options available.

Let us once again look at the above examples. During 1970s and 1980s, TV coverage of cricket matches was quite poor in terms of both quality and the numer of matches covered. Many of the matches did not have a live telecast, so cricket fans were forced to go to the stadium. Even in the case of live TV coverage, the quality of transmission was quite poor in many cases. Because of these reasons, the spectators perceived a very high 'value' of seeing the matches in the stadium compared to watching it at home. All this changed in 1990s. The TV coverage quality improved by leaps and bounds. Technology advances led to multiple cameras, spider cameras, stump vision, Hawk eye, slow motion replays, hotspot, etc. Apart from this, the quality of the TV sets and digital transmission with set-top box had also dramatically improved. The advent of LCD TV, LED TV, HDTV, etc. has made home viewing a pleasure. Having a giant screen LED TV increased the value of watching cricket matches from home. This means that even if the ticket price remains constant, the value of watching the match at the stadium decreases. Given such a scenario, if the price of the ticket also increases, as seen in the above examples, then the value of watching in the stadium goes down further.

Let us once again look at the example of the Indian automobile industry. The prices of Ambassador and Premier Padmini were quite stable and so were the sales. People saw a specific value for these cars that remained unchanged during 1970s. However, during the 1980s, Maruti Suzuki's flagship products—Maruti 800, Maruti Omni, and Maruti Zen, were launched with more features compared to their competitors. Customers began to see a high 'value for money' for Maruti products. This in turn lowered the value for Ambassador and Premier Padmini, though their price remained unchanged.

As Warren Buffet rightly says—Price is what you pay and value is what you get. This means that we need to be sensitive to both these aspects because these are what the customers look at.

Looking at the Bigger Picture

(Sunil Gavaskar, Salim Durrani—Amazon)

'The more you chase the Holy Grail of short-term performance, the less you get in long-term results.'

—Walter Cabot

India played a three match series against Australia in 1981. Australia won the first Test while the second Test ended in a draw. This made the third Test match at Melbourne very important for Indians because they had to win it to level the series. India batted first and scored 237 runs thanks to a brilliant century by G.R. Vishwanath. Australia's Allan Border too scored a century to help his team reach 419 runs. India started off its 2nd innings with a huge deficit of 182 runs, and it needed a good start from its openers when they came out to bat for the second time. Sunil Gavaskar and Chetan Chauhan, by posting a century partnership, gave just the start that India needed.

Unfortunately, disaster struck when the Indian score was 165. Indian skipper Sunil Gavaskar was struck on the pads and was adjudged lbw to fiery Australian fast bowler Dennis Lillee. Gavaskar was upset and stood his ground because he was convinced that he was not out. One of the Australian fielders sledged him and that made matters worse. Gavaskar, who was already fuming, became even more upset. He spoke to his batting partner Chetan Chauhan and forced him to leave the pitch along with him. All the Australian players were stunned to see both Indian batsmen walking back towards the pavilion.

Salim Durani, the team manager realized the gravity of the situation and quickly intervened. He had a long discussion with Sunil Gavaskar, and convinced him that the match should continue to keep the spirit of the game alive. Durani also pointed out to Gavaskar that if the Indians refused to continue the game, the Australians would be declared winners. Gavaskar finally relented and allowed Chetan Chauhan to return to the crease, along with the 'one-down' batsman Dilip Vengsarkar. Helped by useful knocks from Dilip Vengsarkar, G.R. Vishwanath, and Sandeep Patil, India managed to make 324 runs.

When the Australians came in to bat for the second time, they needed a mere 143 runs to win. However, Kapil Dev, in an inspired spell of fast bowling, took 5 wickets and was ably supported by Karsan Ghavri and Dilip Doshi who took 2 wickets each. Australians crashed to 83 runs with only 3 batsmen managing to reach double figures. It is believed that Gavaskar's protest against the wrong decision had fired up the Indians, and that was a major factor in winning the game by 59 runs.

For a moment, think what would have happened if India had not continued and forfeited the game. Australia would have been declared winners. However, both Salim Durrani and Sunil Gavaskar thought that it's better to sacrifice the short-term loss of a wrong decision and think about the match. This long-term vision helped India achieve an incredible victory. India had already lost the 1st match at Sydney and managed to draw the 2nd match at Adelaide. If India had forfeited this match then Australia would have won the series 2–0 but because India won this Test match it leveled the series 1–1. So the team's decision to continue despite the setback not only helped India win the Test match but also square the series.

Years later, Gavaskar himself regretted his behaviour and

apologized for the incident. He said that the game is always greater than the individual and such incidents bring disrepute to both the game as well as the individual. This also demonstrates the greatness of Gavaskar who had the courage to apologize for his behaviour and accept his mistake.

Amazon is an American multinational company headquartered in Seattle, USA. It is the largest online retailer in the world and ships its products to most countries across the globe. It started off as an online bookstore but later diversified into DVDs, CDs, software, video games, electronic items, toys, etc.

Amazon was founded by Jeff Bezos in 1994. He wanted to choose a name that began with the alphabet 'A' so that it would appear early in any list which is in alphabetical order. He chose Amazon because like the river Amazon he wanted his company to become the biggest in the world. The company's logo has an arrow between the 'A' and the 'Z' to indicate his goal to have a product in every alphabet. The other reason why Jeff Bezos chose the name Amazon was because he wanted his organization to be 'exotic and different', just like the famous river and he succeeded in doing just that!

Right from its inception, Amazon was a different kind of an organization. It always believed in long-term strategies rather than short-term gains. The company did not reach profitability during the first few years of its operations but that did not worry Bezos because he was thinking of popularizing the online retailing concept around the world and not just chase short-term profits.

The company has missed Wall Street's estimates on more than one occasion. But it believes in risk taking strategies for growth rather than satisfying the experts at Wall Street. As its CEO and founder Bezos puts it: 'We have a willingness to fail and be misunderstood. If you don't have a willingness to be misunderstood for a long period of time, then you can't have long-term orientation'. He also says that the best way to achieve your long-term strategies is to stick to it and ignore the sceptics and critics.

Normally, a company's dip in revenues and profitability sees employee lay-offs, cuts in R&D budget, slash in advertising budgets, less focus on innovation, and more focus on 'maintaining the existing products'. Amazon works the other way around. It does not hesitate to launch more products and hire more people. It believes in sacrificing short-term profits to create more value for the future.

When Amazon launched Kindle in 2007, many felt that it was a disastrous move.The sceptics felt that Amazon had no experience in consumer electronics products. Kindle's cost of $399 was considered to be very expensive. However, Amazon stuck to its plans and invested heavily into this product and achieved amazing results.

Everyone struggles to balance between short-term gains and long-term returns—be it an individual or an organization. In the cricketing example, India started its second innings with a huge deficit. When Gavaskar was ruled out lbw, his first thoughts were obviously about the immediate disaster. He probably felt that the rest of his teammates would not be able to post a total which would be big enough to defend. So his short-term thinking made him walk off the field and protest against the umpiring decision. This was not a right gesture because in cricket an umpire's decision is always final. Even if a dismissed person stands an extra minute at the crease, it is perceived as dissent and he is fined a percentage of his match fee. To be walking off the field was probably thousand times worse than this. Luckily Salim Durani was able to convince Gavaskar and make him realize the drawbacks of his decision. To give credit to Gavaskar, he realized his folly and the impact that it would have on the match and the series. He allowed the match to continue and India managed to win it and thereby, square the series.

When you have a mature product in the market, like a TV, car, or a phone, there is no need for you to sell the concept of the product. This is because people have already been using your competitor's products or an older version of your own product. In such a case, if a company focuses more on short-term gains, it might probably work. This is because you don't have to invest your time in selling the concept nor is there an incubation period. If your product is good then people will pick it off the shelves.

However, this is not the case while selling an innovative product or a service. You require loads of patience because you have to start right from scratch. You need to first convince your stakeholders and investors that there is a good potential market for your product. Once you are ready with your product, you need to educate your potential customers about the benefits that it offers. You need to focus not only on your product but the concept itself. Majority of the people are resistant to change so asking them to buy your product can be a herculean task. Your initial years will see a lot of investment with very little return. This should not demotivate the organization or its shareholders because you are bound to experience a long incubation period.

When Jeff Bezos started Amazon, online purchase of books was a very new concept. There were many sceptics who were ready to write off Amazon. People always loved to go to bookstores, walk around the aisles, pick up some books, flip through a few pages, chat with the store's manager, and finally buy the book. In an online bookstore, you obviously can't do any of these. How did Jeff Bezos expect to be successful?

Well, he succeeded and how!

Amazon has become synonymous with online shopping and in 2013 it achieved a market cap of around $120 billion. This has been mainly due to Jeff Bezos's philosophy that running a business is like crossing a desert—while crossing the desert, we may feel thirsty but we should not give up if we sincerely believe that we will soon reach the oasis.

While writing this book, USA is going through difficult economic problems. Companies are freezing R&D budgets, laying off people, and looking at only short-term fixes. Amazon is doing just the opposite. There are many economists in USA who believe that if all other American companies began to follow Amazon's strategy of investing heavily to achieve long-term goals then USA would recover from its current economic downturn.

First Mover Advantage

(England Team — Kodak)

'I've always found that the speed of the boss is the speed of the team.'

— Lee Iacocca

Cricket was born in England during the 16th century. For the next few centuries, this game slowly evolved and the first official Test match was played between England and Australia in 1877 in Melbourne. During the initial years, the only countries that played the game were England and Australia. The English took the game to many countries that they ruled and slowly, cricket gained popularity in all those places too.

By the middle of the 19th century, countries such as India, West Indies, Pakistan, New Zealand, and South Africa also began to actively pursue this game. Subsequently Sri Lanka, Zimbabwe, and Bangladesh were also given the 'official status' by admitting them into the ICC fold.

Since the game was invented in England, they had an extremely good infrastructure in place for the development of cricket. Every summer, different English counties participated in inter-county matches. This helped England develop strong bench strength since they had atleast 3–4 good players from each county.

From 1930s to 1970s, England ruled the roost. Most cricketing records were held by Englishmen—highest number of wickets in a match (Jim Laker), highest aggregate of wickets (Freddie Trueman), highest number of runs in an innings (Len Hutton), highest aggregate of runs (Geoff Boycott), highest runs scored by any team in an innings (903–7 vs. Australia), etc.

However, 1970s and 1980s saw the emergence of countries like Australia and West Indies. These countries began to play aggressive cricket and cricket no longer remained a 'gentleman's game'. Australia had the Chappell brothers, Dennis Lillee, Jeff Thompson, Rodney Marsh, Dough Walters, etc. West Indies not only had aggressive batsmen like Gordon Greenidge, Clive Lloyd, Garfield Sobers, and Vivian Richards but also a battery of lethal fast bowlers like Andy Roberts, Michael Holding, Joel Garner, Colin Croft, and Malcolm Marshall.

Though England had the 'first mover advantage', the biggest problem with English cricket was that their game never really changed during the 1970s and 1980s. Most of their Test cricketers were products from county cricket which was still being played in the same manner as in the 1950s. West Indies were repeatedly able to 'whitewash' the England team even when the latter played under home conditions. The Ashes series, once looked upon as the clash among tequals, as turning out to be a one-sided affair because the Englishmen were no match to the mighty Australians.

1980s and 1990s also saw the emergence of South Asian countries like India, Pakistan, and Sri Lanka. It also saw the return of South Africa which had been banned due to apartheid. England, once the best team in the world, had slipped in the world rankings.

In early 1970s, England invented the 'limited overs cricket—also known as ODI (One Day International). Here also, England could never really exploit the first mover advantage. Though the first three World Cup tournaments were played in England, they could not take advantage of the home conditions and didn't win in 1975, 1979, and 1983. Subsequently, seven more World Cup tournaments were played between1987 and 2011 but England has never been able to win the World Cup.

One of the prime reasons for England's lack of success in ODIs has been its inability to adapt to the fast-paced game. English players have always concentrated on the longer version of the game. Only in recent times, has it decided to have separate captains and set of players for the ODIs.

English cricket is an example of how a country that invented a game could not change itself to meet the demands of the modern conditions. In recent times, it had to watch relatively new entrants like Pakistan and Sri Lanka winning the World Cup (in 1992 and 1996 respectively).

In the earlier sections, we have seen the importance of innovation that led to the success of companies like Hotmail, Apple, Google, Facebook, etc. We have also discussed the need to change and adapt according to the situation. Motorola's failure to adapt to the new changing technology in GSM began its downslide. In the case of Motorola, it was primarily driven by complacency and a case of 'resting on its past laurels'. Kodak also makes an interesting case study. It too failed to move into the new technology but in this case, the reasons were different—it was primarily a case of slow speed and the unwillingness to invest in new competencies and technologies.

Eastman Kodak, an American multinational company that produces photographic materials and equipment, was founded by George Eastman in 1892. Popularly known as Kodak, the company was synonymous with photography. Kodak had a near monopoly in most parts of the world. This led to a state of complacency and a sense of arrogance.

The first signs of trouble came in the 1980s when its Japanese rival, Fuji Photo Film Co. launched its 400-speed colour film rolls. The Fuji product was as good as Kodak's and 20% cheaper. This eroded Kodak's market share in the 400-speed film roll segment. However, Kodak didn't take much notice of it since it considered the dent insignificant.

In 1981, Sony launched Mavica, a digital camera that didn't use any film rolls. The output of this camera could be displayed on monitors and TV screens or printed on paper. Since Kodak was a pioneer in the field of film technology and photography, one would have expected it to put all efforts to charge into the digital market. Shockingly, Kodak just sat back and watched. It was not convinced that the expensive digital cameras could ever replace the tried and tested silver halide technology. While Kodak's competitors were busy launching new products based on digital technology, Kodak chose to ignore and continued its investment in obsolete technology.

Apart from its inability to recognize new technology and trends, the other factor that affected Kodak was its inability to take risks. Most of Kodak's workforce had expertise in film technology and conventional cameras. The company did not want to take the risk of exposing its employees to newer technologies. This lack of investment in modern machinery and skills also led to the company's downfall. As in the case of any electronic product, the prices of digital cameras too kept crashing every year. Soon, the cost of a digital camera became low enough for a common man to afford it. On one hand the sales of conventional cameras and films kept falling and year after year on the other, digital cameras kept registering healthy growth.

As business continued to decline, Kodak saw its share prices plummet from $80 in 1997 to $30 by 2003. It was only as late as in 2003 when Kodak's CEO Daniel Carp took serious notice of the photography market and decided to focus on digital technology. It restructured its existing film business and invested in newer technologies. It also laid off around 11,000 workers. Unfortunately it was a case of 'too little too late'. The digital market was flooded with cameras from its competitors and Kodak could not regain its numero uno position. In 2004, it decided to stop marketing film cameras because it was no longer financially viable. In 2009, the company decided to stop manufacturing its legendary 74-year-old product, the Kodachrome colour film.

By 2005, it had hit a low $24 per share and in the year 2011, it was trading at around $1 per share. Its outgoing CEO, Daniel Carp himself confessed that he had seen the first digital camera 20 years ago and realized that his company had to transform itself. However, no one knows why it took 20 long years for this to be implemented. Kodak's case was that of an organization that was unable to judge the future technology quickly enough and even when it later realized it, it was very slow in implementing it.

Both England and Kodak were pioneers in their field—England invented all forms of cricket; Kodak was one of the most well-known companies in the field of photography. Both rose to great heights because they had the 'first mover advantage'. In case of England, they had the advantage of having the best infrastructure and technology. Moreover, competition came only from one country, i.e., Australia. However, they didn't make use of these initial strengths and allowed Australia, West Indies, and the three Asian teams to dominate the game. Today, the game is most popular in India and the high spectator turnout and sponsorship has made BCCI (Board of Cricket for Control in India) one of the richest and most powerful cricketing boards in the world. The rise in Asian power also probably influenced ICC's decision to relocate its headquarters from England to Dubai.

Fotoflash is one of the biggest chains of stores that sell cameras, film rolls, and albums. It had many franchise shops all over the city and there was one such shop close to my home. Till a few years back, this shop used to be bustling with activity. There would be different kinds of customers—people who came to buy film rolls, cameras, albums or get photographed in the shop's studio. With the advent of digital cameras, people neither bought film rolls nor albums since the digital images are transferred from the camera to a CD or hard disk. This drastically reduced the number of customers coming to this shop. Today, this shop is completely deserted and has become a pale shadow of itself. A few weeks back when I made a rare visit to this shop, I noticed that almost three-fourths of the shop space had been converted into a godown to store cement bags! The owner informed me that with dwindling business, it was no longer viable to retain huge space for photography business so he had leased out a major portion of his shop to a cement dealer!

As I walked out of this shop, I was left wondering what would have happened if Kodak had made use of its 'first mover advantage' and equipped itself to the changing technology—probably this shop would have still been a photography shop selling digital cameras, printing digital images, burning CDs, and helping customers design their own albums with the latest software tools.

THE HIDDEN COMPETITOR

(CRICKET — SONY, APPLE)

'I think it's really important to look at the big picture instead of just one competition.'

— Shannon Miller

Know your competition—easier said than done. One of the most common mistakes that people make is to look at companies making similar products as competitors. Nothing can be farther from truth. During 1950s and 1960s, cricket was played in just one format—Test match cricket. When limited overs cricket (ODIs) took birth in 1970s, the traditionalists viewed this form of the game as a 'competitor' to Test cricket. As crowds began to dwindle at Test match venues, it soared at the ODIs. It was fair to say that Test cricket was losing out to its competitor, the ODIs.

By late 1990s, ODI was slowly becoming predictable and hence boring. When the Twenty20 format was introduced, people viewed this format as a strong competitor to both the earlier formats of the game—Test matches and ODIs. This was again a fair statement because if a person had to choose between a 5 day Test match and a short Twenty20 game, he would choose the latter. The purists even moaned that these shorter formats were cannibalising Test cricket.

Though these conclusions are quite logical, are these the only form of competition? What about other forms of entertainment? Aren't they competitors too?

India is a cricket-crazy nation and the game is viewed by over a billion people. However, when important tournaments like Wimbledon Open (tennis) or FIFA World Cup (football) are played, even some of the die-hard cricket fans switch to these games. If Brazil plays Argentina in a football World Cup final, you can bet that there will be far less people at Eden Gardens Kolkata watching India play a test match against England. In this case, the football match is the real competitor for the test match at Kolkata.

In India, apart from cricket, the other great form of entertainment is Bollywood movies. On a Friday afternoon, if a Shah Rukh Khan Blockbuster releases in the movie theatres at Mumbai, won't there be a drop in the number of spectators who come to watch an ODI match between India and New Zealand being played at the Wankhede Stadium? Isn't Shah Rukh Khan's movie a competitor for the ODI match?

Sony is a Japanese multinational company headquartered in Tokyo. It is one of the leading manufacturers of electronics products and operates in six segments—consumer products & services group, professional device & solutions group, pictures, music, financial services, and Sony Ericsson joint venture. In 1946, Masaru Ibuka and Akio Morita founded the company Tokyo Tsushin Kogyo. Twelve years later, the company changed its name to Sony.

Masaru Ibuka and Akio Morita asked their design teams to come up with a revolutionary product that could be targeted towards the youth. The design teams worked very hard on various designs and finally came up with the world's first portable music player. This 1979 product was named Walkman since people could wear headphones and listen to the music even while they were mobile. The conventional music systems were big in size and operated on AC power so they were not portable. However, Walkman was different—it was miniature in size and could be carried anywhere since it operated on batteries.

Walkman was targeted at youth—its advertisements showed young boys and girls wearing the Walkman headphones and roller skating or jogging in a park. Since initially the product did not have a 'record' button, sceptics were not sure of its success. However, an innovative product combined with some clever advertising made Walkman a rage in Japan. Within six months of its launch, it was introduced in other parts of the world. Walkman was the first of its kind product and became synonymous with portable music systems. Soon, it found its way into some of the prestigious dictionaries.

Walkman had created a completely new market and ten years after its introduction, it had sold around 50 million units worldwide. By 1995, Sony had sold more than 150 million units worldwide. Unfortunately, as in the case of many successful companies, Sony too became complacent of its innovation. More importantly, it failed to recognize competition even when it was standing right in the front!

Apple Inc., the American multinational company once famous for its iconic Macintosh range of computers, was struggling in 1990s. During the late 1990s and early 2000, it decided to make a foray into the consumer electronics arena. In 2001, it first opened Apple Retail Stores and subsequently bought Spruce Technologies, a DVD authoring company. The same year, it introduced iPod, a digital audio player. This product was extremely successful all over the world. Its first model had a very user-friendly interface and was equipped with a 5GB hard disk and in Steve Jobs' own words, 'it could store over a thousand songs'.

The basic concept of iPod was very similar to Sony's Walkman. It was a mobile music player equipped with headphones, and the user could use it even when he was 'on the move'. Ideally, we should have expected Sony, with its Walkman range of products, to have come up with such a product since iPod is a logical extension of Walkman. Unfortunately, Sony was unable to recognize the need for such a product.

What made matters worse was the fact that even when Apple introduced iPod, Sony failed to recognize it as a competing product for its Walkman. Sony always looked at other consumer electronics companies such as Panasonic, Sanyo, Samsung, LG, etc. as its competitors. It neither looked at Apple nor its products as a competitor. Based on Apple's iPod's success when Takashi Fukushima, Head of Walkman division, was asked if Sony too would incorporate a hard disk to its product, he reportedly said, 'Hard disks are not interesting because anyone can make them!'

What Fukushima and Sony failed to realize was that the same 'uninteresting' hard disk could store 100 times more songs than a Walkman.

Sony was late in recognizing the market for hard disk based music systems and even when it realized its folly, it continued to make many mistakes. Sony was a traditional consumer electronics manufacturing company and could not match Apple in integrating software in its products. For example, one of the reasons for Apple's success was the introduction of iTunes Stores in 2003. Customers could download music at less than a dollar per song and by 2008, there were over 5 billion downloads. Sony sorely missed a similar product and related software. It introduced a product 'Network Walkman' to compete with Apple's iPod. Unfortunately, this product was built on its proprietary ATRAC format which had no takers. MP3 was the most popular digital audio format and Apple was quick to recognize it and all its iPod models supported MP3 and many other popular formats. However, Sony initially decided not to have the MP3 codec in their products; this lead to frustration among Sony users since they had to convert all MP3 songs into Sony's ATRAC format.

By the time Sony introduced MP3, WMA, and other popular formats, it was too late to make any substantial dent into Apple's market share. Apple had sold over 300 million iPods all over the world by 2011, and was the undisputed king of mobile music players.

The key lesson here is that recognizing your competition is as important as innovation. In the cricketing example, we have seen how the game has repeatedly evolved from one format to another. However, despite the authorities trying to make the game interesting, by making frequent changes to the rules of the game, competition from other forms of entertainment eroded the viewership. Similarly if Sony had been quick to realize that the computer giant Apple's hard disk based product would eat into its market share; it would not have been in such a state. It is important to look at the bigger picture and ask yourself frequently, 'What would make a customer overlook my product? Is there a better product in the market?'

The next time an American or European multinational wants to start manufacturing soft drinks in India, it would do well to remember that its competitors are not just the Cokes and Pepsis being sold in supermarkets and restaurants but also the 'nimbupani', 'chai', and 'tender coconut water' sold by the pyjama or lungi clad hawkers on the roadside!

7

TRAITS FOR SUCCESS

'My manager says that my performance should do the talking so I am converting my graphs and charts to audio files and mailing them to him.'

Proactiveness Pays

(Lasith Malinga, Sachin Tendulkar—Ericsson, Nokia)

'A good hockey player plays where the puck is. A great hockey player plays where the puck is going to be.'

—Wayne Gretzky

Sri Lankan fast bowler, Lasith Malinga bowls with an unusual sling action. This style has earned him his nickname 'Slinga Malinga'. Malinga's most dangerous weapon is his in-swinging yorker. Only Pakistan's Waqar Younis could bowl toe-crushing yorkers with the same ferocity and regularity as Malinga.

What made Malinga a very dangerous bowler was his variety—he had an equally good slower ball and a sharp bouncer. His slinging action made it extremely tough for the batsmen to know whether he'd bowl a yorker, bouncer, or a slower ball.

Malinga could bowl in-swinging yorkers at his will. He could do it at the beginningof the innings with a new ball and do the same with an old ball during the death overs. His bowling was very useful especially in the shorter versions of the games because he could choke one end.

Malinga also represented Mumbai Indians in the IPL tournaments and performed extremely well. During IPL 4, he was the highest wicket taker with 28 wickets and this won him the 'Purple Cap'. He also played a very crucial role for Mumbai

Indians during their victorious 2011 Champions League Tournament. His consistency enabled him to take wickets off consecutive balls. He became the first bowler in the world to take two World Cup hat-tricks. He is the only bowler so far to have taken three hat-tricks in ODI matches. He is also the first player in the world to take four wickets in four consecutive balls.

Many cricketers, commentators, and spectators are amazed at the consistency at which Malinga is able to produce those wicket taking deliveries. What they don't realize is the amount of practise he puts in. It is believed that on the eve of any match, after the Sri Lankans finish their net practice, Malinga stays back at the nets. As the rest of the players return to the comforts of the dressing room and take bath or relax, Malinga continues his practice. He places a pair of shoes in front of the stumps and practises his toe-crushing yorkers. Malinga's net practice sessions are a good lesson of being proactive because the next day, he is able to reproduce his weapons with deadly consistency.

The 1998 Australian series against India was touted as 'Sachin Tendulkar vs. Shane Warne' contest. Cricket is a team game involving eleven players on each side so such an advertisement might seem unfair. However, there was no denying the fact that both Tendulkar and Warne were at the peak of their careers and it promised to be a keen battle between the bat and the ball.

The much awaited contest turned out to be a damp squib, thanks to Tendulkar's proactiveness. He was aware that Shane Warne could spin the ball prodigiously. Before the Australian team landed in India, he vigorously practised the sweep and lofted shots against local leg spinners. In order to make it tough for himself, Tendulkar used wet tennis balls that spun like tops!

Finally when the Australians arrived in India, Tendulkar was more than ready for the battle. He was easily able to handle the spin of the much feared Shane Warne and his spin partner Gavin Robertson as he lofted them to all parts of the ground. Tendulkar was one of the major contributors for India winning the series 2–1. With scores of 4 and 155 in the 1st Test at Chennai, 79 in the 2nd Test at Kolkata, 177 and 31 during the 3rd Test at Bangalore, Tendulkar aggregated 446 runs with an astonishing average of 111.50!

More was to follow as the two teams soon clashed at Sharjah. In a 'must-win' game during the qualifying rounds of the Coca Cola Cup, Tendulkar scored a brilliant 143 runs off 131 balls setting up a finals-clash once again between India and Australia. India won the finals as Tendulkar plundered the Australian attack to score 134 runs off 131 balls.

At the end of the Indian and Sharjah series, Shane Warne, the great Australian leg spinner, was honest enough to admit that he was having nightmares of Tendulkar lofting him for sixes. Both Tendulkar and Warne are among the greatest players in the history of cricket but in that season, it was Tendulkar who won the battle primarily because of his proactiveness. Like Malinga, Tendulkar too understood the importance in being proactive and prepared himself before the big game. No wonder both of them have been match winners for their respective countries.

One of the best lessons of proactiveness in the corporate world is the famous incident involving three global technology giants—Nokia, Ericsson, and Philips. During 1990s, both Nokia and Ericsson were renowned companies in the area of cellular communication devices. The two of them along with Motorola accounted for more than 70% of the global market share. However, a fire at the Philips factory changed everything.

Philips had a semiconductors plant in Albuquerque, Mexico. In March 2000, a fire broke out in one of its manufacturing lines. Initially the engineers at Philips thought that the chips that were damaged were only at the manufacturing line where the fire broke out. They estimated that the affected quantity was in the range of a few thousands. In a high volume semiconductor industry, this did not appear to be too bad. They informed about the fire in the plant, and the expected delay in shipments to their major customers which included Nokia and Ericsson.

Though Philips assured all the customers that the expected delay was going to be around a week, Nokia did not feel comfortable. They realized that the extent of damage could be much more than expected. Nokia was proactive on two counts. Firstly, its senior management worked very closely with the senior management of Philips to ensure that Philips manufactured the chips for them at their other manufacturing sites. Secondly, the Nokia engineers tweaked the design a bit so that they could also accommodate non-Philips chips into their mobile phones. This reduced their dependency on Philips. This proactiveness on the part of Nokia ensured that its sales and deliveries did not suffer. Nokia's performance during this quarter was extremely good as its profits rose by 42% and it captured a market share of 30%.

On the other hand, Ericsson was slow to react. Based on the assurances from Philips, it neither looked for alternate chips from Philips nor redesigned its circuit to accommodate chips from other suppliers. It assumed that the deliveries from Philips would come within a week.

Philips had initially assumed that the only chips that were affected were the ones which were manufactured on the line that had caught fire. However, its engineers were in for a rude shock. They realized that the actual damage was much more than a few thousand chips—it was in the range of a few million chips. This was because the water and gas from the fire extinguishers caused huge damage to the silicon wafers and the finished products. It was an irony that the fire extinguishers, meant to save people and property, had actually caused extensive damage to the equipments and raw materials.

Philips subsequently announced that the delay in shipments would not be just a week, as initially estimated, but would probably take a month or more. Since the Philips plant was running at full capacity, it did not have spare capacity to speed up production. Ericsson had not taken any proactive steps so it had to just wait and suffer.

Ericsson reported an operating loss of $200 million and lost its market share by 3%. These losses forced Ericsson to outsource its manufacturing operations to Flextronics. Thousands of employees lost their jobs. Though the company tried many corrective actions, its fortunes didn't improve significantly. Finally in 2001, it tied up with Sony to form Sony Ericsson—a joint venture.

It is not sheer competence but also proactiveness that makes an individual or an organization successful. It is your ability to judge where you want to be and what needs to be done to reach there that makes all the difference.

Nokia acted in a manner befitting any great leader. There was no way it would allow Philips' fire accident to cause a dent in its deliveries and thereby its sales. Ericsson, on the other hand, was quite reactive in its approach and allowed external factors to control its future. Nokia continued to post profits and became the biggest cellular phone manufacturer in the world. Ericsson lost sizeable market share and posted huge losses for many successive quarters.

When a person meets with a fire accident, the fire can char and change the victim's face. In this case, a simple fire changed the face of the entire global mobile industry!

Let Your Performance do the Talking

(Yuvraj Singh, Zaheer Khan — Vikram Pandit, Citibank)

'Great performers in all fields seem immune to what outsiders think about them. Their sense of themselves never depends on the feedback — positive or negative — they get from the environment.'

— John Eliot

During the 2007 Twenty20 World Cup, India played a very crucial game against England in the Super 8 round. MS Dhoni won the toss and decided to bat first. Virender Sehwag and Gautum Gambhir began the game perfectly, and India was well placed at 171 for 3 at the end of the 18th over. At this juncture, England's star all-rounder Andrew Flintoff accosted Yuvraj Singh and sledged him. Yuvraj Singh despite being a volatile player did not lose his temper. He coolly took strike to Stuart Broad who bowled the 19th over. We will never know what had transpired between Andrew Flintoff and Yuvraj Singh but the latter appeared to be fully charged. He smashed Stuart Broad, the English fast bowler, to all parts of the ground. Each delivery from Stuart Broad was despatched over the ropes and his bowling analysis of the 19th over read 6-6-6-6-6-6! This was the first time in the history of Twenty20 cricket that a batsman had hit six consecutive sixes in an over. India ended up with a mammoth 218/4 thanks to a belligerent half century by Yuvraj Singh. This was the fastest half century in Twenty20 cricket and was scored off just 12 balls. In reply, England could manage only 200 and lost the match. India qualified for the semi-finals and went on to win the Twenty20 World Cup Championship.

There are many instances when you might face hostility and the best way to respond to them is through your performance. Yuvraj Singh responded to sledging by scoring one of the best knocks in Twenty20 cricket. In cricketing parlance, it is known as 'letting your batting do the talking'.

The second instance that comes to mind is again a match involving India and England that was played in the same year. During the 2nd Test match at Trent Bridge, the English players threw jelly beans when tail-end batsman Zaheer Khan came out to bat. Even after he began to bat, they continued to harass him by throwing more sweets towards the stumps. Each time he swept a jelly bean off the wicket, there would be another one thrown at him. With Michael Vaughan, England's captain, briefly off the field, his deputy, Andrew Strauss was leading the English team.

Zaheer was sure that this was a bizarre kind of sledging. It is widely believed that the English players threw jelly beans to indicate Zaheer's stockiness. Zaheer went on to score 10 runs in the innings. When England came in to bat, he had sufficient motivation to bowl one of the best and fastest bowling spells of his career. He took 5 wickets for just 75 runs. India scored the required runs and won the match by 7 wickets.

During the post-match interview Zaheer Khan, with match winning figures of 9 for 134, told the media, 'when I went out to bat, there were some jelly beans near the crease. I just swept one off the wicket, and when I played the next ball there were some more, so obviously someone was chucking them from behind. I was upset about it. I went to speak to them and asked what was going on but they came at me hard. I didn't know exactly where they were coming from, and I just felt it was insulting. When I go out on to the cricket field I am serious. This is a Test match we are playing. It definitely inspired me to do well.' England's bizarre prank had backfired badly on them because it fired up Zaheer Khan to bowl one of his most devastating spells in Test cricket.

How many times have we not faced similar hostilities in our professional life? Instead of getting worked up about it, it is best to give a befitting reply through our performance.

Vikram Pandit was appointed as the CEO of Citigroup in December 2007. In the beginning of his tenure as the CEO, America was hit by a huge financial crisis and recession. The entire banking sector in the US, including Citibank, was badly hit and many of his competitors filed for bankruptcy. Wall Street and other experts were ready to write him off and dubbed him as the worst CEO of the world. Pandit was unfazed by such comments since his entire focus was to bring back Citibank on its tracks.

Vikram Pandit's annual compensation was in an excess of $3 million. He announced that he would take just $1 as a token salary till his company turned around. He was ready to sacrifice a multi-million dollar salary that the head honchos of premier banks normally earn. By refusing to take salary, Pandit not only reduced the operating costs but more importantly, sent out a strong message to his employees that what is applicable to them is applicable to him too.

Vikram Pandit realized that they had lost focus in trying to do too many different things. He decided that it should focus on its core strengths in banking, and in the process, sold off over 30 businesses. He cut annual expenses by $13 billion. These changes turned around the performance of Citigroup by posting profits for 5 consecutive quarters. The company rewarded him with a retention award of $23.2 million and he became one of the highest paid CEOs in the US. The same media had now declared him as one of the best CEOs of the world!

There have been many instances where a player loses his cool and subsequently his focus. This often results in him either getting out (if he is a batsman) or giving many runs away (if he is a bowler). Yuvraj Singh and Zaheer Khan are both aggressive players and do not hesitate to retaliate when confronted with sledging. Thankfully both of them responded to their English counterparts by turning in strong performances with the bat and ball respectively. Similarly Pandit ignored strong criticism from the detractors and instead went about his tasks silently and completely turned around the performance of his organization. In 2008, the Government of India awarded him with Padma Bhushan, one of the top civilian awards in the country.

Focus on Core Competency

(Irfan Pathan — Texas Instruments)

'Focus is a matter of deciding what things you're not going to do.'

— John Carmack

Irfan Pathan was one of the most talented cricketers to burst into the international cricket scene at a young age of 19. He made his debut in the Indian team as a left-arm fast bowler in 2003. He started his career on a promising note, grabbing 18 wickets in 2 Tests against Bangladesh. In 2004, the ICC (International Cricket Council) named him as the 'Emerging Player of the Year'. He was no bunny with the bat and played many crucial innings for India. His ability to bowl left-arm swing and bat as a useful lower order batsman evoked comparisons with the great Pakistani cricketer, Wasim Akram.

Greg Chappell became the coach of the Indian cricket team in May 2005. He recognized the batting skills of Irfan Pathan and asked him to focus on this aspect to make him an all-rounder. Pathan followed his coach's advice. On a few occasions, he either opened the Indian batting or went in at No.3 as a 'pinch hitter'. Initially Pathan met with a fair amount of success as he scored three Test fifties in four innings. He became the first bowler to take a hat-trick in the first over of a Test match. He also quickly rose to the No.2 position in ICC's ODI ranking. Most Indians declared that India had finally found an all-rounder who could fill the void left by the legendary Kapil Dev.

Unfortunately Pathan's initial success with the bat proved to be his nemesis. Seeing him score heavily with the bat, Chappell focused more on improving his batting skills. The flipside was, Pathan's bowling suffered. His pace vanished, and so did the prodigious swing that he used to get with a new ball. He lost his wicket taking abilities and with that his place in the Indian national team. Pathan had started as a specialist left-arm swing bowler but by end of 2006, he lost his place in both formats of the game.

Pathan returned to international cricket for the inaugural World Twenty20 in 2007. His 3 wicket haul earned him the Man of the Match award in the nail-biting final and India's victory against Pakistan. This helped him make a comeback into the Test and ODI side. Unfortunately he could not cement his place since he was more of a 'first change' who was played only as the third seamer. Unfortunately for Pathan, the Indian team played most of the Test matches with two fast bowlers.So he struggled to make it into the final eleven. He has been in and out of the Indian team since the last five years. Though Irfan Pathan started his career on quite a high note, he could not sustain for long. For a person of his talent and cricketing abilities, he played just 29 Tests and 120 ODIs. In his brief Test career he took 100 wickets and scored 1,105 runs at an average of 31.57 runs. In the 120 ODIs, he took 173 wickets and scored 1,544 runs at an average of 23.39 runs.

Wasim Akram, one of the greatest left arm fast bowlers of Pakistan, was an extremely dangerous bowler who had the ability to bowl reverse swing with the old ball. He had a fantastic record in both Tests as well as ODIs. Akram was a pretty good batsman and even had a double hundred to his credit. However, he never considered himself an all-rounder in the mould of an Ian Botham or a Kapil Dev. He knew that like Shaun Pollock and Richard Hadlee, he was more of a bowling all-rounder. He realized that his primary task was to lead the Pakistani bowling attack. This clarity of thought helped him focus on his bowling, and he remained Pakistan's No.1 bowler for more than a decade.

Irfan Pathan was like Wasim Akram in many ways—a young handsome lad who bowled left arm pace and was also a good batsman. Pathan considered Akram as his role model and frequently consulted him for bowling tips. Unfortunately, Pathan did not have his mentor's ability of recognizing core competency. His was a classic example of an extremely talented cricketer who lost focus of his core competency, and allowed his career to drift into oblivion. If Pathan had concentrated on honing his bowling skills, he could have probably been India's answer to Pakistan's Wasim Akram.

In the corporate world also, too much diversification can lead to a loss of focus and downfall of the organization. There are numerous examples of corporate failures where the CEO or the management board diversified into completely unconnected areas with disastrous results. Though there have been a few success stories, but such cases are too few in number. There have also been many instances where a cash rich organization had diversified into many unrelated areas but when the hard days came by, the topmost priority of the organization was to hive off unrelated businesses and retain only the core businesses.

Tom Engibous, former president and CEO of Texas Instruments, understood the importance of focusing on core competence and this helped his organization become one of the biggest semiconductor companies in the world. Engibous completed his master's degree in Electrical Engineering from Purdue University. In 1976, he joined Texas Instruments as an IC Design Engineer. For the next seventeen years, he held various technical and management positions in the company. In 1993, he was elected as the executive vice president of the organization.

The year 1996 saw the semiconductor industry go through downswing because of steep fall in chip prices. The woes of Texas Instruments increased when James R. Junkins, the company's president, CEO, and chairman, died suddenly. The company took a bold decision to promote 43-year-old Tom Engibous to the post of president and CEO.

When Tom Engibous took over, he found that the company, over the years, had diversified into divergent areas and had lost its focus on its core competence. He realized that the company should not remain a broad based conglomerate, but instead it should focus on its core products. Unlike his predecessor James Junkins who was an easy going CEO, Engibous was ambitious and aggressive. He had no hesitation in selling off unprofitable businesses or laying off people. During his tenure, he sold off many businesses including its custom manufacturing and notebook computer businesses, defence electronics operation, and Enterprise Applications Software.

Engibous decided to focus only on two areas—Digital Signal Processors (DSPs) and Analog ICs. These were not only Texas Instruments' core competence but also the fastest growing segments in the field of semiconductors. He was shrewd enough to realize that one of the most effective ways to make the DSPs popular was to tie up with universities. The university students, during the course of their study, were taught to use and program the DSP. Since a majority of these students had done programming using the DSPs of Texas Instruments as a part of their curriculum, they had no hesitation in using DSPs from the same manufacturer when they took up jobs as Hardware Design Engineers!

Around the same time, the entire communication industry across the world was undergoing a swift revolution. Modems, mobile phones, and other Internet based products were becoming fast moving consumer commodities. All these products needed DSPs and Analog ICs, and by 2000, Texas Instruments had a market share of nearly 50% in the $4.4 billion industry of DSPs. The decision that Engibous took in mid-1990s was visionary because the company continued to reap rich benefits in these two fields. He can be credited with bringing focus into an organization that had been drifting aimlessly during 1990s.

In 2007, Dallas based Texas Instruments received the 'Manufacturer of the Year for Global Supply Chain Excellence' Award by *World Trade* magazine. It is now ranked No.1 in the field of DSPs and Analog ICs. It is currently the 2nd largest manufacturer of semiconductor chips used in mobile phones and the 3rd largest manufacturer of semiconductors.

Before Tom Engibous took over Texas Instruments, the company had made the mistake of diversifying into too many areas instead of focusing on a vital few. Luckily for Texas Instruments, Engibous was quick to recognize this problem and tried to reverse it as much as possible. His decision to focus on DSPs and Analog ICs as the core areas proved to be one of the best judgements in the semiconductor industry. For his rich contribution in the field of semiconductor business, Engibous was listed among the 'Top 25 Executives of the past 25 Years' by *Electronic Business* and also listed among the 'Top 25 Managers' by *Business Week* in 2000.

Adaptable Like a Chameleon

(Mohinder Amarnath—Motorola, Toyota)

'I am a man of fixed and unbending principles, the first of which is to be flexible at all times.'

—Everett Dirksen

Whether you are playing cricket or developing a product, it is always good to have multi-skilled people—known as all-rounders in cricketing parlance. One of the most valuable roles in the game of cricket is that of an all-rounder. The game has produced many great all-rounders like Ian Botham, Kapil Dev, Imran Khan, Jacques Kallis, and Richard Hadlee.

Certain all-rounders are better in batting compared to bowling—like Jacques Kallis, Mohinder Amarnath, and Yuvraj Singh. These cricketers are known as 'batting all-rounders'. Similarly there are a few all-rounders who are more famous for their bowling abilities. Examples of these 'bowling all-rounders' are Imran Khan, Richard Hadlee, and Shaun Pollock. Then there are exceptionally talented all-rounders like Ian Botham and Kapil Dev who are equally good at batting as well as bowling.

Mohinder Amarnath's all-round ability of providing solidity to the middle-order, and at the same time snaring wickets with his innocuous looking medium-pace helped India clinch the World Cup for the first time at Lord's, England, in 1983.

Mohinder had two match winning performances in the World

Cup tournament and both came in the most critical matches—the semi-finals and finals. India played against England in the semi-finals and Mohinder's all-round performance of 42 runs and 2 wickets for just 27 runs led India into the finals of the World Cup for the first time. In the low scoring finals, Mohinder scored 26 runs and grabbed 3 crucial wickets for just 12 runs. He was one of the prime architects of the India's victory against the mighty West Indians. For his superb all-round performance, Mohinder Amarnath was adjudged the Man of the Match in both these matches.

India won its second World Cup in 2011, after a gap of 28 years. This time too, it was an all-rounder who played an important role in India's march towards victory. Yuvraj Singh scored a stupendous 362 runs at an average of 90.50, taking 15 wickets at 25.13 runs apiece. It was fitting that he was at the wicket when Dhoni hit the winning six to bring back the Cup after 28 years. His multi-dimensional skills helped him garner four Man of the Match Awards and Man of the Tournament in the World Cup.

The biggest advantage of an all-rounder is the flexibility he provides to his team. Having an all-rounder bat at No. 7 position can allow the captain to have four more specialist bowlers, apart from the all-rounder himself. Similarly, the captain can have seven specialist batsmen, including the all-rounder.

In corporate world too, flexibility is the key to success. This flexibility can be in terms of product design, manufacturing lines, organization structure, or people's competency and skills.

In 1994, Motorola setup a manufacturing plant in Bangalore to manufacture numeric and alphanumeric pagers. Pager like any consumer electronics product, had an extremely short shelf life. Motorola, being the market leader had to ensure that it brought out many new products every year. This was the only way it could stay ahead of competition. However, this also brought about a number of problems in setting up the manufacturing lines.

Motorola had a front end manufacturing line to populate the PCBs and a back end manufacturing line to assemble and test the pagers. Each manufacturing line was dedicated to a specific product. This meant that whenever Motorola designed a new product, it had to setup a new manufacturing line. This had major disadvantages like cost of new capital goods, additional space for new manufacturing lines, training, etc. Since the entire front end manufacturing line was automated with robots, the cost of setting up a new manufacturing line for every product was unthinkable. Though it was a problem that plagued all the Motorola manufacturing plants worldwide, it was more severe in India because the low pager volumes in the Indian market could not justify having dedicated manufacturing lines.

In 1995, a team of Motorolans formed a taskforce 'Chameleons' to address this issue. Their leader announced, 'just like a chameleon changes its colours when it moves from one environment to another, we should make our manufacturing lines flexible to move from one product to another with ease.'

During the next few months the team went about studying the existing equipments on all its manufacturing lines. The team members redesigned the software, hardware, pickup tools, jigs, and fixtures. This was to ensure that all the product dependant items were now made universal, flexible, and product independent. With these changes, the Motorola paging operations at Bangalore could manufacture multiple products on the same manufacturing lines. It resulted in saving millions of dollars. The team presented this project at a competition of different Motorola teams at Dallas, Texas. Needless to say, the 'Chameleons' won the Gold Award for this innovative project.

The idea of having a flexible manufacturing line in the automobile industry was implemented by Toyota in 1996. It introduced the concept 'Global Body Line' at its Vietnamese manufacturing plant that assembled Camrys. As in the case of

Motorola, here too, it was possible to swap robots, change the software, and exchange people for robots and vice versa. This gave Toyota the flexibility to manufacture different models on the same manufacturing line. Like Motorola, Toyota too saved millions of dollars on capital goods and shopfloor space. By early 2000s Toyota implemented this concept at its other plants too.

At its Kentucky plant, it was possible to build Toyota's Camry, Solara Coupes, and Avalon on the same manufacturing line.

At Toyota, this kind of flexibility was not restricted to its manufacturing lines. It introduced 'all-rounders' in its product development functions too. Toyota had a role named 'chief engineer' who was responsible for the entire new product introduction. This person was responsible not only for the product design but even other areas like identifying the right markets, defining manufacturing process that had to be adopted, supplier identification, and even marketing strategies! This not only ensured a high degree of accountability but also minimal problems arising due to inter group co-ordination.

This was a far cry from the setup at other conventional automobile manufacturers that had different groups working on each of these aspects. These companies suffered from bureaucratic delays, improper coordination, and poor communication—each affecting the timeliness and quality of the product. The 'chief engineer' concept of Toyota was a clear winner.

Though it may appear that there is a contradiction between the previous chapter and this one, in reality it is not. The previous chapter does not say that the game should have only specialists and no 'all-rounders'. Rather, it deals with a situation where a player focuses on developing a secondary skill but at the cost of losing focus on his prime skill. If Irfan Pathan had concentrated on his bowling and looked at his batting as an additional skill to be used in critical times, he might have succeeded. Mohinder Amarnath and Wasim Akram succeeded in this regard. As mentioned in the previous chapter, Akram considered himself a 'bowling all-rounder' and never lost focus on his bowling. His high scores with the bat came only in situations of crisis. Mohinder considered himself a 'batting all-rounder' and was well aware of the fact that he was in the team mainly for his batting ability. He bowled mainly under favourable conditions or when the regular bowlers were unable to break a long partnership.

This chapter is about being flexible to the changing needs of the environment. Moninder knew that his gentle medium-pace was harmless in the Indian subcontinent but he could swing the ball prodigiously under favourable English conditions,. He realized that he would be expected to play a major role with the ball in the World Cup. He reposed the faith that his captain had in him by taking 2 wickets in the semi-finals and 3 wickets in the finals.

Similarly, Motorola and Toyota were aware of what the customers expected from them. They knew that different consumers preferred different models so there was a constant need to upgrade their products and manufacturing lines. They were also aware of the high costs involved in setting up dedicated manufacturing lines. The situation demanded them to be flexible to the customer's needs. American, European, and Chinese markets needed high volumes of pagers to be manufactured; so having dedicated lines was not a major problem. However, in the Indian context where the volumes were low, Motorola had two options—either to manufacture fewer types of products or invest in more manufacturing lines. Both were not acceptable to the local management and this gave birth to the innovative concept of flexible manufacturing lines. Whether it is cricket or the corporate world, we should always understand the demands of the situation and be flexible enough to meet them with great agility.

STAY FOCUSED

(AMIR SOHAIL, VENKATESH PRASAD — OLDSMOBILE)

'Concentrate all your thoughts upon the work at hand. The sun's rays do not burn until brought to a focus.'

—Alexander Graham Bell

It is important that even under the most challenging and adverse circumstances, one should remain focused. There are many who show flashes of brilliance but that is not enough. What is expected of a good professional is the ability to sustain the focus for long periods of time.

India played against Pakistan during the second quarter-finals of the 1996 World Cup at Bangalore. Batting first, India made 287 for the loss of 8 wickets. At the innings break, this appeared to be a match winning score. However, Pakistan had other ideas. They were off to a blistering start and were well in control of the required run-rate.

The left handed talented Amir Sohail was going great guns and it looked as if India's 287 runs was grossly inadequate. On one occasion, he smacked the local boy Venkatesh Prasad effortlessly for three consecutive fours. Pakistan's score had reached a healthy 113 and they needed just 174 runs with 9 wickets still in hand. The Indian spectators began to wonder if this would be India's first loss to Pakistan in a World Cup match.

However, very soon everything changed. What happened next

will forever remain etched in the memory of 50,000 spectators in the stadium and another hundred million Indians who watched it on TV. After hitting Venkatesh Prasad for the third consecutive four of the over, Amir Sohail suddenly lost his focus and cool. He pointed his bat threateningly first at the bowler and then to various points in the stadium. He was signalling to Venkatesh Prasad that he would despatch the remaining balls of his over to various parts of the ground.

Amir Sohail misjudged Venkatesh Prasad's cool exterior and assumed that he would buckle under pressure. However, Venkatesh Prasad, like Anil Kumble, was a smiling assassin! The cool headed fast bowler, with the support of 50,000 local fans rooting behind him, bowled an indipping yorker and Sohail took a wild swing at it only to watch his timber shatter. This was the turning point of the match from which Pakistan never recovered. Pakistan seemed to be coasting towards a comfortable win, but suddenly they lost a few quick wickets, and from 113 for 1 they were reduced to 184 for 5. The Indians won the match by 39 runs as Pakistan could make only 248 for 9 in their allotted 50 overs.

It has been seventeen years since this incident took place. Ask any Indian the top three moments he cherishes in an Indian victory against Pakistan and he will fondly remember this incident as one of them. However, what remains unanswered is—what made Amir Sohail behave in this manner? Having done all the required groundwork initially, he just threw it away in one moment of indiscretion, and with it his team's chances of entering the semi-finals of the World Cup

Oldsmobile was founded by Ransom E. Olds in 1897. In its 107 year history, it produced 35.2 million cars. It was acquired by General Motors (GM) in the year 1908. Oldsmobile was a classic case of an American automobile which had a very successful run for many decades till it lost its focus and innovativeness.

Let us look at some of the pioneering works that Oldsmobile did during its initial years.

In 1937, it was one of the first automobile companies in the world to introduce a four-speed, semi-automatic transmission called the 'Automatic Safety Transmission'.

In 1940, it became the first auto manufacturer to offer a fully automatic transmission which featured four-forward speeds.

During 1949, it was once again a pioneer when it introduced the Rocket engine. This engine produced far more power than the engines that were popular during that era, and found favour with car racers. They were considered as the fastest cars in the market.

Oldsmobile was among the first companies to introduce a wraparound windshield—a trend that became very popular in America.

In 1962, it was also the first to introduce turbo charged engine, and in 1966 it became the first car manufacturer to introduce a front-wheel drive car.

Oldsmobile became extremely popular in 1970s and 1980s and was called 'Change Leaders' because of its continuous innovations. It became the third best-selling brand in the US.

Unfortunately, after a few decades of success, Oldsmobile slowly began to lose focus and thereby its grip over the market. In 1977, since Oldsmobile was unable to meet the market demands, it began to equip its automobiles with the Chevrolet engine instead of the V8 Rocket engine. Many loyal Oldsmobile customers specifically wanted the Rocket V8 engine but were not aware that their vehicle was fitted with a Chevrolet engine until they performed maintenance and discovered that the purchased parts did not fit. The customers felt cheated and slowly moved away from their once preferred brand. This resulted in a drop in Oldsmobile sales.

By 1990, the brand had lost its place in the market. It was squeezed between other GM divisions, with competition from new upscale import makes like Acura and Lexus. GM increased its focus on the performance of Chevrolet and Pontiac. It looked at Oldsmobile only as a car to showcase futuristic designs and as a guinea pig for testing new technology.

In spite of Oldsmobile being one of the most popular and innovative cars of America, continuous shortfall in sales and overall profitability prompted the company to announce its plans to phase out the Oldsmobile brand in December 2000. The final production day for Oldsmobile was April 29, 2004. It was a poignant moment as the division's last car was signed by all Oldsmobile's assembly line workers.

These two examples express the pitfalls of losing focus when you are in a winning position. In the cricketing example, though India had posted a good score, Pakistan was well ahead of the required run-rate and had many wickets in hand. They just had to maintain their momentum and they would have won the match. However, for no apparent reason, Amir Sohail, the highly talented but volatile Pakistani batsman suddenly lost focus and this resulted in his and his team's downfall.

The case of Oldsmobile was also quite similar. During 1940s and 1950s, it was one of the most innovative automotive companies in the world—a company that could do no wrong. It had many differentiating features that its faithful customers loved. Unfortunately, the company lost its innovative edge and with it, its market share.

In our professional life too, it is not sufficient to have a good start. A good beginning is only half the work done—sustaining the momentum for long period of time is equally important. One of the hallmarks of good finishers of the game is the high degree of concentration and focus that they exhibit till the end. A sudden lapse in concentration has been the undoing of many great innings in cricket. Similarly, a sudden lapse in vision and direction has spelt doom for many companies. The loss in focus can happen due to numerous reasons—over confidence, influenced by external factors, inability to move out of the comfort zone, the feeling of insecurity, etc. Oldsmobile is a classic example of an American car which was once considered the most innovative automobile brand in the US, but which now ceases to exist.

Risk Taking Ability

(MS Dhoni—Azim Premji, Wipro)

'Behold the turtle. He makes progress only when he sticks his neck out.'

—James Bryant Conant

One important quality that great leaders exhibit is their ability to take calculated risks. If you look up the dictionary for the definition of risk, it says: 'A situation that could be dangerous or have a bad outcome. The possibility that something unpleasant will happen. Exposed to danger or loss.'

With such a severe negative connotation, why would anyone want to take risks?

India played against Sri Lanka in the finals of the 2011 World Cup at Mumbai. Sri Lanka batted first and scored 274 runs for the loss of 6 wickets, thanks to a classy century by Mahela Jayawardene. 274 is a very good score to defend in any match and may seem even tougher when a team has to chase it in a 'pressure cooker' situation during a World Cup.

India disastrously lost its key batsmen Sachin Tendulkar and Virender Sehwag with the scoreboard reading 31 for 2. When India lost its 2nd wicket, in walked the skipper, MS Dhoni. The entire Wankhede stadium let out a gasp, just as the billion viewers did while watching the match on TV. What made an out-of-form Dhoni take the bold decision of promoting himself up the order ahead of the in-form Yuvraj Singh—this was the question on most of our minds. It was a brave but risky move, especially since Dhoni was not in his best form. Dhoni took the gamble because he wanted to lead from the front, which he did quite admirably, and in fact he was one of the main architects of an Indian victory.

Dhoni, with a mix of aggression and defence, scored 91 runs off 79 balls. He was involved in a match winning partnership of 109 runs with Gautam Gambhir who scored 97 runs.

The winning shot came from Dhoni—the huge six that he hit over long-on off Nuwan Kulasekara's bowling is etched in every Indian's mind and will remain so for the next few decades.

Why did Dhoni promote himself up the batting order? What made him take such a great risk? Dhoni himself told during the post-match award ceremony: 'I took lots of unusual decisions. If we had lost then questions would have been asked.' In a country where every citizen is a cricket coach, expert, and commentator, he was aware that if he had been dismissed cheaply then a billion Indians would be screaming at him—'we told you so!'

Azim Hashim Premji is one of the most famous leaders in the IT Industry. He is the chairman of Wipro Limited. According to Forbes, he is currently the third wealthiest Indian with a personal wealth of $12.2 billion in 2012.

He completed his initial education at St Mary's School, Mumbai, and later went to Stanford University, California, USA to study Electrical Engineering. However, he was forced to leave his studies and take over the family business when his father suddenly died in 1966. His father's net worth was estimated to be $1 million.

One of the hallmarks of Azim Premji's leadership was his ability to take many calculated risks. When he took over the reins of the company at the tender age of 21, the company was in the business of hydrogenated vegetable oil and cooking fats and it had a steady turnover from these businesses. There are lots of leaders who would have been quite contented and remained in the comfort zone—but not Premji. He realized the need to diversify and so he made forays into the field of toiletries, hair care soaps, lighting products, and hydraulic cylinders.

The biggest turning point of his life came when he decided to venture into the IT arena, a relatively unknown field in the 1970s and 1980s. His company was involved in the manufacture of computer hardware, computer peripherals, and software development. Later, he tied up with the US giant GE to enter the field of Medical Electronics and Healthcare.

Not only was Premji a risk-taker, he also encouraged his team members to imbibe that quality. He believed that self-confidence is an essential part of leadership and having confidence in turn allows a person to take risks. He stressed that risk-taking can lead to occasional failures but it's important to learn from that failure. During one of his speeches, he said, 'self-confident people assume responsibility for their mistakes and share credit with their team members. Remember, no one can make you feel inferior without your consent.' On another occasion, he said, 'you must fail sometimes else you are doing something wrong, not experimenting, not taking risks, or not being bold enough.'

Azim Premji was responsible for turning Wipro into a global Information Technology Services company and among the Top 3 in India. As on June 2013, it has around 1,47,281 people worldwide spread across different segments.

He was voted among the '20 Most Powerful Men in the World' by *Asiaweek* in 2000. TIME Magazine listed him twice among the '100 Most Influential People'. In 2009, Wesleyan University, Connecticut, awarded him with an honorary doctorate. The Indian Government honoured him with Padma Bhushan in 2005 and Padma Vibhushan in 2011.

A great leader not only likes to take risks but prefers to be in the thick of things to monitor the situation and mitigate the risk. When India was struggling at 31 for 2, Dhoni knew that he had to be right there, in the middle of the pitch, dictating the game in a manner that he liked. Though Gambhir and Yuvraj Singh were seasoned campaigners, Dhoni preferred to go to the centre and take charge. In order to achieve this he had to take the risk of promoting himself up the batting order ahead of the in-form Yuvraj Singh.

One of the most important aspects of risk management is performing periodic risk assessment. This can be done by knowing the probability of occurrence and the impact if it occurs. In the above example, as the Indian innings progressed, and India inched towards victory, the severity of the risk that Dhoni had taken kept reducing. As in cricket, in the corporate world too, the magnitude of these two parameters keeps changing with time. So it is essential to assess the risk periodically.

When Azim Premji took over as the chief of Wipro, the organization was quite stable in terms of revenues, growth, and profitability. He could have well-maintained status quo, however, he aspired to build one of the biggest IT companies in the world. Over the next few years he worked very hard towards fulfilling his dreams. Under his leadership, his company grew from $2.5 million to $7.95 billion. What started off as a company manufacturing hydrogenated cooking fats and consumer products, has today become one of the largest software companies in the world.

Every risk has a probability of failure but if you don't take risks, you don't achieve anything. There is a famous saying: 'A ship is safe in harbour but that is not what ships are built for.' The purpose of a ship is to transport people and goods across seas and oceans. During its journey, it frequently encounters bad weather, storms, hurricanes, etc. However, it needs to overcome these and reach its destination safely. A ship is probably safest when it is anchored at the harbour but it serves no purpose. Similarly, a good leader—be it a cricket captain or a CEO of an organization—needs to come out of the comfort zone occasionally to achieve his goals.

OVERCOMING HANDICAPS
(B.S. CHANDRASHEKHAR, M.A.K. PATAUDI – THOMAS ALVA EDISON)

'Success is to be measured not so much by the position that one has reached in life as by the obstacles which he has overcome.'

– Booker T. Washington

B.S. Chandrashekhar is considered as one of the greatest leg spinners of the world. Despite his unorthodox style, he had an amazing strike rate and captured 242 wickets in just 58 Test matches. His most well-known feat is his 6-wicket haul against England at the Oval in 1971 which resulted in the famous Indian series victory on English soil. However, what is less known is the fact that he had to overcome a serious handicap during his childhood before becoming one of the greatest spinners in the world.

Chandrashekhar was born and educated in Mysore. Right from his childhood, he had a strong passion for cricket. However, he was afflicted with polio and that resulted in the withering of his right wrist. While any child would have been disheartened with such a handicap, Chandrashekhar took his illness in his stride. He not only overcame his disability but actually turned it into his greatest strength.

Since his right wrist was affected with polio, he was able to move it much more than normal-leg spin bowlers. He could spin the ball like a top even on the flattest tracks of the world. What made him extremely dangerous was his unpredictability. There were occasions when even he was unable to control his wrist movement and the spin that it imparted.

Chandrashekhar along with E.A.S. Prasanna, Bishen Singh Bedi, and Venkataraghavan constituted the famous Indian spin quartet that dominated spin bowling in 1960s and 1970s.

Chandrashekhar, for whom playing cricket seemed doubtful during his childhood days, went on to become one of India's greatest bowlers, and he was named as a Wisden Cricketer of the Year in 1972. He also won Wisden's 'Best Bowling Performance of the Century' award in 2002 for his 6 wickets for 38 runs against England at the Oval in 1971.

Mansur Ali Khan Pataudi, popularly known as Tiger Pataudi, was a former captain of the Indian cricket team. Like Chandrashekhar, he too had to overcome a major physical handicap before becoming one of India's shrewdest cricket captains.

Tiger Pataudi spent his childhood in England. In 1957, he made his first-class debut at a young age of 16. He captained his school team in 1959, and broke the record for the highest number of runs scored in a season. Pataudi went abroad to study and play at the prestigious Oxford University.

Soon tragedy struck. Pataudi had a major car accident in England. The windscreen shattered and a piece of glass pierced and damaged his right eye. Initially, he had a tough time performing even normal tasks. This made people believe that he would no longer be able to play cricket. However, Pataudi was made of tougher stuff. He was back on the cricket field, batting with one eye.

Pataudi was able to overcome his handicap quickly. Within six months, in 1961, he made his Test debut against England in New Delhi. He scored a brilliant century in the Madras Test which helped India achieve its first series win against England. The following year, he was appointed the vice captain of the Indian team. During the series against the West Indies, Indian skipper Nari Contractor was struck and injured by a Charlie Griffith bouncer. Pataudi became the youngest Test skipper when he took over from Nari Contractor.

During the initial days of Indian cricket, it was quite common to see many princes and people with a royal lineage representing the country. Unfortunately, many of them maintained a distance from their teammates which led to poor team spirit and bonding. Pataudi was different—though he was also a prince, he mixed freely with his teammates. Not once did the players feel that their captain belonged to a royal family.

Pataudi was not only a stylish batsman but also one of the best Indian fielders during 1960s and 1970s. Despite his visual handicap, Pataudi played 46 Test matches and scored 2,793 runs. Under his captaincy, India achieved its first Test series win in an overseas match. During his distinguished test career, he won many awards. He won the Arjuna Award in 1964 and the Padma Shri in 1967. A year later, he was awarded the Wisden Cricketer of the Year.

Cricket, as in case of most sports, expects its players to have a high degree of physical fitness. In such a scenario no unfit player can dream of making it to the top. B.S. Chadrashekhar had a major handicap, but that did not deter him from pursuing his passion. He used his handicap to his advantage and became one of the best leg spinners in the world. Vivian Richards, the greatest batsman West Indies ever produced, had stated in an interview that Chandrashekhar and Dennis Lillee were the most difficult bowlers he had ever faced. Pataudi lost his right eye even before he had made his Test debut. However, this did not prevent him from becoming one the best batsmen of 1960s and 1970s.

Thomas Alva Edison too had to overcome his learning disabilities and hearing impairments in his childhood to become one of the greatest inventors in the world.

During his childhood days, his mind often wandered, and he was unable to concentrate in class. Along with this disability, Edison also developed hearing problems at an early age. There are different versions regarding the cause of his hearing problems. One theory attributes the cause of his deafness to a bout of scarlet fever during childhood and recurring untreated middle-ear infections. Another version states that he became deaf because he was struck on the ears by a train conductor, when his chemical laboratory in a boxcar caught fire, and he was thrown off the train along with his apparatus and chemicals. Later, Edison modified the story to say that the injury occurred when the conductor, while helping him onto a moving train, lifted him by the ears. Though there are different versions related to the cause of his hearing impairment, the fact remains that he had to overcome this major handicap. This resulted in his official schooling, ending within three months. However, his mother was convinced about his intelligence and continued to educate him at home.

Edison's young days were full of difficulties. He had to earn money by selling candy, vegetables, and newspapers on trains. In a way these helped him discover his inherent talent as a businessman. It helped him to eventually found 14 companies, including General Electric, which is currently one of the largest and most respected companies in the world.

Despite a difficult childhood, Edison did not lose his motivation and confidence. He went on to become the third most prolific inventor in history. In US alone, he holds 1,093 patents and apart from this he also holds patents in UK, Germany, and France. He is credited with numerous inventions that include a mechanical vote recorder, a battery for an electric car, electric light bulb, recorded music, and motion picture camera. He originated the concept and implementation of electric-power generation and distribution to homes, businesses, and factories.

When Edison dropped out of school, not many would have believed that he would have a distinguished professional career, leave alone becoming one of the top inventors of the world. The president of the Third French Republic, Jules Grévy, designated Edison with the distinction of an 'Officer of the Legion of Honour' (Légion d'honneur). In 1983, the United States Congress designated February 11, Edison's birthday, as the National Inventor's Day. In 1890, he was elected as a member of the Royal Swedish Academy of Sciences. Fantastic achievement for a person who had to drop out of school within three months and also suffer from hearing impairment!

These are examples of people who overcame their initial handicaps to become one of the best in their respective fields. It should motivate us to believe that if we have self-belief and passion then even the worst handicap cannot become a deterrent for success.

8

TEAMWORK

'We believe in teamwork and sharing the workload. Each morning I toss the coin. If it is "heads", then the team on my left works. If it is "tails", then the team on my right works. If the coin falls in an upright position, then I work.'

Teamwork and Synergy

(Rajasthan Royals, Deccan Chargers — HP, Compaq)

'Coming together is a beginning. Keeping together is progress. Working together is success.'

— Henry Ford

Shane Warne is considered as the best captain Australians never had! In the inaugural IPL T20 Tournament in 2008, he was made the skipper of the Rajasthan Royals team.

All the knowledgeable people of India, and we don't have scarcity of them, had written off Rajasthan Royals even before the first ball had been bowled.

How could an IPL team which just had Shane Warne, Graeme Smith, and Shane Watson as its stars win the tournament?

How would Shane Warne get the best out of Graeme Smith? Their professional rivalry and relationship was a well-known fact in the cricketing circles.

Would Warne be able to integrate Sohail Tanvir, a Pakistani player, into an Indian domestic team?

Most importantly, how would he be able to communicate with his Indian teammates? Shane Warne spoke only English — a language that some of the Rajasthan Royals players struggled with.

However, as the IPL tournament progressed, Shane Warne's leadership stood out. His ability to motivate and communicate with people from different cultures was outstanding. While some of the local captains of the other IPL teams struggled, despite knowing the local culture, Shane Warne used his excellent people management skills to overcome his lack of local language and cultural skills.

Warne was able to define the roles and responsibilities for each and every player and more importantly, he knew how to communicate it to them. Graeme Smith, one of the senior most batsmen in his team, was an opener whose job was to anchor the innings together. Swapnil Asnodkar was a relatively unknown cricketer from Goa. When he was recruited by Rajasthan Royals, cricket fans asked, 'Swapnil, who?' However, Shane Warne was quite impressed by what he saw at the nets. He realized that Asnodkar had the ability to hit the ball hard and also loft it over the close-in fielders, so he asked him to open the innings for Rajasthan Royals. Shane Warne's move paid rich dividends as Asnodkar and Graeme Smith formed a formidable opening partnership and by the end of the tournament they had scored 418 runs together at an average of 59.71—the highest in the tournament. In the seven IPL matches that he played, Asnodkar scored 244 runs at 34.86 with a strike rate of 127.08.

Yusuf Pathan was another relatively unknown cricketer whose career was shaped by Shane Warne and IPL. He scored 435 runs and took 8 wickets. He recorded the 2nd fastest half century from 21 balls against the Deccan Chargers.

Shane Watson was a very talented Australian cricketer who had never done justice to his potential. He had the potential to become one of the best all-rounders in the game but unfortunately, he could never become a regular member of the Australian team. However, the inaugural IPL tournament changed all that. Like Asnodkar and Pathan, Shane Watson too had a fantastic season. He scored four half centuries and took 17 wickets. He won the Man of the Match award on four occasions. He was rated as the Most Valuable Player of the tournament for his consistent performance, both with the bat and ball.

Apart from these players, Shane Warne set a high bar for himself. Knowing very well that he had an inexperienced squad, he always led from the front. Whenever he felt that the opposite batsmen were dominating the proceedings and snatching the game away, he would bring himself to bowl, and either break the partnership or slow down the scoring. His performance with the ball rubbed off on his teammates which helped Rajasthan Royals win many close encounters.

Rajasthan Royals had a disastrous start to the tournament, losing the first match against Delhi Daredevils by 9 wickets. However ,they won their next game against Kings XI Punjab. They continued their winning streak by winning the next five games in a row. At the end of the 14 preliminary qualifying rounds, they had won 11 matches. It also included an undefeated record on their home ground. They not only topped the points table but also became the first team to reach the semifinals with a 65 runs victory over the Royal Challengers, Bangalore.

At the start of the tournament, no one had given Rajasthan Royals a chance. However, Shane Warne proved everyone wrong and his team won the first IPL tournament when they defeated Chennai Super Kings by 3 wickets in the June 2008 finals. Many of the Rajasthan Royals' players won individual awards for their performances during the tournament; Yusuf Pathan bagged the Man of the Match award for the final match. Sohail Tanvir won the Purple Cap, given to IPL's leading wicket taker. Australian all-rounder Shane Watson was declared the Man of the Series. Shane Warne's captaincy and coaching was praised and appreciated by everyone, including the opposition teams.

At this point, it would be appropriate to compare Rajasthan Royals with Deccan Chargers.

Deccan Chargers probably had the strongest team on paper.

In Twenty20 format, the ability to hit hard and score fast is of prime importance. In this regard, Deccan Chargers had some of the most destructive batsmen in the world—names like Shahid Afridi, Adam Gilchrist, Andrew Symonds, and Herschelle Gibbs could send a chill up the spine of even the best bowlers in the world. Each of them was a match winner of his day and to have all of them in one team was any captain's dream!

Unfortunately, the Deccan Chargers could never convert their potential into victory. They won only two matches and finished at the bottom of the table. A team which was expected to win the tournament didn't even qualify for the semi-finals!

The above two examples featuring Rajasthan Royals and Deccan Chargers have proved two important points:

1. With great leadership and good teamwork even a team of ordinary people can become winners.
2. It is not sufficient to have stars. A bunch of brilliant individuals but poor teamwork is of no use.

There have been numerous cases where two great companies have merged but the resultant company did not live up to the expectations. The best example of this was the purchase of Compaq by HP in 2002. HP with a turnover of around $47 billion was the 2nd largestcomputer company in the world, next only to IBM. Compaq had a turnover of approximately $40 billion and was ranked as the 3rd largest computer company in the world. When HP first announced its decision to purchase Compaq, industry experts felt that the new company with annual sales of around $87 billion would finally be able to match IBM in size and turnover.

Unfortunately, the merger seemed to create more problems than solve the existing ones. Since HP and Compaq worked in the same field, there were many overlapping products, technology services, and competence. This led to severe downsizing in different areas including headcount reduction. This in turn resulted in a severe dip in employee morale. The other problem that the new organization faced was the vast differences in culture between Compaq and HP—while Compaq was an aggressive player in the PC market, focusing primarily on sales, HP was an engineering company that lay great emphasis on engineering excellence and innovative products. This aggravated the problems at all levels in the merged organization.

The HP-Compaq merger was also opposed by Walter Hewlett and David Packard (the kins of the late founders) because they felt that the merger ran counter to 'The HP Way' which defined the core values of the organization. In their opinion, the massive layoffs because of this merger, was against the core values that their fathers had established. They also felt that HP would struggle in the low profit PC market due to severe competition and price erosion. They wanted HP to focus on the profitable printer business.

When HP bought Compaq, some of the market analysts expected the merged company to become the best computer company in the world. It was expected to have the highest market share and become a major threat to IBM and Dell. Unfortunately, the merger of two computer giants failed to make any inroads into the market share of IBM or Dell. The biggest IT merger had gone sour.

The cricketing example showed how Rajasthan Royals won the inaugural IPL tournament despite having the least number of star players in its squad. It also showed how Deccan Chargers, even with the best talent, struggled throughout the tournament and finished at the bottom. The case of HP–Compaq merger was similar to the Deccan Chargers' performance—in both cases it was proved beyond doubt that a group of talented individuals cannot guarantee the success of a team or an organization. Having good teamwork and synergy is more important than bringing a bunch of brilliant individuals or great products together.

Cross Cultural Teamwork

(Clive Lloyd — Bob Hoekstra, Philips)

'Diversity may be the hardest thing for a society to live with, and perhaps the most dangerous thing for a society to be without.'

—William Sloan Coffin, Jr

Cultural Intelligence or Cultural Quotient (CQ) is the ability of a person to understand the cultural differences and the impact it has for proper functioning of that individual. People with high CQs are regarded as those who can easily blend in any environment in a seamless manner compared to those with lower CQ.

West Indies was one of the best cricketing teams in the world in 1970s and 1980s. There are a lot of people who are not aware that West Indies is actually not a single country but a group of different nations such as Barbados, Guyana, Jamaica, Port of Spain—to name a few. West Indies cricket team is a multinational team that represents around 15 English speaking countries in the Caribbean.

Clive Lloyd is regarded as one of the best captains in world cricket. He was one of the most successful West Indian captains. He won 36 out of 74 test matches. In the ODIs, he was the most successful captain, winning 64 outs of 84 matches. Known popularly as 'Super Cat', what distinguished him from the other West Indies captains was not just his match-winning record bu this ability to not only unite players from different countries and play under the Windies flag but also to get them to perform to their best potential. It was no easy task to lead players coming from different nations. The team consisted of big stars like Gordon Greenidge, Desmond Haynes, Alvin Kallicharan, Vivian Richards, and temperamental fast bowlers like Colin Croft, Michael Holding, Andy Roberts, Joel Garner, and Malcolm Marshall. Though they had their own differences, either due to cultural diversities or personal preferences, when they stood near the 22 yards of the cricket pitch, they represented one country, one voice.

Many decades ago, there were very few true multinational companies. Each organization did business only in its country or on certain occasions, with its neighbours. It was enough for a leader to understand his local employees and the local culture.

However, all of this has undergone a sea change. In today's scenario, there are thousands of multinational companies, with many of them having establishments or doing businesses with hundreds of countries.

Each and every country has its own culture, its own flavour. The first challenge that a leader faces is to unite people from different nationalities and inspire them to work for a common cause.

The second challenge is the ability of the leader to understand and appreciate the cultural differences among his team members. There is a famous saying: One man's food is another man's poison. What works very well for one culture may be totally unacceptable to another culture. A good leader should never be judgmental. The moment he declares, 'this is the right way to do it because this is the way we do it in my country', you can safely assume that he has alienated majority of his workforce.

A leader is bound to unearth lots of strange traits and behaviours when he works in a different country. He should be able to understand those differences and use them to his advantage.

In today's context, where the world is shrinking in terms

of distances due to the communication infrastructure and technology advances, it is very common to see projects that are spread across different parts of the world. For example, in the field of software development, majority of the projects are multisite in nature. Different modules are developed in different countries, and the final product integration happens at the parent site. The overall project manager or the program manager is responsible for the final product in terms of timeliness and quality. He would be expected to lead different functional teams from different countries.

During the past few years, a large chunk of Software Development has been transferred from the 'high cost countries' like USA, UK, France, Germany, etc. to 'low cost countries' like India, Poland, China, Philippines, etc. Though this has been beneficial to the organizations and the shareholders in terms of cost reduction, it has caused a lot of heartburn to the employees from the downsized organizations. It has led to a feeling of insecurity among them because they feel the Damocles sword constantly hanging on their heads. In a high technology industry where Knowledge is Power, such employees like to cling on to their knowledge and refuse to share it with others. For them, becoming indispensable is a means of survival. The biggest challenge for a leader is to motivate and inspire such insecure and non-cooperative team members.

In today's corporate world, each multinational company operates from many countries and this necessitates key leadership positions at each of its centres. It is quite common to see an organization which has its corporate headquarters in USA, have major development centres in USA, India, and Europe, manufacturing in China, and sales offices around the world. It may not be always possible to have local talent at each of its centre. This demands global mobility. A high performing manager from Bangalore may get promoted and transferred to California.

Similarly, a top manager from China may have to take up a challenging assignment in London.

Apart from the usual challenges that a leader faces in any organization, he now faces the challenge of having to perform as an expat in a different country, in a different environment. The high performing manager from China may suddenly face language problems in London. The manager from Bangalore may not be aware of the people issues in Cupertino, USA. The Chinese who might have had the best communication skills in his Shanghai office may suddenly realize that English is not his forte. Similarly the Bangalorean might face a strong revolt from his Cupertino team members if he does not understand the American culture.

The success of a leader depends on the speed at which he adapts to his new surroundings. In such circumstances having a high cultural quotient really helps.

Every expat has two options:

1. Look at his expat term as a necessary evil that he needs to suffer for a better future later. This is truer if the expat is going from a rich nation to a developing country that might not have the same materialistic comforts. These leaders look at every difference with shock and dismay, with a feeling of: 'Back home, it was not like this.'
2. Look at his new adopted country as a new challenge. Learn to appreciate and enjoy the differences. He should fall in love with his new workplace, culture, and country. When you fall in love, you don't notice the flaws.

Bob Hoekstra, the former CEO of Philips Software Centre, Bangalore, definitely belonged to the second category of people. He was born in Netherlands and spent his formative years there. In 1968, he graduated from the Technical University Delft with an MS in Technical Physics. The same year, he joined Philips

Research. He worked in various divisions of Philips, some of them in leadership positions. The turning point of his life came when he was transferred to India to head the Philips Software Centre in Bangalore. Bob was neither an expert in Software Engineering nor the most knowledgeable person in the domains that Philips worked in. However, he still managed to grow the company from 300 engineers in April 1999 to 1700 by February 2006. The company had an annual growth rate of 35%—much higher than the industry average of 10%for R&D centres and captive Software Product Development multinational companies. The company which was developing low-end software in 1999 was accounting for over 30% of software for Philips in 2005. It owned complete software stacks for many consumer electronic products. No wonder that the company's name changed from Philips Software Centre to Philips Innovation Campus.

What made Bob Hoekstra one of the best expat CEOs in the Indian IT Industry?

It was his ability to soak in the Indian culture and love everything Indian. He travelled through the length and breadth of the vast country and mingled freely with the local population everywhere. Every weekend saw him cycle to the scenic Nandi Hills, around thirty miles from the IT city. He was extremely fond of Indian customs and traditions and even had an Indian naming ceremony for his grandchildren. They were given Indian names—Kavitha and Bhaskaran! He also devoted his spare time for many NGOs that helped underprivileged children. He wrote two books about India and the impact that the country had on him.

Bob Hoekstra also played a significant role in trying to improve the infrastructure in Bangalore. Unlike other expat CEOs who focused primarily on business growth and their corporate activities, Bob was in constant touch with the other local CEOs and local Government bodies to improve the image of Bangalore. He was regularly meeting ministers and bureaucrats, giving speeches at various local forums, trying his best to put Philips and Bangalore on the IT world map. In short, he was everywhere!

Bob also pioneered the Indian Business Creation Centre which was a greenhouse for ideas to serve rural India (and other developing countries), applying technologies and business models which fit the needs and ability to spend on people just rising out of poverty.

In 2002, Philips Innovation Campus was ranked as Indian IT's 5th Best Employer. The following year, it was ranked 5th in *Businessworld*'s survey on 'Great Places to Work'. In 2004, Bob was honoured with the 'International Understanding Award' by the Rotary Club of Bangalore Cantonment. He came to India in 1999, and by the time he left his adopted country in 2006, he had become the most loved and familiar face in Bangalore.

Bob wrote two books about his Indian experience. They are collections of short stories titled *An Exemplary Family in Bangalore* and *Our India*. He left the shores of India in February 2006 but still continues his strong relationship with the country by helping Dutch companies leverage on Indian talent. During his stay in Bangalore, had he stood for the Mayor's post, he would have probably won hands down! Bangalore has seen hundreds of expats from USA, UK, Netherlands, Germany, Sweden, France, China, Singapore, Japan, Korea, etc. but none of them was as colourful and popular as Bob Hoekstra!

A jigsaw puzzle consists of various pieces—each one is of different shape and size. However, when it is assembled properly, it creates one picture. Similarly, a team may consist of people coming from diverse cultures and backgrounds, but a good leader should be able to bring them together and make them work towards a common goal. This can happen with a leader exhibiting a high degree of Cultural Quotient, as seen in the case of Clive Lloyd and Bob Hoekstra.

Relationship between Management and Employees

(Chris Gayle — Premier Automobiles)

'Whenever you're in conflict with someone, there is one factor that can make the difference between damaging your relationship and deepening it. That factor is attitude.'

—William James

Chris Gayle is a former West Indian captain and one of the most destructive batsmen in the world. This great Jamaican is one of the only four players to have scored two triple centuries in a Test match. In 91 Tests he has scored 6,373 runs at an average of 41.65, and in 223 ODIs he has scored 7,917 runs at an average of 39.

With such a fantastic record, we would have imagined Chris Gayle to be the key figure of West Indian cricket. Unfortunately, he has periodically been in and out of the West Indian squad. This will not come as a surprise to those following cricket. Chris Gayle and some of his other teammates have been frequently involved in disputes with the West Indies Cricket Board. Some of the controversies surrounding them were related to sponsorship issues.

Initially Cable & Wireless were the sponsors for West Indies cricket. The company also had individual deals with many West Indian players. Subsequently, the West Indies cricket sponsors changed to Digicel. Since Digicel were rivals to Cable & Wireless, they insisted that the West Indies Cricket Board ask its players to drop their Cable & Wireless deals. Some of the West Indies players, including Chris Gayle, refused to sever their deals with Cable & Wireless, and this resulted in them getting dropped for the first match in a Test series against South Africa. However, Gayle later dropped his Cable & Wireless deal and rejoined his side for the second Test.

This did not end Chris Gayle's confrontation with the authorities. During a Test match against New Zealand in 2006, he was charged with violating the spirit of the game, though he was later declared 'not guilty'. During October 2006, he was fined 30% of his match fee for having verbal exchanges with Australian batsman Michael Clarke. During West Indies' 2007 tour in England, he criticized the West Indies Cricket Board for which he received an official warning. His disputes with the West Indies Cricket Board continued in 2011 which led to him being dropped for the West Indies Twenty20 and ODI series against Pakistan.

In one of the interviews, Chris Gayle mentioned that he had written off IPL 2011 since he was expecting to play for West Indies in the home series against Pakistan. He remarked that it was unfortunate that he was not included in the national team. A hurt Chris Gayle decided to join the Royal Challengers Bangalore team for the fourth edition of IPL, India's premier Twenty20 tournament. Clearly, West Indies' loss was Royal Challengers Bangalore's gain.

Chris Gayle announced his arrival in India with a scintillating 102 off 55 balls, consisting of 10 fours and 7 sixes against his former team Kolkata Knight Riders. A few days later, he scored a quicker century against Kings XI Punjab. He hit a brilliant 107 runs off 49 balls with 10 fours and 9 sixes. He was not done yet! Against Kochi Tuskers Kerala, he scored 37 runs in one over which consisted of 3 sixes, 3 fours, and a no-ball which he hit for a 6. Chris Gayle had joined the Royal Challengers Bangalore team after the tournament had already commenced so he missed the initial matches. Despite this, he won the Orange Cap Award for scoring most number of runs in the tournament—608 runs in 12 matches. He played a key role in many victories of Royal Challengers Bangalore that resulted in him receiving the Man of the Match Award on five occasions.

After a miserable performance in the 2011 World Cup, West Indies played host to the Indian cricket team. Chris Gayle refused to sign the contract because he felt it had too many restrictions. The West Indies Cricket Board, in turn, decided not to consider him for national duty. One could see the most destructive batsman in the world watching and cheering his teammates merely as a spectator in the stands. It was indeed strange but a sad sight that while the West Indians were struggling against the Indians, their best batsman was watching from the sidelines. Chris Gayle helplessly watched his team lose the Test series 1–0 and ODIs 3–2 against a second string Indian team.

This is an example of how unresolved disputes can harm both the country and the player. If Chris Gayle had played all those matches then West Indies' performance would have been far better and the final result would have told a different story altogether. For Chris Gayle too, it would have been much more satisfying playing international matches against Pakistan and India rather than turning up against domestic Indian teams like Kolkata Knight Riders, Kings XI Punjab, Kochi Tuskers, etc.

Premier Ltd, formerly known as Premier Automobiles Limited is a Mumbai based company and till a few decades ago, it was one of India's premier car manufacturers. The company was founded in 1944 and it built vehicles under license from Dodge and Plymouth. In 1951, it tied up with Fiat and began to produce Fiat 500. In 1954, it launched the Fiat 1100 model. Following the success of these models, in 1973, it decided to use 'Premier' name for its vehicles and launched 'Premier President' and later 'Premier Padmini'. In 1978, the company decided to enter the premier car segment by launching Premier 118NE. This car had an 1180cc Nissan Engine and was based on Fiat 124 model.

When the Indian Government decided to open the doors for foreign car manufacturers, both Hindustan Motors and Premier Automobiles, till then the 'kings of Indian Automobile Industry' suffered huge competition especially from their Japanese counterparts. Premier Automobiles also faced frequent labour problems and the recurrent disruptions affected its production and delivery.

Premier Automobiles wanted to get back into its earlier profit making days. It tied up with Peugeot to build the Peugeot 309 model in India. Though the demand was quite good, the company faced severe labour problems. This coupled with poor dealer service affected the Peugeot car production. The last straw for Peugeot came when Premier decided to tie up with its old partner Fiat for the production of Fiat Uno. In 2001, Peugeot decided to pull out of the venture with Premier Automobiles.

The tie up with Fiat didn't prove any better for Premier Automobiles. Problems related to labour unrest continued and the plant shut down in 2001. These problems, along with poor customer service issues, damaged the brand name of Fiat and Premier Automobiles Ltd. They had to face the ire of thousands of angry customers. It is believed that several customers who had booked the vehicle were neither given the vehicle nor refund for non-delivery. These angry customers filed complaints against Premier Automobiles at the Consumer Courts of India. It was indeed sad to see Premier Automobiles Ltd, once the most reputed brand in Indian automobile industry, being nowhere in the list of top brands of automobiles in India.

The problem faced by West Indian cricket was akin to that faced by Premier Automobiles. West Indies cricket board was unable to smoothly resolve its disputes with one of its greatest batsmen, Chris Gayle. Though West Indies tried various cricketers, none of them helped the nation get back into its winning ways. West Indies cricket's woes were further compounded by the lack of proper bench strength and succession planning—described in another chapter of this book. Premier Automobiles too went downhill and tried various options to bring back the golden days of 1960s and 1970s. It tied up with different car manufacturers and introduced various models to address different market segments. Nothing helped. The company continued to struggle because it did not address its inherent problem of people management. West Indies was swamped with other problems like poor planning for future and people changing their preference towards other sports. Premier Automobiles faced problems related to new government regulations and customers changing their preferences. West Indies cricket board and Premier Automobiles probably failed to realize the importance of having good relationships with its players and employees respectively.

TEAM VS. SELF

(SACHIN TENDULKAR, ANIL KUMBLE, RAHUL DRAVID — MICHAEL DELL, DELL INC.; ANU AGA, THERMAX LTD)

'It is under the greatest adversity that there exists the greatest potential for doing good, both for oneself and others.'

— Dalai Lama XIV

During the 1999 World Cup being played in England, Sachin Tendulkar was struck with a major personal tragedy. His father passed away quite unexpectedly and a shattered Sachin immediately rushed back to India to perform the last rites of his father.

The media, quite expectedly, began to talk about Sachin's departure from the Indian team, and how it would affect India's fortunes. Sadly, there were very few people who seemed to care about the great loss that Sachin had suffered. No one talked about the thoughts going on in Sachin's mind. For most Indian cricket fans, it was just winning the World Cup that mattered.

Sachin was considered as the main pivot around which the entire team revolved. The opposition often believed that if they got Sachin out, the rest of the batsmen would follow. Sachin too was aware of this perception and realized the importance of his presence in the Indian dressing room. He was also fully conscious of the team's dependency on his all-round abilities in the ODI matches. Apart from the strength that he provided to batting, he often served as the fifth bowler.

After Sachin's return to India, Zimbabwe played and won against India—a game that the Indians threw away due to some reckless batting. Sachin's calming presence in the dressing room was sorely missed. He returned to England in time for India's match against Kenya at Bristol. He scored a brilliant 140 and was one of the main architects of the Indian victory. When he reached his century, he looked heavenwards and raised his bat towards his departed father. This emotional gesture had the entire crowd at its feet and even the most 'stiff upper-lipped' Englishmen could be seen wiping a tear or two.

India toured West Indies in 2002. During the 4th Test match at Antigua, Anil Kumble broke his jaw when he was hit by a ball from West Indian fast bowler Merv Dillon. Those who expected to see him returning to his hotel or taking rest in the comforts of the dressing room were in for a shock!

Anil Kumble, the gutsy Indian leg spinner, with his jaw strapped into place with a bandage, came onto the field. Despite a broken jaw and the excruciating pain, he bowled fourteen consecutive overs and managed to dismiss Brian Lara. The sight of a bandaged Anil Kumble celebrating the dismissal of one of the greatest batsmen in the world was worth beholding.Though the match ended in a draw, everyone complimented his sincerity and dedication. Former West Indian great Vivian Richards was all praise for Anil Kumble's heroic efforts as he remarked, 'It was one of the bravest things I've seen on the field of play.'

The next day, Anil Kumble, while boarding the flight to Bangalore for his surgery, said, 'It was very tough but I wanted to try. I didn't want to just sit around. I didn't feel the pain while bowling but I did when the match ended. Now I can return home thinking I gave my best shot.'

Rahul Dravid is probably the best example of being a team

player. As one of the most selfless cricketers in the Indian team, there are numerous instances where he has put the team's interests ahead of his own personal preferences. Though Rahul Dravid was essentially a middle order batsman, he has played multiple roles, as per the demands of the situation.

It is a well-known fact that Dravid is one of the best Indian players of short-pitched bowling, especially on hard bouncy tracks. He is also technically very sound and offers the best defence to a moving ball. Unfortunately, his biggest strength has also continued to haunt him because he was often been asked to open the innings to negotiate the new ball. Dravid was one of the best No. 3 batsmen in the world, and loved to bat at that position. However, this has not stopped the Indian team from asking him to open the innings for India in Test matches. Dravid has donned the mantle of an opener and played many remarkable innings for India as an opener. His primary task has been to see off the shine of the new ball before the stroke players come in to bat. During the 2006 series against Pakistan, he opened the Indian batting along with Virender Sehwag. Both of them were involved in a mammoth 410 run partnership for the first wicket. Only Pankaj Roy and Vinoo Mankad have a better partnership for India, 413 versus New Zealand in Chennai.

If the Test matches tested his skills as an opener, the ODIs were no less challenging!

In order to accommodate an extra batsman or a specialist bowler, there were numerous instances where Rahul Dravid was asked to play the dual role of a wicket keeper–batsman. He had kept wickets during his college days in Bangalore but had never done it even in domestic Ranji Trophy matches. However, since the Indian selectors knew of his wicket keeping abilities, they asked him to take up this additional role.

Rahul Dravid performed admirably as a wicket keeper–batsman. His ability to lend flexibility to the Indian team helped it reach the 2003 World Cup finals. He had the second highest score (145 runs) by a wicket keeper in a World Cup, just four runs less than Adam Gilchrist. Rahul Dravid clearly showed the importance of putting the team ahead of the self. He was ready to handle additional roles, even if he didn't enjoy them. What makes Dravid truly great is the fact that not once did he air his grievances openly to the media. He went about his tasks in a truly professional manner.

These are some of the finest examples of cricketers putting their team's interests ahead of themselves. In corporate life too, we need to be extremely flexible to the needs of the organization. We may have to play different roles depending on the situation. There are lots of examples in different organizations where people have changed roles to help the organization achieve its objectives.

Michael Dell was the founder of Dell—one of the biggest computer companies in the world. He became the CEO of Dell and remained in this position till March 2004. In 2004, Kevin B. Rollins, then the president and COO, became the president and CEO of Dell. Michael Dell became the chairman of the board. Unfortunately for Rollins, in 2006, Dell's profits and market shares slowly eroded. It began to face stiff competition from its arch rival HP. As the revenues, profits, and market shares dropped, the stockholders began to put tremendous pressure on the board. It saw the exit of Kevin B. Rollins and on 31st January 2007, Michael Dell, at the request of the board, returned as the CEO of Dell.

Michael Dell knew that no one knew Dell better than him. He was aware of his organization's strengths. He was also aware of what was going wrong and what had to be corrected. He knew that recruiting someone from outside for the CEO's role would mean a long delay in getting the company back on its track because the new CEO would have his own learning curve in understanding the organization and its businesses. Considering all these facts, he himself took over as the role of the CEO.

Michael Dell is a classic example of a person who was ready to leave the comforts of the boardroom and take over an earlier role because the situation demanded it.

Let us take another example, closer home.

Thermax Ltd is a multinational energy and environment engineering company that has its operations in India and UK. It manufactures boilers, vapour absorption machines, and installs captive power projects. The company was started by the late A.S. Bhathena in 1966 with a manufacturing unit in Dadar, Mumbai. During those days it was known as Wanson (India) because it had collaboration with Wanson, a Belgian company. The company first started manufacturing small baby boilers to cater to the steam requirements of hospitals. It has grown considerably since then, and currently has four manufacturing centres and operates in 75 countries.

A.S. Bhathena's daughter, Anu Aga did her B.A. in Economics from St Xavier's College, Mumbai and post-graduation in medical and psychiatric social work from the prestigious Tata Institute of Social Sciences (TISS), Mumbai. She was also a recipient of the Fulbright Scholarship and studied in the United States for four months. Her husband, Rohinton Aga, joined Wanson (India). The company was renamed Thermax in 1980, after A.S. Bhathena retired, and Rohinton Aga took over as the chairman and managing director.In 1995, it became a public company on the Bombay Stock Exchange. Unfortunately, soon disaster struck. Rohinton passed away in 1996. His wife Anu Aga was shattered. Her husband's untimely death was a great loss for her but she realized that this was not the time for grieving. She quickly took over as the executive chairperson of the Thermax Group. Luckily for her, she had begun her career in Thermax in 1985, and later was in charge of the company's human resources function from 1991 to 1996. So she was quite familiar with the organization, its vision, strategy, and products.

The company diversified into various businesses and was going through a very successful phase when it was hit by economic slowdown. Initially, Aga was concerned about the dipping numbers but her team convinced her that this was to be expected due to the economic downturn. However, a letter from an anonymous shareholder acted as a catalyst for a change at the top. The shareholder wrote that Aga had probably felt she had made enough money and didn't care to make more, thereby, letting the shareholders down. This prompted her to move to a non-executive role as the chairperson of the organization. But before moving into her new role, she hired Boston Consulting Group to overhaul the entire business. Based on Boston Consulting Group's advice, the company decided to exit from all non-core businesses and reconstitute the board. The number of working executives on board were reduced and more independent directors were inducted into the company. As the chairperson, Anu turned around the company and helped transform it into a high performance organization with a bigger presence in international markets, and a turnkey player in energy / environment projects.

Anu Aga was also active in other activities connected with the Indian industry. She served as chairperson of the Confederation of Indian Industry's Western Region. She has written extensively and given talks on corporate governance, corporate social responsibility, the role of women and education, etc. She figured among the eighth richest Indian women and in 2007, and was a part of '40 Richest Indians by net worth' according to Forbes magazine. In 2004, she stepped down from her role as the chairperson and handed the post to her daughter, Meher Pudumjee. She involved herself actively in social work and was awarded the Padma Shri by the Government of India.

Sachin Tendulkar and Anu Aga are examples of people who could quickly put behind their personal heartbreaks for the sake of their team and organization. When his father died in an untimely manner, Sachin returned to his team after a very brief visit to India. Anu Aga took up the reins of Thermax when her CEO–husband died quite unexpectedly. Anil Kumble too put his team's interests ahead of his own as he bowled with a broken jaw. Rahul Dravid and Michael Dell showed that they were ready to give up their existing roles in the interests of the team. They were the people who could get out of their comfort zones whenever the situation demanded it. The most important quality that we need to learn from them is their selflessness and putting the team or organization ahead of themselves.

Development of Ecosystem

(Wasim Akram—YouTube, Texas Instruments)

'One man can be a crucial ingredient on a team, but one man cannot make a team.'

—Kareem Abdul-Jabbar

In cricket, it is quite common to see many great players willing to share their skills with their junior teammates. It is not rare to see a senior batsman walk up to his junior and instruct him on how to play a short-pitched ball. Similarly, it is a common sight to see a senior bowler advising his junior on how to contain the flow of runs when the latter is being hammered all around the field.

There are also a few rare heart-warming sights of great cricketers helping players from other countries. This is extremely good for the game of cricket because it helps to raise the level of the game. Wasim Akram, former Pakistan captain, is undoubtedly one of the greatest fast bowlers in the world. Known as 'Sultan of Swing', he had the capability to prodigiously swing a ball that was more than 70 overs old.

Indian speedsters Zaheer Khan and Irfan Pathan were also left-arm fast bowlers like Wasim Akram. These two players always considered Akram as their idol and mentor. It was a common sight to watch Akram helping the Indian duo during his frequent visits to India. There were many instances when Zaheer and Pathan would not hesitate to call up Akram and take tips from him to iron out chinks in their bowling. Zaheer Khan went on to become one of the most important strike bowlers for India. Irfan Pathan, despite bowling with a slower pace, developed his outswingers very well, thanks to the guidance that he received from his mentor.

The above instances show that sharing between players, irrespective of the nationality, can increase the competence of the players, and thereby raise the level of the game. A genuine cricket lover would love to watch Zaheer or Pathan bowl with the same degree of pace and swing as Akram.

In the corporate world too, sharing has lot of advantages—as can be seen by the success story of YouTube. This San Bruno (California) based company has a video sharing website where users can upload and share videos. It has a broad variety of professional videos like movie clips, TV clips, and songs sung by famous singers. It also allows amateurs to create their own videos and upload them on the website. Hence the website contains videos uploaded by individuals and media corporations.

YouTube was founded by Chad Hurley, Steve Chen, and Jawed Karim—all former employees of PayPal. The popular story is that in 2005, Hurley and Chen shot a video at a dinner party at Chen's apartment but had difficulty in sharing it with their friends. This led to the idea of creating YouTube—a website for sharing videos.

In April 2005, Jawed Karim created and uploaded the first YouTube video that shows him at the San Diego Zoo. This became extremely popular so within a month, YouTube launched a beta test site for the general public. It was officially launched in November 2005. YouTube allows all users to watch its videos and registered users to upload and share videos. Any person who is 18 years or more can register as a YouTube user. It also has a very powerful search engine for searching any video that has been uploaded on the website.

In the past few years, YouTube has grown beyond its initial

purpose of sharing videos. It has become similar to various social networking sites. It allows registered users to create their own channels, write their profiles on their wall, and post comments. It also allows registered users to send invitations to other registered users, befriend them, and exchange information. It allows them to subscribe to others' videos and post comments on them.

These days, YouTube has become a tool for open communication (by posting comments) and private mails (popularly known as PMs). In this regard, it has many capabilities that are normally associated with social networking sites like Facebook, Orkut, etc.

Before the arrival of YouTube, consumers had to purchase audio and video CDs and DVDs. In many poor and developing countries, music and entertainment market grew at a sluggish pace due to the high costs of CDs and DVDs. However, with the advent of YouTube, videos started being uploaded and shared free of cost. This has not only made the videos accessible to everyone but also completely changed the media and music industry. It has indirectly benefitted the celebrity singers and musicians too because their music has become accessible to millions of people around the world. These celebrities have now become household names.

YouTube is able to generate huge revenues through online advertisements. In November 2006, Google bought YouTube for $1.65 billion. More than 65,000 new videos are uploaded and more than 100 million views are received every day. It is the most dominant provider of online videos not only in the US but around the world. YouTube is a great example of how a new market can develop and explode with the simple concept of sharing your assets with others.

Texas Instruments (India) Pvt. Ltd is a subsidiary of the American semiconductor company, Texas Instruments. In 1985, it became one of the first semiconductor companies to commence operations in Bangalore, India. Till the entry of

Texas Instruments, Bangalore was known for its public sector companies like BEL, HAL, NAL, ISRO, HMT, etc. However, the entry of Texas Instruments changed the face of Bangalore. Within a short span of time, it ramped up their headcount with the best software engineers in the country. Unlike many software services companies that were primarily providing resources, Texas Instruments (India) was involved in developing the latest cutting-edge technology.

Many other software product development companies saw the kind of activities that Texas Instruments were doing in Bangalore and the kind of people they hired. These companies wanted to visit Texas Instruments and learn from their experiences of setting up a software development centre in Bangalore. Texas Instruments had a choice of refusing their request but it didn't. It welcomed anyone who wanted to visit them. It patiently explained to them the journey that they had embarked on since 1985. When other companies heard and saw the progress made by Texas Instruments, they felt confident of setting up operations in Bangalore. Slowly, one by one, many multinational companies came and setup software development centres in Bangalore—IBM, Motorola, HP, Philips, Robert Bosch, Intel, Infineon, Siemens, Nokia, SAP Labs, Dell, Tesco, Target, AMD, Analog Devices, Samsung, LG, NDS, Honeywell, Sony, Google, Yahoo, Microsoft, Huawei, etc. Bangalore was named 'The Silicon Valley of India' due to the presence of all these high-tech companies.

What is common between Wasim Akram, YouTube, and Texas Instruments? Wasim Akram selflessly shared his tips and raised the level of the game by improving the bowling skills of bowlers from other countries. YouTube encouraged sharing of videos that helped setup a sound infrastructure for social networking which in turn generated revenues for the company. Texas Instruments was open to helping all new entrants who established operations in Bangalore. Today Texas Instruments and other software companies have built the rich ecosystem of Bangalore. This in turn has helped these companies have a wider pool of skilled resources and infrastructure. Who says sharing doesn't pay?

No One is Bigger than the Game
(Shoaib Akhtar—Carly Fiorina, HP)

'Don't measure yourself by what you have accomplished, but by what you should have accomplished with your ability.'

—John Wooden

Shoaib Akhtar is considered as one of the fastest pace bowlers Pakistan ever produced. This is a great achievement considering the fact that this country had produced some genuinely quick bowlers like Imran Khan, Sarfraz Nawaz, and Wasim Akram. He set the record for bowling the fastest delivery in the history of Test cricket when he bowled at a speed of 161.3 km/hr (100.2 mph). His inswinging yorkers bowled at such a furious pace made him one of the most dangerous bowlers in world cricket.

Shoaib made his debut for Pakistan in 1997 and announced his retirement in 2011 after a poor performance in the World Cup. Despite representing Pakistan for fourteen long years, he played just 46 Tests and 163 ODIs. This was partly because of the frequent fights that he had with his cricket board which resulted in him getting banned a few times on grounds of indiscipline. His career had been ridden with several controversies. He had poor interpersonal skills with his teammates, his coach, and the Pakistan Cricket Board. He was accused of having poor attitude and not being a team player.

During the 2005 Pakistan tour to Australia, he was sent home due to attitude problems. In 2006, he was involved in a drug scandal after testing positive to a banned drug. Luckily for him, the court lifted the ban. Unfortunately, within a year, he was involved in a few more controversies. During the national cricket camp at Karachi, he was fined ₹3,00,000 for lack of discipline. Shoaib protested and used foul language against the Pakistan Cricket Board. A week before the World Twenty20 tournament, he hit his teammate Mohammad Asif with a cricket bat, bruising the latter's thigh.

Shoaib never learnt from his past mistakes and continued to court controversies. In 2008, he was banned for five years for criticizing Pakistan Cricket Board. Within a few months, the Lahore High Court suspended the ban and he was once again chosen to represent Pakistan.

Even after Shoaib's retirement from all forms of the game, he continued to create controversies. In his book, aptly titled *Controversially Yours*, he made disparaging remarks about some of the best cricketers in the world, his teammates, and Pakistan Cricket Board.

Shoaib Akhtar was a celebrity in Pakistan. This made him feel that he was bigger than the game. However, he failed to realize that cricket is a team game and at the end of the day, it is teamwork and not individual heroics that matter. Shoaib is not an exception. There are many celebrity sportsmen, actors, and CEOs who fall into a similar trap. As they gain popularity, they begin to believe that they are bigger than the industry that they represent. I would like to take the example of Carly Fiorina, former CEO of HP.

When Carly became the CEO of HP in 1999, she considered herself as nothing short of a celebrity. Unlike her predecessor Lew Platt, she was an extrovert and extremely media savvy. She starred in many of HP's commercials, and paired up with entertainment celebrities like Matt Damon, Ben Affleck, and Sheryl Crow. She was hailed as the most powerful businesswoman in the US. Her pictures appeared on the covers of leading business magazines and she became one of the most recognized faces in the corporate world. However, all these activities also created a perception among her employees that she promoted herself more than the organization.

HP was always known to be a very people-friendly organization but Carly's style of functioning changed all that. She felt that 'The HP Way' was a major cause for the company's ills. She began to change many of the company's rules and policies. She was seen as a self-centred manager who was not open to feedback from her employees. Her leadership style resulted in severe attrition of key roles in the organization.

It is widely believed that Carly Fiorina stopped the electronic bulletin board because she felt that the employees were using it to attack her and tarnish her image. She rarely mixed with other employees of the organization. She even hired a bodyguard which distanced herself further from her employees. When she took over as the CEO of HP, the organization was completely decentralized and each line of business was operating like an independent unit. She changed the organization's structure and centralized most of the decision making. The consolidation of business units and centralization of decision making made Fiorina very powerful but it greatly affected the company's performance. From being one of the most agile companies in the world, HP began to suffer from great inertia because none of the important business decisions could be taken at lower levels. This was a classic case of a 'larger than life' CEO—a person who probably put her interests ahead of the company's. The results were there for everyone to see.

Shoaib Akhtar and Carly Fiorina were extremely talented individuals. Both promised a lot but sadly didn't meet the expectations of the public. Shoaib entered the cricketing scene with a bang. Who can forget his devastating spell in the Asian Test Championship at Kolkata in February 1999? The look of disbelief on the faces of Sachin Tendulkar and Rahul Dravid when a rookie Shoaib bowling at full steam uprooted their stumps off consecutive balls is etched in everyone's memory. It was one of those rare instances when Tendulkar got out to a first-ball duck. It was a clear signal to the cricketing world that one of the most dangerous bowlers had arrived, and would soon be sending shivers up the spine of some of the best batsmen in the world. Pakistan won that match by 46 runs with Akhtar taking 4 wickets in each innings. Unfortunately, he never understood the importance of teamwork and always considered himself to be above the rest of his teammates. His career was mired with controversies and injuries. Because of this, he played far less matches than what he deserved. His raw talent ensured an excellent strike rate—he took 176 wickets in just 46 tests and 247 wickets in 163 ODIs. Had he played as much as Kapil Dev or Wasim Akram, he might have ended up being one the highest wicket takers in the world.

The case of Carly Fiorina was quite similar. She joined AT&T as a sales manager but soon drew the attention of senior management. She was able to handle tough assignments and became one of the best salespersons of AT&T. She rose rapidly to become the president of North America sales. She also played a key role in AT&T's spin off of Lucent Technologies, and became the head of Lucent's sales and marketing group. She was rated as one of the top performers in the corporate world. It was no surprise when she was hired as the CEO of HP. The shareholders, the customers, and employees of HP—practically everyone expected this lady to make HP the biggest and the most profitable IT company in the world. And why not? She had the past credentials. Unfortunately, as the CEO of HP she considered herself bigger than the organization. She also failed to recognize the importance of teamwork and people management. It was always her ideas, her decisions, her image. Her six year tenure was one of the most turbulent periods for HP in recent times.

Having a talented bowler like Shoaib, Pakistan could have become the top cricketing nation in the world. Unfortunately it didn't. Just like HP could not become the biggest computer company in the world despite having an achiever and a go-getter like Carly Fiorina at the top.

9

ATTITUDE

'I hope my positive body language scares this monster.'

Tenacity and Perseverance
(Steve Waugh — Karsanbhai Patel, Nirma)

'To make our way, we must have firm resolve, persistence, tenacity. We must gear ourselves to work hard all the way. We can never let up.'

— Ralph Bunche

Steve Waugh is considered one of the best Australian players in the modern era of cricket. When he first appeared in the international scene, not many felt that he had the required expertise and talent to make it to the top.

When he made his debut he was considered as a 'bits and pieces player'—'a batsman who could bowl a bit' or 'a bowler who could bat a bit'! This led to a perception that he was more suited for limited overs cricket rather than Test matches.However, he proved the cricket pundits wrong and went on to become not only one of the leading batsmen of Australia but also one of the most successful captains in the world.

Steve Waugh made a very modest start to his Test career. He made his debut against India in 1985–1986, and scored just 26 runs in four innings. He was retained for the tour of New Zealand. His performance did not improve much, scoring 86 runs with an average of 17.40 runs. His tour to Pakistan in 1988 yielded just 92 runs at an average of 18.4 runs.

Steve Waugh was probably not as flamboyant as some of his

teammates. However, what he lacked in style and finesse, he more than made up with his self-belief, tenacity, and hard work. His solid performance in the 1993 New Zealand tour saw him scoring 178 Test runs at a healthy average of 44.5. This enabled him to get selected for the Ashes tour in England being conducted in the same year. He amassed 416 runs at an awesome average of 83.2 runs and helped Australia clinch the Ashes series 4–1 against England. Within a year, he was ranked as the world's leading Test batsman.

Steve's twin brother Mark Waugh was also an all-rounder, and he too represented Australia in both forms of the game. Though Mark Waugh was a far more attractive batsman to watch and immensely gifted with abundanant natural talent, he could never match his brother Steve in terms of performance and output. Mark Waugh scored 8,029 runs at an average of 41.81. Compare this with Steve Waugh's record of 10,927 runs at an average of 51.06 and 92 wickets from 168 Tests. Steve also had an incredible ODI record in 325 ODIs he scored 7,569 runs at an average of 32.9 runs and took 195 wickets. He was not only a great batsman but also a shrewd captain. In the 57 Tests that he led, he won 41 matches, drew 7, and lost only 9 matches at a success rate of 71.93%. He led in 106 ODIs and won 67, lost 35, and the remaining were either drawn or no result.

Dr Karsanbhai Patel was born into a farmer family in the northern part of Gujarat. After his studies, he started his career as a lab technician in New Cotton Mills, Ahmedabad. He later joined the Geology and Mining Department of Gujarat State Government.

In the year 1969, he setup a small workshop in a suburb of Ahmedabad and began to manufacture a detergent powder named Nirma—named after his daughter Nirupama. He would work at the State Government office the whole day and after his office hours he would focus on his business. He would visit neighbourhoods, selling his handmade detergent powder on his bicycle! His product was priced at one third the cost of leading detergent powders so it became an immediate success. In 1972, he quit his job to focus completely on Nirma.

Karsanbhai was aware that a large percentage of India's population was middle-class or lower middle-class. Most of them found detergents made by multinationals to be quite expensive so they were looking for a product that was inexpensive but of good quality. Nirma met the expectations of millions of Indians and soon became a household name for the Indian middle-class. It also became a leading detergent powder in India, overtaking some of the biggest multinationals in business! Subsequently, Karsanbhai entered the premium soap and detergent segments with products like Nirma Beauty Soap and Super Nirma Detergent. At one point in time, Nirma had a 20% market share in soap cakes and 35% in detergents. For all his efforts, Karsanbhai was awarded a honourary doctorate by Florida Atlantic University in 2001 and Padma Shri in 2010.

What made Steve Waugh and Karsanbhai so successful?

Steve Waugh rarely displayed the classy off-drive of Greg Chappell or the sweet-timing of Mark Waugh. However, he was more successful than most Australian cricketers because of his sheer doggedness and hard work at the wicket. He probably understood the value of his wicket more than anyone else, and batted as if his life depended on it. It is not surprising that some of his best innings came at the time of crisis. He batted relatively lower down the order. There were numerous incidents when Australians lost a few quick wickets at the top. The opposition would feel that they had the game firmly in their clutches. Then Steve Waugh would walk into the wicket and with just the tail-enders for company, he would slowly rebuild the Australian innings. He would bring respectability to the Australian score not through flashy strokes but through tenacity and resolve. He would keep nudging for 1s and 2s, and keep the score board ticking. The opposition would feel completely frustrated because he would play a very safe game, without giving the bowlers and fielders too many chances.

Karsanbhai's success came from similar tenacity and hard work. When he started Nirma it was a 'one-man-show'. He was himself involved in manufacturing and packaging the product. He would go from door to door on his bicycle and sell his products. He knew that low cost of Nirma had played a major role in his success. Normally for an organization, cost control becomes an issue as it grows in size. Karsanbhai did not want his organization to fall into the same trap. Even when the organization grew bigger, he knew how to manage the costs. He optimized the distribution network, and manufactured the raw materials to keep costs and lead times well under control. Initially, his competitors did not take him seriously. How could a 'one-man-show' company with hardly any past record, brand image, or advertising, challenge them? Slowly, as Nirma began to eat into their market shares, the competitors woke up. They struggled to overcome Karsanbhai's challenge because his products were not just cheap or inexpensive; they were also of good quality. Like Steve Waugh, Karsanbhai too played within his limitations and more importantly, knew how to overcome them through a never-say-die attitude.

Self-belief and Conviction

(MS Dhoni — Dhirubhai Ambani, Reliance Industries)

'If I have the belief that I can do it, I shall surely acquire the capacity to do it even if I may not have it at the beginning.'

—Mahatma Gandhi

Mahendra Singh Dhoni, popularly known as MSD, is the current captain of the Indian team and one of the most popular cricketers in India. He endorses many of India's leading products and in the last couple of years; his advertisements have helped him earn more than any other sportsman in India. Today MSD is the most recognized cricketer in India. But what may not be known to many is the humble beginning he had during his early part of life.

Dhoni was born in Ranchi (Jharkand) and during his initial years, he played badminton and football. Ironically, it was his football coach who sent him to play cricket for a local cricket club. Dhoni impressed everyone with his wicket keeping skills and soon became the wicket keeper for Commando Cricket Club. Based on his performance, he was selected for Vinoo Mankad Trophy Under-16 Championship.

A.K. Ganguly, the Divisional Railway Manager of Kharagpur Division was also a great cricket enthusiast. He saw Dhoni's game and recognized his ability through a talent spotting recruitment drive. He was instrumental in Dhoni getting a job as a ticket collector at Kharagpur Railway station.

Unfortunately for Dhoni, Kharagpur was neither blessed with a cricket academy like Bangalore nor was it a Mecca of cricket like Mumbai. He had to make the best use of limited infrastructure that the town offered. Playing matches in east zone also meant that he would not get easily noticed by the Indian selectors. However, these handicaps did not diminish his passion for the game or his desire to succeed. Kharagpur residents love Dhoni and fondly recollect how he would cycle around the town, playing cricket with tennis balls on different grounds in and around Kharagpur.

Dhoni made his Test debut in December 2005, and became the captain of the Indian Test team in the year 2008. Today he is one the most destructive batsmen in the world of cricket. Under his shrewd captaincy, India won the 2007 ICC World Twenty20, CB Series of 2007, Champions League Twenty20 Tournament, and Border Gavaskar Trophy against the Australians. The biggest feather in his cap was the 2011 World Cup victory.

Despite these successes, Dhoni has not forgotten his humble beginning at Kharagpur. When he is not playing for India, he can be seen hanging out with his old friends. It does not come as a surprise that whenever Dhoni and India have a crucial match, the Kharagpur residents perform Yagnas and pray for their former ticket-collector of South Eastern Railways.

There are numerous rags to riches stories in the corporate world too—people with very humble backgrounds who made it big through sheer hard work and dedication. The best example is Dhirajlal Hirachand Ambani, popularly known as Dhirubhai Ambani. This small time worker with Arab merchants went on to become the founder of Reliance Industries which is a conglomerate in the areas of petrochemicals, textiles, power, and communication.

Like Dhoni, Dhirubhai Ambani too had a very humble childhood. His father was a village school teacher with a low income. Dhirubhai had the spirit of anentrepreneur right from his childhood which saw him setup bhajiya (onion and potato fries) stalls at village fairs to make extra money. Though as a child he was very intelligent, he had to discontinue his studies after his matriculation because of his father's poor health.

He went to Aden(Yemen) and worked there as a clerk at A. Besse & Co.

Aden was one of the busiest trading and oil bunkering port in the world. A. Besse& Co. was involved in different aspects of trading like cargo booking, shipping, forwarding, and merchandising. It was a trading agent for a large number of European, American, Asian, and African companies that dealt in sugar, spices, textiles, tools, machinery, and petroleum products. This enabled Dhirubahi to learn the ways of commodity trading, sales, marketing, distribution, currency trading, and finance management. During lunch breaks he would roam around the streets of Aden where traders from different continents bought and sold goods worth millions. He met traders from all parts of Europe, Africa, India, Japan, and China.

To learn the tricks of the trade he worked free for a Gujarati trading firm. He learnt accounting, book keeping, preparing shipping papers and documents, and dealing with banks and insurance companies—skills that would come in handy when he launched himself into trading about a decade later. Though Dhirubhai had an option of migrating to London and settling for an easy life, he chose to return to India because he could visualize many exciting years for India. He soon started 'Majin'—a company that imported polyester yarn and sold spices. Later, he setup Reliance Commercial Corporation and started a textile mill in Ahmedabad in 1966. His 'Vimal' brand of textiles soon became a household name in India.

In 1982, Ambani set up a plant to manufacture polyester filament yarn. He subsequently diversified into chemicals, petrochemicals, plastics, power, and telecommunications. Reliance as a whole was described by the BBC as: 'a business empire with an estimated annual turnover of $12 billion and an 85,000-strong workforce'. Dhirubhai Ambani was among the select Forbes billionaires and also figured in the list of Top 50 Businessmen in Asia. In June 1998, he became the first Indian to receive the Wharton School Dean's Medal. It is believed that Dhirubhai Ambani started his business with just ₹1,50,000, and at the time of his death, Reliance Group had a turnover of approximately ₹75,000 crores!

Dhoni started his career as a ticket-collector at theKharagpur railway station and soon worked his way to become India's cricket captain, and one of the richest sportsmen in the country. Dhirubhai too started his career with an insignificant job but then became the captain of the Indian industry. Dhoni could have easily settled down in his railway profession like most of his peers but he had the burning desire to change tracks and become one of India's most successful captains. Similarly, Dhirubhai Ambani had the easier option of migrating to England but he chose to return to India and pursue his dreams. He too changed tracks and went on to become one of India's most successful entrepreneurs.

There was a perception that if you have to get selected in the Indian cricket team, you need to be from one of India's top cities. This perception was common because during 1970s and 1980s, most of the cricketers in the Indian Test team were from Mumbai, Bangalore, New Delhi, and Chennai. On a similar note, when we see successful industrialists, we have a tendency to attribute their success to the well-known family names that they carry. We assume that to achieve success, we need to be born in a rich industrial family.

However, people like MS Dhoni and Dhirubhai Ambani proved this hypothesis wrong. Their phenomenal rise in their respective careers motivate youngsters with a belief that even if you are born in an ordinary family with a modest beginning, you can rise to become one of the best in the business.

Positive Body Language

(Vivian Richards, Sunil Gavaskar—Steve Ballmer, Microsoft)

'The most important thing in communication is hearing what isn't said.'

—Peter F. Drucker

Cricket was dubbed as a 'gentleman's game'. It is still known as that though in the past few decades, it has lost much of its sheen. Though sledging has been a part of the game for many years now, in recent times, it has crossed acceptable norms.

Anil Kumble, the affable former Indian skipper was one of the most aggressive players, despite having a gentle exterior. His steely resolve, despite a cool face, earned him the nickname 'The Smiling Assassin'. He once remarked, 'aggressiveness means the desire to take a wicket off every ball. It does not mean abusing a batsman or his family.'

Among the batsmen, there is no better 'smiling assassin' than the great Sir Vivian Richards. When Vivian Richards used to come in to bat, his aggressive walk, famously known as 'the swagger' would send a chill down the bowler's spine. Richards loved to dominate the best bowling attacks right from the first ball he faced. Richards's body language could dishearten the best bowler in the world—his approach to the wicket, the way in which he took his stance, the way he gazed at the fielders, and the even manner in which he munched his chewing gum!

It is believed that Richards would look at the fielders who were guarding the boundary rather than those standing in close-in fielding positions. This was a message to the fielding side that he expected to dispatch most of the balls to the boundaries.

Many cricketers believe that hurling abuses at the opponents is a sign of aggression. They feel that sledging is the best form of attack. Though Vivian Richards has been regarded as one of the most aggressive batsmen in the history of cricket, he had a different approach. He believed in an aggressive style of batting and rarely indulged in verbal abuse. He loved to decimate the best bowling attacks in the world through sheer destructive batting. You could see him smiling as he despatched the ball to the boundary. The more the bowler tried to intimidate him with verbal abuse, the more he smiled and the farther the ball travelled on the ground! Very soon, the bowler would realize the futility in trying to sledge Richards, and would get down to getting his basics right.

Richards was not only a devastating batsman but also an excellent fielder and a part-time spin bowler. He made his debut against India in 1974 at Bangalore, and in his 17 distinguished years, he has scored 8,540 runs in 121 Test matches at an average of 51. He also scored 6,721 runs in 187 ODIs at an average of 47.

Sunil Gavaskar, former Indian captain, and one of the best openers in world cricket played without a helmet. This was one of the best examples of body languages that an opening batsman could display. Imagine taking guard against the fastest bowling attacks in the world such as those in West Indies and Australia. When someone like Sunil Gavaskar comes to the crease without a customary helmet, he sends a strong message to the opposition that he doesn't believe he will miss any ball and get hit on his head.

While speaking at a felicitation function, Gavaskar told the audience that Imran Khan, former Pakistani captain, had advised him to wear a helmet since any batsman could miss a ball and get hit. Gavaskar confessed that he was subsequently hit by a Malcolm Marshall bouncer but he believed that 'the one ball' mentioned by Imran was done with! Gavaskar was widely admired for his technique against fast bowling, with an excellent average of 65 against the West Indies, that possessed the most vicious fast bowling attack in Test history. Vivian Richards was another great batsman who did not use a helmet.

In corporate life too, there is a misconception that to be aggressive, you need to abuse your peers, team members, and other colleagues in the organization. The general perception is that: 'nice men finish last'. However, some of the best performers have been those who have shown aggressiveness through results and not through abusive behaviour. For a sales manager, it could be the sales figures. In the case of an engineering manager, it could be the 'design to manufacture' lead time. For a project manager it could be the way he manages the project within the budgeted cost and exceeds the expected performance and quality.

Steve Ballmer has been the CEO of Microsoft Corporation since January 2000. As of 2011, he had an estimated wealth of around $14.5 billion. He is well-known for his high energy levels and positive body language. Steve Ballmer comes on stage for many Microsoft events. His behaviour and body language are much talked about in media and the Internet. His emotion-packed energetic speeches have made him hugely popular. There are countless YouTube videos showing him performing on stage, including his 'monkey dance'. During the past decade, his body language on stage has been compared to that of many celebrities, motivational gurus, and evangelists.

Dr Peter Langford, a senior organizational psychologist with Macquarie University described Steve Ballmer's events as 'an evangelist movement'! He said that though Ballmer's body language was bizarre, it was a calculated and deliberate performance to attract people.

The media and the audience love Ballmer's gesticulations, tongue-poking, finger-pointing, and other facial expressions which are both funny and aggressive! During Microsoft's 25th anniversary celebrations, Steve Ballmer popped out of a cake, much to the amusement of the onlookers.

This kind of body language is mostly inherent rather than consciously acquired. For example, Richards was genuinely surprised when he was told that his swagger from the pavilion to the wicket was the most talked about walk in the history of cricket!

This is probably why among all the skills—body language is one of the toughest to change because it is a 'soft skill rather than a hard skill. It is not a competency that can be easily acquired through class room training. The general belief is that you either have it or you don't. However, these days there are lots of corporate trainings where body language training is one of the key elements. People are taught to have the right mix of body language, not to look too dominating and intimidating and at the same time, not to appear too submissive. Positive body language is one of the most important aspects for any good professional. It shows the kind of self-confidence and self-belief that you possess.

Ownership and Passion

(Sachin Tendulkar—Bob Galvin, Motorola)

'Without passion you don't have energy, without energy you have nothing.'

—Donald Trump

This chapter consists of two attributes—ownership and passion. It is my personal belief that both are strongly linked to each other. People who display a strong sense of ownership are those who also are very passionate about their work and vice-versa. They appear to be two sides of the same coin.

It is a common belief that words like 'leader' or 'manager' indicate designation or titles. In reality, these don't represent just the designation but the attitude as well. A person may not have such a designation but can still show leadership or managerial qualities. This attribute can be seen among those people who display a high degree of 'ownership'.

In cricket it's a common sight to see players exhibiting behaviour that goes beyond the roles that they are expected to perform. How many times have we not seen wicket keepers like Adam Gilchrist rushing towards the bowler, in the middle of an over, suggesting him on how to bowl the next ball? How many times have we not seen bowlers like Alan Donald, while standing at mid-off, run to a rookie fast bowler and share tips? It was also a common sight to see an experienced Sunil Gavaskar, as a non-striker, walk up to the struggling batsman and tell him how to handle the short-pitched balls.

These are all examples of players who have contributed to the success of the team by showing ownership.

One of the best examples of this trait is Sachin Tendulkar. He has played under different captains and he has always contributed as a leader by constantly mentoring and coaching other players—both on and off the field. Irrespective of who the captain is, he has been the main anchor of the Indian team for the past two decades. Sachin played under different captains like Saurav Ganguly, Rahul Dravid, Anil Kumble, MS Dhoni, etc. One of his his best acts of ownership came under the captaincy of Mohhamed Azharuddin.

During the 1993 Hero Cup semi-finals at Kolkata, India played against the mighty South Africans which boasted of star cricketers like Alan Donald, Hansie Cronje, Darryl Cullinan, Fanie de Villiers, and Brian McMillan.

Batting first, India coul d muster only 195 runs. At the end of the 49th over, South Africa needed just six runs to coast to the finals. Anil Kumble had already finished his quota of 10 overs. Even as Azharuddin was contemplating whom to choose between Srinath, Kapil Dev, and Manoj Prabhakar to bowl the last over, Sachin walked to the Indian skipper and had an animated discussion with him. Sachin was ready to bowl the final over. This gamble by Sachin and Azharuddin had the Eden Gardens crowd up on its feet. Sachin daring to take on South Africa's most destructive batsman was truly remarkable.

In order to retain the strike, McMillan attempted two runs off the first delivery, but it resulted in Fanie de Villers getting run out. This brought in Alan Donald whose batting skills are nowhere near his bowling ability. Sachin bowled three successive dot balls. Donald managed to steal a single of the penultimate ball. South Africa now needed a boundary off the last ball to win the match. The noise and din from the 1,00,000 strong crowd at Eden Gardens and playing in a high-pressure semi-finals choked McMillan. The hard hitting batsman could manage just a single. India had won by 2 runs and entered the finals of the Hero Cup which they won against West Indies.

Every budding professional should realize from this cricketing example that you need not be the captain to be a leader. Everyone in the team should show leadership qualities, irrespective of their designation. As managers, how many times have we not seen young employees with eight to ten years of experience walk up to us and ask for leadership or managerial roles? When the employee says, 'I want to become a manager', he does not mean, 'I want to show leadership qualities', or 'I want to take responsibility of leading the company towards greater heights'. He simply means, 'I want the designation of a manager', or 'I want the manager tag attached to my name.'

Every employee in India wants to become a manager within a decade of his professional existence. This is true in all the areas—sales, customer support, software development, manufacturing, etc. This could partly have something to do with the Indian culture—we love to chase fancy designations and titles. Some of the American and European expats based in India are at a loss on how to handle such people, probably because such instances are rare in their countries.

In the area of R & D, it is indeed sad to see brilliant design engineers and architects change tracks and leave their technical roles to take up roles in the line management. This is done to get a managerial tag. These days, many companies have come up with innovative solutions to retain such talent in technical roles. We now have designations like technical manager, technical product manager, etc. It won't be long before an R & D organization evolves designations like scientist manager or research manager!

No other cricketer in the world has received as much accolades as Sachin Tendulkar. While the Oxford dictionary might be running short of adjectives to describe this greatest cricketer of all times, what is the one word that comes to our mind when we think of Sachin Tendulkar? It is his *passion* for the game.

How many cricketers can boast of a cricketing career spanning over 23 years? He has not only been performing consistently at the top and establishing new records, but also displaying the same degree of passion that he had as a 15-year-old boy while playing cricket at Shivaji Park, Mumbai.

Today he is the leading run-scorer and century maker in Test matches and ODIs. He became the first player to score a double century in the history of ODI cricket. In 2002, Wisden ranked him the second greatest Test batsman of all times, behind the Australian star Donald Bradman, and the second greatest ODI batsman of all time, behind the former West Indian Vivian Richards.

Inspite of playing so many Test matches and ODIs, he still takes each and every match with the same seriousness as a player making his debut. Not one to shy away from net practice, he can be seen batting, bowling, fielding with the enthusiasm of a young teenager. There was a recent instance where he was described as; 'a young school boy who hates to stop batting because the evening darkness is soon going to set in'—and this remark was made when Sachin was 37 years young!

Since the past two decades, there have been endless debates and comparisons between Sachin Tendulkar and the West Indian great Brian Lara. Both are extremely gifted players and have set records that would be very difficult to break. However, there is one major difference between the two. While Brian Lara was an extremely talented batsman and one of the best in the world, there were very few instances of him rubbing off his passion on his teammates. It was a common sight to see Brian Lara play an extraordinary innings but his team lose the match.

In the case of Sachin, he is everywhere. While batting, he constantly advises his batting partner. While fielding, he can be seen running to the bowler and telling him how to bowl the next ball. The opposition too knows the amount of passion and enthusiasm he brings into the Indian side. There was a time in the early 90s when the opposition would feel that getting Sachin out was more than half the job done. They knew that the moment Sachin walked back to the pavilion, Indians would be demoralized and give up without a fight.

Many people have asked me what I look for while hiring professionals. I always tell them that 'passion is the key'. If a person has passion, the rest can be acquired through training. However if a person lacks passion and enthusiasm then no amount of training, coaching, or mentoring can help.

Robert 'Bob' Galvin was the son of Paul Galvin, founder of Motorola. He served as the CEO of Motorola that developed various products in the area of cellular communication, pagers, TVs, semiconductors, networking & data communication equipments, two way radios, and other wireless equipments. Under his leadership, Motorola sales grew from $216.6 million in 1958 to $6.7 billion in 1987 and cash flow per share grew from 89 cents to $6.10.

In 1986, Bill Smith, a senior engineer at Motorola's communications division decided to introduce the concept of Six Sigma. A product operating at Six Sigma level meant that it would have just 3.4 defects per million opportunities! Smith took the idea to Bob Galvin who immediately recognized that this was the most innovative concept to improve product quality. With high passion, Bob Galvin made Six Sigma the main theme and all his corporate strategies were centred on it. Motorola won the prestigious Malcolm Balridge National Quality Award in its inaugural year 1988. It soon became the most respected American company with respect to the quality of its products.

Six Sigma had its own share of sceptics at Motorola. Though Galvin was the CEO, he had to struggle to convince everyone about the potential of this new initiative. He formed lots of cross functional task forces that had subject matter experts from different areas of the organization. Some of the cross functional teams also had members from different sectors. This speeded up the institutionalization of the revolutionary concept. Success stories of various task forces were given visibility across the organization. When the employees began to see the passion with which Bob Galvin drove this newly launched initiative, and the success stories that followed, they too were willing to jump into the Six Sigma bandwagon. Within a few years, General Electric too realized the importance of Six Sigma, and took it to even greater heights.

To build a great company, it is extremely important not only to have fire in your belly but also the zeal to light fire in others' bellies! The difference between a good company and a great company is in the passion that its employees have. When the leader displays the passion that Bob Galvin showed, then it inspires the rest to follow suit. Passion is probably the only attribute which is infectious. Even your biggest sceptics will be willing to join you in your challenging journey.

There is one difference between Sachin Tendulkar and Bob Galvin. Tendulkar was not the skipper during the Hero Cup episode whereas Galvin was the chief of Motorola during his Six Sigma drive. However, the sense of ownership and passion that they both displayed helped them win against all odds.

Failure: a Stepping Stone to Success
(Anil Kumble, Chetan Sharma—Thomas Alva Edison)

'Perseverance is the hard work you do after you get tired of doing the hard work you already did.'

—Newt Gingrich

In 1990, India played against England at Old Trafford, Manchester. Anil Kumble was on the field, playing as a substitute player. Those were still initial days for the leg spin bowler. On one occasion, during the course of the match, the 18-year-old allowed the ball to slip between his legs. Kapil Dev, the skipper of the Indian side expressed anger and displeasure in the most explicit manner. Anil Kumble was completely devastated because his ability to perform at the highest level was questioned. During the break, when Kapil Dev went to the dressing room, he found Kumble crying his heart out.

Any other cricketer would have been completely demoralized. Seeds of doubt would have been sown into his mind with thoughts like, 'Am I good enough to play at this level?'

Though Anil Kumble was shattered momentarily, he did not allow this incident to affect his confidence and self-belief. He sincerely believed that he had the ability to become a great leg-spin bowler for India. His tremendous self-belief, hard work, and perseverance helped him become the leading wicket taker for India in both Test matches and ODIs. He took 619 Test wickets in 132 Tests to become the third highest wicket taker in Test cricket. He also took 337 wickets in 271 ODI matches. Apart from becoming one of the greatest leg spinners in world cricket, he also went on to become one of India's most respected skippers in his brief tenure. It is indeed an amazing record for someone who was written off even before he had donned the Indian cap!

Contrast this with the career of Chetan Sharma, one of the fastest Indian bowlers in 1980s. He made a brilliant start to his career by capturing a wicket in his very first over against Pakistan in 1984. He played many match winning innings both with the ball and bat and was also a key member of the Indian squad that defeated England in 1986.

The turning point of Chetan Sharma's career came at Sharjah when India played against Pakistan in the 1986 Australasia Cup. He was asked to bowl the last over of the innings. Pakistan needed four runs off the last ball. Chetan Sharma bowled a low full-toss outside the leg stump which was effortlessly carted over the boundary for a six by Javed Miandad. This incident had a huge impact on both Chetan Sharma and the Indian team. After this shocking incident, Chetan Sharma was never the same bowler again. His form took a massive dip and he was dropped from the Indian team The Indian team also struggled against Pakistan at Sharjah for the next few years. This single incident left a deep scar on Chetan Sharma as well as the Indian team.

Thomas Alva Edison was an American inventor and scientist. He is well-known for many famous inventions—one of the most famous being the electric light bulb. It is believed that Edison struggled for a very long time before he could make a light bulb that could work. Any normal scientist would have felt frustrated and stopped his experiments but he did not. Finally when he succeeded he said, 'I now know a thousand ways not to build a light bulb!' This is one of the most famous quotes of the century and shows the kind of dedication and big heart that Edison had.

One of the most important aspects for any young and budding professional is the ability to handle criticism and failure. In the case of Anil Kumble,even before he made his international debut, his captain made disparaging remarks about his fielding. It is not easy to handle criticism when you are young, immature, and at the start of your career. However, Anil Kumble had the mental toughness to handle it. He was also able to stop thinking about his bad experience. There were also many cricketing pundits who questioned his ability to spin the ball. Though Kumble was not a great turner of the ball, he had the required guile and aggressiveness to become one of India's leading strike bowlers.

Let us now study the other cricketing incident that involved Chetan Sharma. His talent and skill were never in doubt. However, what he probably lacked was mental toughness and the ability to overcome failure. One incident at Sharjah demoralized him and never again was he the same wicket taking bowler for India. In limited overs cricket, the game is heavily loaded against the bowlers so there are bound to be many incidents of the bowlers being taken to the cleaners and this was one of them. After the Sharjah incident, he could have consoled himself that this was just a one off incident and that too against Javed Miandad, one of the best batsmen in the world. Sadly, he didn't and his bowling slowly deteriorated.

Thomas Edison showed the same qualities like Anil Kumble. He had the desire to succeed despite the initial setbacks. Most scientists would have probably given up half way through their struggle, but not Edison. He took the failures in his stride and finally came up with one of the most famous inventions of the century—the electric light bulb.

Can you imagine how the world would have been if Edison had given up after the initial rounds of failure?

Patience and perseverance are important qualities that every professional should be equipped with. Unfortunately, in today's jet age, both these qualities are becoming increasingly rare. Everyone wants to make a quick buck—promotions, fast track growth, money, house, cars, etc. If people don't succeed in one particular area, they are not ready to work hard and try to overcome their deficiencies. They take the easy path of changing their role or function. There are numerous examples of incompetent software developers who switch over to testing because they feel that this is the fastest way to overcome their deficiencies in programming. In certain cases, the middle or senior management is also equally guilty. They have no time for failures. I have heard many project managers and program managers say, 'X is not good in Java programming, move him to testing!' This is not the right approach because there is no guarantee that an incompetent developer will shine as a test engineer. Moreover, such a move also sends wrong signals to the organization. It may lead to employees developing a misconception that testing is easier and inferior compared to software development—and nothing could be farther from truth. The right approach for both the employee and his manager would be to identify the gaps in his competence and work towards rectifying them.

In sports and corporate life, people are bound to experience failures during certain phases of their career. The employee should have the mental toughness and self-belief to overcome these setbacks. The employer or manager should play his part too—by showing patience and confidence in his struggling employee. In the long run this is beneficial to everyone. The failed individual is willing to stretch and run the extra mile to succeed. His manager wins the respect and confidence of his employee. The organization too gains in terms of not only building competence but also self-belief and fighting spirit among its employees.

10

CHALLENGES OF SUCCESS

'We believe in the concept of "Survival of the Fittest". We ask all employees to swim across a shark infested river. The survivor gets to do a victory lap in the river.'

Complacency Kills

(West Indies Team—General Motors)

'Success is a lousy teacher. It seduces smart people into thinking they can't lose.'

—Bill Gates

There is a very thin line between confidence and complacency. While it is good to have self-belief and confidence, when it begins to border on over confidence then it can lead to complacency and ultimately to one's downfall.

The West Indies cricket team, led by the great Clive Lloyd, was invincible in 1970s and 1980s. Just imagine a batting lineup that had Gordon Greenidge and Desmond Haynes as the opening pair, followed by the aggressive Vivian Richards, stylish Alvin Kallicharan, and skipper Clive Lloyd. If the batting was aggressive then the bowling was absolutely unplayable with fearsome fast bowlers like Andy Roberts, Michael Holding, Joel Garner, and Colin Croft!

The great West Indian side beat the Australians to win the World Cup in 1975, in its inaugural year in England. In its second edition in 1979, West Indies defeated the hosts to retain their crown. By the time the teams came to England in 1983, the West Indies side had gained the reputation of being the best cricketing team in the world.

As initial rounds progressed in the 1983 World Cup, West

Indies went about their business, beating most of the teams they faced. In sharp contrast, the Indian team started the tournament as one of the biggest underdogs. Having fared very poorly in the first two editions, no one gave them a chance to even qualify for the semi-finals.

However, India did manage to play a few brilliant matches and qualified for the semi-finals. In the semi-finals against England, India started off as underdogs since the England team was not only stronger but had the advantage of familiar home conditions. It was a big surprise when India beat England to qualify for the finals.

The West Indies team too won their semi-finals and entered the finals. The entire cricketing world had written off India even before the first ball was bowled. It was considered as a David versus Goliath encounter.

India batted first and scored in paltry 183 in 60 overs. During the innings break, even the biggest Indian supporters had written off the Indian team. Victory was out of question—everyone was just hoping that the Indian team should go down fighting and not surrender tamely. However, Kapil Dev and his boys, popularly known as Kapil's Devils, had different ideas.

The West Indies openers, brimming with confidence, briskly walked to the pitch. Unfortunately, they had a disastrous start as Gordon Greenidge shouldered arms to an excellent inswinger delivery from Balwinder Sandhu that sent his off stump cart-wheeling. However, the entry of Vivian Richards spelt disaster as he went about his business in his usual aggressive fashion. Those were the days when Doordarshan was the only TV Channel and the live telecast was interrupted due to the daily news program. I vividly remember the scene when the live telecast resumed after the news program. Narottam Puri, the Doordarshan commentator informed the viewers that West Indies, especially Vivian Richards, was going great guns and India had absolutely no hopes of winning the match. Our hearts sank as we watched Richards display his array of shots all around the field.

Luckily for the Indians, Richards got out and that turned out to be the turning point of the match. Kapil Dev ran many yards to take a great catch off Madan Lal's bowling. Most of the West Indian batsmen had good starts but threw their wickets away to some disciplined Indian bowling. Chasing 183 and that too in 60 overs was not a difficult task but West Indies, due to their complacency and over-confidence, crashed to 140 and lost the World cup finals by 43 runs!

Complacency is one of the prime reasons for failures of many successful companies. Haven't we seen numerous profitable organizations going bankrupt? We have seen numerous instances where companies that were the darling of the share market, later had their share value crash by more than half. We have also seen the most innovative companies getting into a rut due to their resting on past laurels

One of the best examples of a leading company that suffered from complacency was General Motors, an American multinational automotive company headquartered in Detroit, USA.

In 1950s, General Motors was one of the biggest automobile companies in the world. It brought out great products and during 1970s, it had a market share of almost 50% in the US market.

Unfortunately, complacency stepped in. While the rest of the world was moving forward, General Motors was caught up in its legacy practices. The Japanese automotive industry made swift inroads with a very high degree of focus on cost and quality. They introduced lots of innovative practices, both in the shopfloor and in their supply chain process. General Motors remained complacent of their market share and refused to see and understand the changing market scenario. By the mid-1980s, its market share had fallen to around 40% and by 1990 it further fell to around 36%.

During 1990s, General Motors lost further focus and direction. It refused to look at the best practices of the Japanese automobile industry and replicate them in its own backyard. General Motors was suffering from low productivity, its inability to introduce new models at the speed of its Japanese counterparts, labour problems, and bureaucracy.

In June 2009, General Motors filed for Chapter 11 reorganization. Since only the US Subsidiary was forced into bankruptcy, it had no access to assets from GM owned assets in Asia or Europe. On July 10, 2009, General Motors emerged from Chapter 11 reorganization. It was unbelievable that one of America's most respected automotive companies had such a steep fall.

What we see are classic examples of complacency. The West Indians, having won the earlier two editions of World Cup in 1975 and 1979, believed themselves to be invincible. They made the cardinal mistake of underestimating their opposition and allowing competency to take better of them. During those days, apart from West Indies, the only other strong team in the ODI format was Australia. When a weak team like India (yes, during those days India was one of the weakest teams in limited overs cricket!) surprisingly qualified for the finals, the West Indies would have felt they had already won the tournament for the third consecutive time. During the first half of the game, the West Indians did everything right. They bowled like champions and got the Indians out at a low score. When the West Indians came out to bat, the asking rate was just a little above three runs an over. Unfortunately, they batted like spoilt millionaires squandering their wealth away.

The case of General Motors was no different. Being world leaders like the West Indies team of 1980s, General Motors grew complacent and never realized that the new entrants could upstage them in their own game. American automobile industry had always been at the forefront right from the World War days. Among the American automobile companies, GM was the leader. It had different products—each a leader in its respective segment. During those days, Japanese cars were not viewed seriously. The new entrants commanded as much respect as the Indian cricket team of 1983. GM considered only Ford and similar American companies as worthy competitors—just like West Indies considered only Australia as serious challengers to their throne. However, the Indian team, like the Japanese cars, came and threw the king off the throne. They showed what complacency could do to the best in the world.

Survival of the Fittest

(L. Sivaramakrishnan, Narendra Hirwani, Vinod Kambli — Sipani Automobiles, Maruti Suzuki)

'In the struggle for survival, the fittest win out at the expense of their rivals because they succeed in adapting themselves best to their environment.'

— Charles Darwin

L. Sivaramakrishnan was a right-arm leg spinner who served the Indian team for a very brief period. Popularly known as LS Siva, he burst into the cricketing scene at a very young age. He first made headlines when, as a young 12-year-old, he took 7 wickets for 2 runs in an inter-school championship. In 1980, he became the youngest member of the Under-19 India team that toured Sri Lanka.

He was just 16 when he made his first class debut against Delhi in the Ranji Trophy quarter-finals. His remarkable performance with the ball ensured a place in the South Zone team for the Duleep Trophy. He was picked up for India's tour to the West Indies and made his debut at 17 years.Unfortunately, his test debut was quite ordinary and went unnoticed.

However, he was absolutely brilliant in his second Test. It was the 1st Test match of the series between England and India being played at Mumbai. Batting first, England could manage just 195 runs thanks to Siva's magnificent spell of 6 wickets for just

64 runs. India replied with a strong score of 465 runs. England played much better in the second innings, however, Siva's 6 for 117, ensured that they were restricted to 317 runs. India reached the target with the loss of just two wickets. Siva's 12 wicket haul had played a major role in India's 8 wicket victory. He took 6 more wickets in the next innings at Ferozshah Kotla, New Delhi.

During the 1985 World Championship of Cricket in Australia, Siva was the leading wicket taker with a rich haul of 10 wickets. He also played a key role in India's final match against arch rival Pakistan. Batting first, Pakistan could manage just 176 runs for 9 wickets, thanks to Siva's spell of 3 wickets for 35 runs. India comfortably won the match by 8 wickets. Siva and Ravi Shastri were the key architects of India winning the championship.

Unfortunately, Siva was unable to sustain his success for long. In the next season, surprisingly he lost his wicket taking ability. He played one Test in Sri Lanka and two Tests in Australia but did not have much success with the ball. It marked an end to a promising but very brief Test career. He made a comeback to the ODI squad during the 1987 World Cup. Here too, he did not meet with much success, taking just 1 wicket in 2 matches.

Though Siva had become a national icon when he made his debut as a 17-year-old, he played just 9 Tests where he took 26 wickets. His ODI performance was slightly better, taking 154 wickets in 76 ODIs.

Narendra Hirwani was another Indian cricketer who started his career in a brilliant fashion but could not sustain his success. Coincidentally, like Siva, he too was a right-arm leg spin bowler. At the age of 16, he made his first class debut for Madhya Pradesh where he took 5 wickets. This was followed by a 23 wicket haul in an Under-19 three Test series against Australia. In 1987–88, he had a successful tour of West Indies in the Under-25 squad. The selectors had noticed the discomfort of the West Indies batsmen while playing his leg spinners so they selected him for the home series against them.

Hirwani had a dream debut in the final Test match at Chennai. Electing to bat first, India scored 382 runs. Hirwani's devastating spell of 8 wickets for 61 runs restricted the West Indians to just 184 runs. India scored 217 runs in the second innings. Set to score 416 runs to win, West India managed just 160 runs, thanks to another destructive spell by Hirwani where he grabbed 8 wickets for 75 runs. With match figures of 16 wickets for 136 runs, he had beaten Bob Massie's record of 16 wickets for 137 runs. The most noteworthy feature of his rich haul was his ability to get the great Vivian Richards out in both the innings. A few months later, Hirwani won the Man of the Series in a 3-nation tournament at Sharjah. The next home Test series was against New Zealand where he took 20 wickets in three Tests.

Unfortunately, like Siva, Hirwani too was unable to sustain his initial success. He had a poor tour of the West Indies in 1989–90. Though he had tormented the West Indians during the earlier series, this time he failed to make an impact. The opposition had studied his bowling and learnt how to tackle his leg-spin. Moreover, he began to bowl much slower through the air, allowing the batsmen to attack him.

Hirwani did not adjust his game by ironing out the deficiencies in his bowling and this partly led to his downfall. By then, Hirwani was no longer a regular member of the Indian team. Four years later, he was surprisingly selected for a Test match against New Zealand. On a rain-affected match, he took 6 for 59. Subsequently, he toured England in 1996 and played two more Tests against South Africa at home. After this series, he was once again out of the Indian team. In 2001, in the home series against Australia, he was picked in the fourteen but he did not make it into the final eleven. At the end of his cricketing career, he had played just 17 Tests and 18 ODIs, taking 66 and 23 wickets respectively.

Sachin Tendulkar and his schoolmate Vinod Kambli made their Test debuts within a gap of few years. Vinod Kambli not only had a meteoric rise but also crashed swiftly like a shooting star. Kambli had abundant talent. The stylish left-hander made his Test debut against England in 1993 and within a year, he had scored two double centuries—224 vs. England at Wankhede Stadium, Mumbai, and 227 vs. Zimbabwe at Ferozshah Kotla, New Delhi. At one point, he was scoring better than even Tendulkar. He had scored four Test centuries in his first seven Tests and looked all set fora great future. Unfortunately, Kambli quickly lost his way. His name began to figure in newspapers for reasons other than cricket. He soon lost his form. His Test career, which had started on such a promising note, ended within two years, at the young age of 24. Despite repeated failures during the later part of his career, he had a Test batting average of 54.20. His performance in first class cricket was even better—he had an average of nearly 60, consisting of 35 hundreds and 44 fifties in just 129 matches. It is indeed sad that though both Sachin Tendulkar and his best friend Vinod Kambli had brilliant starts to their respective careers, one of them played for more than two decades whereas the other represented India only for a very brief time.

Sipani Automobiles Ltd's Dolphin is an example of a product that showed a lot of initial promise but could not live upto the expectations of the customers. It was a case of initial hype that did not convert into sustained performance and results.

Sipani Automobiles was started as Sunrise Automotive Industries Ltd in 1974 by Mr R.K. Sipani. This Bangalore based automotive company, with the help of British manufacturer Reliant, developed its first product, the 3-wheeler Badal. This was based on Reliant Robin model of 1970s. Unfortunately, the organization could not sell it as a car because as per Government regulations, only autorickshaws were allowed as three wheeler automobiles.

Subsequently Sunrise Automotive Industries Ltd was

restructured and renamed as Sipani Automobiles Ltd. The company decided to replace Badal with a 4-wheeler car named Dolphin. Dolphin was based on Reliant Kitten model.

After having witnessed only heavy cars like Premier Padmini and Ambassador, Dolphin's 848cc engine combined with light fibre glass body was an instant hit. People welcomed the light bodied compact car with its designer looks. Its bright colours made it a head-turner in the 1970s. Dolphin was dubbed as a city car because its compact size and good manoeuvrability was a big boon on the congested Indian roads.

Unfortunately Dolphin could never live upto its initial hype, primarily because it could not meet the customer's expectations in terms of quality and timeliness. It was unable to convert 'low volume' prototypes into 'high volume' manufacturing. Moreover it had one major flaw—the Dolphin was a 2-door model whereas Indians always preferred 4-door cars. What adversely affected Sipani Automobiles further was, it could sell its cars only in South India due to certain Government regulations.

By early 1980s, Maruti Suzuki introduced its flagship product Maruti 800. Backed by sound Japanese technology of Suzuki, Maruti 800 had none of the disadvantages of Dolphin. The 4-door Maruti 800 with its superior quality, delivery, and service was soon seen as the 'common man's car'. With a body looking quite similar to Dolphin, Maruti 800 completely ate into the former's market. Unlike Dolphin, Maruti 800 was allowed to sell across the entire country. This low-cost product took the Indian industry by storm.

In order to match the 4-doored Maruti 800, Sipani launched the 4-doored Montana. Unfortunately, it was nowhere near Maruti 800 in terms of quality and service. Within a couple of years of its launch, Montana was overhauled and a new variant, the Montana D1, was launched. Montana D1 was a mix of several automobiles—it had parts from Daihatsu, Maruti, Mahindra, and Mitsubishi. It too was nowhere close to Maruti

800 in terms of quality and hence could not challenge the latter.

Sipani decided to move into the high-end automobile market. It imported Rover Montego kits from UK and assembled them in India. Unfortunately this also did not improve the performance of the company. By now, Maruti-800 and Maruti Esteem had well entrenched as the market leaders and none of the models from Sipani Automobiles could make even the slightest dent into the market share of Maruti Suzuki. Finally, in 2000, after many failed attempts, Sipani Automobiles declared bankruptcy.

In cricket, as in many other games, there is a strong belief that retaining the No.1 position is tougher than reaching the top spot. This is true not only for the cricket teams but also the players. Both Sivaramakrishnan and Narendra Hirwani reached the pinnacle at a very young age but could not sustain their success. They had all the ingredients to reach to the top but what they lacked was the ability to sustain their performance. When you play the game at the highest level, you should realize that the strength that took you to the top may not be sufficient for you to remain there. In today's technology-driven world where videos of all important matches and players are freely available, it is very easy for the opposition to study your bowling and modify their batting style accordingly. Today's mystery bowler may appear a pedestrian tomorrow. The only answer to this unavoidable problem is to keep enhancing your game with new tricks.

Sipani Automobiles too started with all the right intentions—introducing a compact car with a light fibre glass body which had very good maneuverability to suit Indian roads. Unfortunately, when Maruti Suzuki launched a similar product—the Maruti-800—Sipani did not have the capability to upgrade its products. The only way Sipani could have survived was to match the quality and service capabilities of Maruti. However, Sipani could not improve upon its existing performance and its demise was as swift as its ascent.

Arrogance of Success

(Hershelle Gibbs—Digital Equipment Corporation)

'The arrogance of success is to think that what we did yesterday is good enough for tomorrow.'

—William Pollard

The final match at the Super Six stage of the 1999 World Cup was played between Australia and South Africa at Headingly, England. Batting first, South Africa scored 270 runs thanks to a brilliant century by Hershelle Gibbs. Chasing any score above 250 runs is a difficult task under English conditions. What made it tougher was the fact that this was a high-pressure game because they had to win this match to qualify for the semi-finals.

Australia had a disastrous start, losing its first 3 wickets for just 48 runs. With Adam Gilchrist, Mark Waugh, and Damien Martyn back in the pavilion, few would have given hopes of an Australian recovery. When Australian skipper Steve Waugh walked into the middle, South African Hershelle Gibbs fresh from his scintillating century greeted him with taunts, hoping to unsettle the batsman. However, Steve Waugh was too experienced to take the bait. He played his normal game—pushing and nudging the balls for 1s and 2s but at the same time, not hesitating to smack the odd bad ball to the fence.

When Steve Waugh was batting on 56, he gave a simple catch to Hershelle Gibbs at midwicket off Lance Klusener's bowling.

Gibbs was thrilled to see a simple catch coming towards him. He caught the ball and tried to hurl it upwards but unfortunately, before he could complete the catch, it slipped from his hand and fell on the grass! Stunned silence enveloped the field because the best fielder of the South African team had dropped the most important catch of the match.

Gibbs was shocked. He could not believe that he had dropped such an easy catch. Neither could the bowler and the rest of his teammates. Waugh didn't take any more chances after that and went on to score a match winning and unbeaten 120 runs off just 110 balls. Australia qualified for the semi-finals and went on to win the championship.

It is widely believed that Steve Waugh smiled at Hershelle Gibbs and remarked, 'you have dropped the World Cup mate!'

There are different versions of this anecdote—some believe that Waugh actually spoke these words but others think that he did not say anything. However, that is not important. The crux of the matter is—Gibbs' overconfidence led to this disaster and South Africa, despite being one of the best cricketing teams in the world, had to return home empty-handed once again.

Digital Equipment Corporation, popularly known as DEC, was an American multinational company and a leading manufacturer of Computers, peripherals, and software. It was most well-known for its PDP and VAX series of minicomputers.

In 1960s, DEC introduced the PDP series of minicomputers which became famous worldwide. It first introduced PDP-8 and followed it up with PDP-11. Subsequently, it introduced the 32-bit microprocessor based VAX-11 series in 1980s. The VAX series known for its high speed was called 'Supermini'. It could compete even with powerful mainframes like IBM System/370. DEC had a very high growth rate and it soon became the second largest computer company in the world.

During 1970s and 1980s, DEC had developed the Midas

touch, turning whatever it touched into gold. This also led to a high degree of overconfidence and arrogance within the organization. Its competitors had developed the first set of microcomputers around 1975, but DEC was not convinced about this new revolutionary product.

In 1981, IBM launched its microcomputer IBM PC, which took the world by storm. This was a wake-up call for DEC and it decided to introduce an equivalent product to tackle the IBM PC. Unfortunately, DEC made the mistake of introducing systems which were built on proprietary architecture. It first introduced DEC Professional in 1982 but it failed in the market because it was incompatible with IBM PC hardware and software. It also had a user-interface which was completely different from the one provided by IBM PC so it was intimidating to the new users. DEC next introduced DECmate II but this was more of a word processor than a computer. Finally, DEC realized the importance of having a system based on CP/M and Intel 8086 processor, and introduced Rainbow 100. Unfortunately this product too bombed because it was priced much higher than IBM PC. The IBM PC also came loaded with many applications that were not available on DEC systems. Though DEC's products were probably better engineered, compared to many of its competitors, the company failed to capture the market because of its desire to retain proprietary architecture.

DEC's arrogance and complacency also made the company believe that it should be different and exclusive. Despite having failed earlier with proprietary systems, it continued to make peripherals based on proprietary systems. It introduced RX50 floppy disk drive which was based on proprietary disk format. Though the DEC format had a higher data capacity, it was not compatible with the floppy drives of its competitors. Due to this, its floppies were not interchangeable with that of IBM PCs, leading to low usage and sales. DEC also decided to copyright its proprietary disk format which meant that whoever wanted to use it, had to pay royalty to DEC. We may never understand DEC's thought process and condescending attitude but that's how it treated its customers.

Highly successful products like PDP and VAX minicomputers made DEC feel that it was invincible. It neglected the low end PC market. Unfortunately early 1990s saw the emergence of IBM–Microsoft–Intel which made PCs the fastest selling products in the world. In 1977, when DEC's President Ken Olsen was asked if his organization had any plans to design and manufacture PCs, he laughed, 'there is no reason for any individual to have a computer in his home.' Fifteen years later, almost every home in the US had atleast one PC!

Following years of low performance and revenues, Ken Olsen finally stepped down in 1992 and Robert Palmer became the company's president and CEO. Palmer tried his best to revive the company's fortunes but met with very little success. He laid off thousands of employees, introduced new products, sold off non-core businesses, but none of this had a major impact on the company's profitability.

In 1998, Digital Equipment Corporation, the inventor of minicomputers and formerly the second biggest computer company in the world, was sold to Compaq which itself was later acquired by HP in 2002.

Hesrchelle Gibbs was one of the best fielders in the world but he was flamboyant with a mercurial temperament. On numerous occasions, after taking difficult catches, he would celebrate wildly by throwing the ball high in the air. During this particular match, Gibbs was more pumped up than usual. It was an important match and that too against the mighty Australians. A defeat here for Australia would signal their exit from the tournament. He had himself scored a scintillating century earlier during the day, and was on the verge of becoming the hero of the match. All he had to do now was to take the simple catch given by the Australian skipper.

All these thoughts were probably playing on his mind and led him to a mix of overconfidence and arrogance. He made a mess of a simple catch which allowed the opposition to claw back into the game and finally win it. At one stage, South Africa was right on the top and it appeared as if they would beat their arch rivals. Unfortunately, Hershelle Gibbs's complacency was the turning point of the game that ultimately led to their defeat.

DEC's fate was quite similar to that of South Africa's. The computer giant had tasted success during 1970s and 1980s. Its PDP, VAX, and Micro VAX series of minicomputers made DEC the second biggest computer company in the world. Though DEC's rival IBM was the biggest computer company in the world, it was still struggling with its heavy and obsolete mainframes. At one point, it looked as if DEC might overtake IBM since the latter's revenues and profitability was shrinking. Unfortunately, complacency struck DEC which led to its downfall. Its high revenues in minicomputers made it reluctant to jump onto PC bandwagon and that had a major as well as adverse impact on the company.

These are clear examples of arrogance creeping into highly successful individuals or organizations—ultimately leading to their downfall. If we do not guard against it then it is a sure shot recipe for disaster.

Don't Rest on Laurels

(West Indies Cricket—Motorola)

> **'It isn't the incompetent who destroy an organization. The incompetent never get in a position to destroy it. It is those who achieved something and want to rest upon their achievements who are forever clogging things up.'**
>
> **—F.M. Young**

During 1980s, West Indies, under the shrewd leadership of its skipper Clive Lloyd, became the best cricketing team in the world. It had the best and most fearsome fast bowling attacks, with Andy Roberts, Michael Holding, Colin Croft, and Joel Garner. It also had one of the best opening pair in the world in the form of Gordon Greenidge and Desmond Haynes. The middle order consisted of the classy Alvin Kallicharan, destructive Vivian Richards, and Clive Lloyd at number five. The team played 27 matches that included 11 successive wins!

By the time Colin Croft and Andy Roberts retired in 1982 and 1983 respectively, Malcolm Marshall had made his debut, followed shortly by Curtley Ambrose and Courtney Walsh. Due to the constant supply of fast bowlers, Clive Lloyd and West Indies cricket didn't face any problems.

Clive Lloyd retired in 1984 and was replaced by Vivian Richards and subsequently, Ritchie Richardson. Though Michael Holding and Joel Garner had retired by 1987, the West Indies attack was still a formidable one, consisting of Malcolm Marshall, Curtly Ambrose, and Courtney Walsh. However, one could already sense the decline of West Indies cricket. It was not just the fast bowlers, great batsmen too were ageing and retiring one after the other.

Around the same time, the sports scenario was changing in West Indies. Since West Indies had been a British Colony, the British brought cricket to these islands and it was the most popular game till 1980s. However, 1990s saw a slow but major change creeping into the society. Young West Indians began to watch TV programmes and most of the sports channels broadcasted popular American sports like baseball and basketball. These games were also more commercially lucrative so the youngsters were weaned away from cricket. In short, West Indies cricket was suffering from two problems—on one hand, its legendary stars were ageing and on the other hand, they were facing with a short supply of young talent.

Unfortunately, West Indies was resting on its past laurels and never saw the writing on the wall. It never focused on succession planning for its players. It was well aware that Vivian Richards, Desmond Haynes, Gordon Greenidge, Alvin Kallicharan, Clive Lloyd, and Ritchie Richardson would not be able to keep batting forever. They probably lacked the foresight and vision to tackle a potential crisis.

Due to poor succession planning, they did not have a strong 'bench strength' which is essential to sustain winning. When Curtly Ambrose and Courtney Walsh retired in 2000 and 2001 respectively, to be soon followed by the great Brian Lara in 2006, the West Indies team was in deep crisis. Its bench strength had completely dried up. A team which once boasted of the best and most consistent opening batting pair of Gordon Greenidge and Desmond Haynes, was now struggling to find an opening pair who would last more than twenty Tests together. A team which had the most destructive middle-order consisting of Vivian Richards, Alvin Kallicharan, and Clive Lloyd, was now a pale shadow of itself. In the bowling department, it had no fast bowler who was even half as good as the earlier greats. Within a few years, they declined in all forms of cricket and dropped heavily in the cricket rankings. A team which had won two successive World Cups in 1975 and 1979 was now struggling to even qualify into the knockout stage of the tournament.

West Indies cricket is a case of a once great side that failed to see the changing scenarios and believed that what worked for it in the past would work for it in the future as well. It never had a strong domestic structure but went on to become one of the best international sides in the world. However, it failed to realize that this past success can no longer be repeated in future if it didn't introduce some drastic changes in its basic structure.

Motorola is a great example of a highly successful company that lost its way because it rested on its past laurels. During 1970s and the 1980s, it was a darling among its employees, customers, and shareholders. The company had a Midas touch since whatever it touched turned to gold. It was one of the world leaders in the different areas like semiconductors, pagers, cellular phones, two-way radios, and data communication.

During 1980s, pagers were the most popular means of communication. Motorola was a world leader in the field of numeric and alphanumeric pagers. With a market share of over 80%, it developed such a high degree of complacency that it never saw the writing on the wall. They didn't realize that cellular phones had made a strong entry into the communication market and was slowly eating into the pager market.

During 1990s, pager users in developed countries like the US and Western Europe were slowly replacing their pagers with cellular phones. Motorola had banked a lot on developing countries like China and India. Given the high population in both these countries, Motorola felt they would be able to sell millions of pagers every year. Unfortunately for Motorola, the pager market never took off in these developing countries. Countries like India transitioned from landline directly to cellular phones. The paging market was killed even before it could mature.

Luckily for Motorola, it was the world leader in the field of cellular communication too. It had a market share of over 50%. The loss in paging business was offset by the cellular market. The company was able to introduce new and sleek models at an aggressive pace that kept Nokia a distant second. However, complacency once again crept in. Motorola repeated its earlier mistake of resting on its past laurels. It failed to understand the changing market scenario.

During early 1990s, USA was the biggest market for cellular phones. Most of these cellular phones were designed for analog networks. However, the rest of the world was slowly moving towards digital technology. GSM, the protocol for digital cellular communication, was becoming the buzz word. Competitors like Nokia and Ericsson were quick to jump into the GSM bandwagon. It was shocking that Motorola, despite being the world leader in cellular phones failed to recognize the need to go digital. Since they had been so successful in the US analog market, they never felt the need to change. They believed in the adage, 'What is good for USA is good for rest of the world.'

The result of this behaviour was disastrous—when Europe and Asia embraced digital technology, Motorola initially struggled in the digital market! Companies like Nokia and Ericsson ate into Motorola's market share which fell from 50% to 30% during 1998. By 1999, Motorola's market share was a mere 13% and had lost its place to Nokia.

During 2000s, Motorola gallantly tried to revive its fortunes but it was a case of 'too little too late'. What affected Motorola the most was the fact that between 2000 and 2010, the fastest growing market in the world was the Asian market and this was predominantly digital. Competitors like Nokia, Apple, and Samsung were far ahead of this erstwhile cellular giant. Meanwhile, Motorola sold off many businesses including its semiconductor business but it did not make significant improvement to its profitability.

Motorola's losses kept accumulating and in fourth quarter of 2007, it had losses worth $1.2 billion dollars and its market share was less than 10%. Finally in August 2011, Motorola sold off its Mobility division to Google for approximately $12.5 billion. Motorola's cellular story is one of the saddest tales in the history of corporate world—something that could have been avoided if the company had not sat on its past legacy and laurels.

The story of West Indies cricket and Motorola are so strikingly similar. During 1970s and 1980s, West Indies had the greatest team in the world and Motorola was a world leader in the area of electronics and communication. Early 1990s saw both of them become complacent, leading to a steady decline in the late 1990s. 2000s saw further decline and today, both are a pale shadow of themselves. West Indies cricket is fighting for survival whereas Motorola has sold off its major division to Google.

In the earlier chapters we have seen the need to constantly innovate. Here we have seen what happens when innovation stops and complacency sets in. Ironically, only successful teams and organizations suffer from this syndrome. Top American automobile companies like General Motors, Ford, etc. suffered from a similar syndrome giving rise to the growth of Japanese automobile manufacturers like Toyota, Honda, etc. However, it is interesting to note that even the Japanese were not spared from this syndrome! In the field of consumer electronics once successful Sony, Matsushita, etc, are today facing stiff competition from their Korean counterparts Samsung, LG, etc.

Don't rest on laurels—'Rest' can lead to 'Rust'!

EPILOGUE

Walk into any bookstore and you will find numerous management books stacked on the shelves. What differentiates *Pitch It!* from the others is its innovative approach of teaching management lessons by drawing analogies between the game of cricket and the corporate world. It consists of several fascinating stories from cricket wherein each cricketing anecdote is linked to a corporate case study.

At first, you might wonder—what could be similar between cricket and the corporate world?

However, as you peruse this book, you will realize that there are lots of similarities between the two. The parallels are very well elucidated while dealing with different management aspects like leadership, teamwork, ethics and values, attitude, execution, innovation, and competition.

There are many similarities between cricketing and the corporate worlds in the matter of leadership. The book contains numerous examples of great captains and top CEOs who exhibited similar leadership traits such as visionary leadership, ability to take risks, effective communication skills, humility, and the ability to handle crisis and challenges. For every Kapil Dev, Saurav Ganguly, MS Dhoni, and Clive Lloyd in the cricketing arena, we have the likes of Tatas, Birlas, Ambanis, and Bill Gates in the corporate world.

A cricket team demands various roles like batsman, bowler, fielder, and wicket keeper; its success depends on how well the different roles are integrated. It is imperative that each player not only does well in his area of expertise but also exhibits teamwork by contributing to the success of others in the team. For example, it is not enough for a batsman to score a century. His role as a fielder is equally important to the bowlers of his team. Similarly, it is not sufficient for a bowler to take a 5 wicket haul if he is unable to contribute with the bat, especially in critical situations. Similarly, an organization also consists of a variety of functions and teamwork is equally important for the success of the organization.

Attitude is another important factor for success in both cricket and the corporate world. There were lots of successful cricketers who were probably not the most stylish and elegant players, but they had tons of confidence, self-belief, and the passion to win. Companies like Nirma, Reliance, and Hewlett Packard started from humble beginings but were successful because their founders showed the same kind of tenacity and determination.

Cricket is a gentleman's game but it has been repeatedly rocked by various scandals like match fixing and sledging. Many organizations too have been shaken by unethical practices. Whether it is a cricket team or an organization, there should be zero tolerance towards violation of ethics and principles. In this regard, cricketers like G.R. Vishwanath, Sachin Tendulkar, Anil Kumble, and Rahul Dravid have been role models for youngsters. In India, the Tata group of companies evoke the same kind of awe and respect.

Nowadays the buzzwords in companies are vision, mission, and strategy and these are probably the most misused and misunderstood terms. While it is good for any organization to have visionary leadership and evolve good strategies, it would do well to understand the importance of good execution. The mammoth partnership between Rahul Dravid and VVS Laxman against the mighty Aussies in the famous Kolkata Test showed how a seemingly impossible mission was achieved through flawless and clinical execution.

Innovation and change are also equally important to cricket and to any organization. The cricket boards that have applied the 'horses for courses' theory for different formats of the game, different types of pitches, different kinds of opposition, etc. have been more successful than the conventional ones. Similarly, those captains who have been creative with respect to flexible batting order, bowling changes, field placements, etc. have been more successful than their conservative counterparts. This is also true for organizations that have been extremely successful primarily because of their creativity and innovativeness.

Every cricketer aspires to win matches for his country and feels blessed to share the hallowed dressing room with the all-time greats. Every corporate professional wants to be the major driving force behind the company's success and rise to the highest echelons in the organization and enter the hallowed corporate boardroom.

The truth that comes through this book is: whether it is a game of cricket or corporate world, the core values, ethics, and success factors remain unchanged.

I would like to congratulate Dev on this fascinating book which is a unique bridge between the cricket and the corporate worlds.

Venkatesh Prasad
Former Indian cricketer and
former Indian cricket team coach

BIBLIOGRAPHY

General:

- *Seduced by Success* by Robert J. Herbold
- *Built to Last* by Jim Collins and Jerry I. Porras
- *The HP Way* by David Packard
- *Execution* by Larry Bossidy and Ram Charan
- http://www.espncricinfo.com
- http://www.wikipedia.org
- http://www.brainyquote.com
- http://www.thinkexist.com

Leadership:

- http://www.thehindu.com/news/article388837.ece?homepage=true
- http://articles.timesofindia.indiatimes.com/2010-06-08/holistic-living/28302878_1_pyarelal-bundle-gods
- http://forum.spiritualindia.org/a-lesson-in-humility-t30775.0.html;wap2=
- http://www.zoroastrian.org.uk/vohuman/Article/JRD%20Tata%20--%20On%20the%20Islands%20of%20Tata,%20In%20the%20Ocean%20of%20India.htm
- http://www.businessweek.com/magazine/content/04_40/b3902020.htm ('A Spin with Carlos Ghosn')
- http://www.icmrindia.org/casestudies/catalogue/Leadership%20and%20Entrepreneurship/LDEN020.htm

('Carlos Ghosn-The Turnaround Specialist')

- http://www.thinkingmanagers.com/management/effective-leadership.php ('Effective Leadership: Mike Brearley'sTeam Management' by Robert Heller)
- http://leadership.wharton.upenn.edu/digest/02-03.shtml ('Leading the Turnaround: Lou Gerstner of IBM' by Paul Sheppard)
- http://markettorrent.com/community/viewtopic.php?f=10&t=4397 ('Leadership Lessons and Turnaround Tactics of IBM's Lou Gerstner')
- http://markettorrent.com/topic/6230?page=20
- http://findarticles.com/p/articles/mi_m0SMG/is_n8_v17/ai_19615298/ ('Master of the Game Lou Gerstner' by Patrick L. Forter)
- http://articles.timesofindia.indiatimes.com/2011-07-11/top-stories/29760876_1_anil-kumble-sehwag-and-gambhir-kumble-and-ganguly ('A Jumbo Secret behind Team India's Success' by K ShrinivasRao)
- http://mind-value.blogspot.in/2011/10/least-known-strength-of-steve-jobs.html ('The Least Known Strength of Steve Jobs—Standing On Others Shoulders')
- http://en.wikipedia.org/wiki/Xerox_Alto
- http://www.espncricinfo.com/ci/content/story/154458.html ('Cricketer of the year 1985: Larry Gomes')
- http://www.siliconindia.com/magazine_articles/BioconA_Bionic_leadership_story-AXS185745072.html ('Biocon-A Bionic LeadershipStory' by Kiran Mazumdar-Shaw)
- http://www.biocon.com/biocon_aboutus_history.asp ('Biocon: History')
- http://www.merinews.com/article/in-conversation-with-kiran-mazumdar-shaw/147114.shtml ('In conversation with Kiran Mazumdar-Shaw' by Kanika)
- http://www.britannica.com/EBchecked/topic/1089319/Kiran-Mazumdar-Shaw ('Kiran Mazumdar-Shaw' by Sherman Hollar)

- http://knowledge.wharton.upenn.edu/india/article.cfm?articleid=4257 (ICICI's ChandaKochhar: 'Whenever There's a Challenge, I See an Opportunity')
- http://articles.economictimes.indiatimes.com/2010-07-31/news/27599836_1_sandeep-bakhshi-icici-group-shikha-sharma ('ICICI Life MD VaidyanathanResigns')
- http://www.business-standard.com/india/news/lunchbs-chanda-kochhar/448875/ ('Lunch wth BS: ChandaKochhar' by ShyamalMajumdar and SomasroyChakraborty)
- http://www.moneycontrol.com/news/management/kumar-mangalam-birla-believesmeritocracy_190083.html ('Kumar Mangalam Birla Believes in Meritocracy')
- http://www.adityabirla.com/the_group/km_birla_profile.htm ('Profile: Mr Kumar Mangalam Birla')
- http://india-australia.cricket.deepthi.com/harbhajan-singh-andrew-symonds-racism-hearing.php
- http://www.business-standard.com/india/news/singur-to-sanand/444956 ('Singur to Sanand' by A.K. Bhattacharya)
- http://infolona.com/news/popular_business_leaders/find ('Popular Business Leaders in India')

Team Building and People Development:

- http://money.cnn.com/2009/01/26/news/international/gumbel_porsche.fortune/index.htm ('The man who outfoxed the market' by Peter Gumbel)
- http://christophe.benavent.free.fr/IMG/pdf/PorscheDossier2007.pdf ('Porsche's success in the automobile sector and its involvement in VW' by Christina Dietz)
- http://www.toyota-forklifts.co.uk/EN/company/tmhephilosophy/Pages/The-Toyota-Way.aspx ('The Toyota Way')
- http://www.scribd.com/mike734/d/33247373-The-Five-Key-Principles-of-the-Toyota-Way ('The Five Key Principles of the Toyota Way')

- http://www.thetoyotasystem.com/lean_concepts/kaizen.php ('Kaizen/Continuous Improvement' by Greg)
- http://www.slideshare.net/musicoholic/g-case-study ('GE Succession Planning Case Study')
- http://75.125.242.10/view/mq5xl ('Jack Welch')
- http://www.forbes.com/2007/11/07/succession-ceos-governance-lead-cx_sm_1107planning.html ('Best Practices in Succession Planning' by Stephen A. Miles and Nathan Bennett)
- http://www.khelopakistan.com/163-gods-left-arm.html ('WasimAkram: God's Left Arm' by SwarajdeepMohanty)
- http://www.motoart.com/aviation-history/aircraft-history-b-707
- http://www.referenceforbusiness.com/businesses/A-F/The-Boeing-Company.html ('The Boeing Company')
- http://businesstoday.intoday.in/story/yash-birla-goes-to-school/1/5630.html ('Yash Birla goes to School' by SumanLayak)
- http://markettorrent.com/topic/7321?page=15
- http://abidian.com/articles/Bossidy02310.pdf ('Thought Leader' by Randall Rothenberg)
- http://hbr.org/1995/03/the-ceo-as-coach-an-interview-with-alliedsignals-lawrence-a-bossidy/ar/1 ('The CEO as Coach: An interview with AlliedSignal's Laurence A. Bossidy')
- http://www.crn.com/news/channel-programs/18825964/lew-platt-harry-stonecipher-take-reins-at-boeing.htm;jsessionid=WVZQ5Mkn+FuP2wEQz2J4jA**.ecappj01 ('Lew Platt, Harry Stonecipher take reins at Boeing' by Barbara Darrow)
- http://money.cnn.com/2003/12/01/news/companies/boeing_condit/index.htm ('Boeing CEO out')
- http://www.time.com/time/specials/packages/article/0,28804,2009445_2009447_2009459,00.html ('Harry Stonecipher, Boeing' byFrances Romero)

- http://www.referenceforbusiness.com/biography/A-E/Condit-Phil-1941.html

Ethics and Values:

- http://www.mid-day.com/sports/2011/jul/180711-India-England-Golden-Jubilee-Test.htm ('Mid Day recalls Ind-Eng Golden Jubilee Test' by Sai Mohan)
- http://news.bbc.co.uk/sport3/cwc2003/hi/newsid_2740000/newsid_2747600/2747627.stm ('Warne out after failed drugs test')
- http://online.wsj.com/article/SB10001424052748704268004575417800832885086.html ('Mark Hurd neglected to follow H-P Code' by Ben Worthen and Joann S. Lublin)
- http://www.managementparadise.com/forums/human-resources-management-h-r/219000-employee-retention-hewlett-packard.html ('Employee Retention of Hewlett Packard')
- http://www.abcofcricket.com/A_Legend_Is_Born/Bodyline/bodyline.htm ('Bodyline Cricket')
- http://whatreallyhappened.com/WRHARTICLES/enron.html ('The Enron Scandal')
- http://www.instantshift.com/2010/02/03/22-largest-bankruptcies-in-world-history/ ('22 Largest Bankruptcies in World History' by Anders Ross)
- http://www.cpa.org.au/resources/global-issues/enron-capitalism-nutshell.pdf ('Enron: Capitalism in a Nutshell' by Anna Pha)
- http://www.espncricinfo.com/nzvsl/content/story/271912.html ('No regrets on controversial run-out: Fleming')
- http://www.telegraph.co.uk/sport/cricket/international/india/8674845/England-v-India-Anil-Kumble-and-Gundappa-Viswanath-praise-MS-Dhonis-gesture-to-Ian-Bell.html ('England versus india: Anil Kumble and

GundappaVishwanath praise MS Dhoni's gesture to Ian Bell')

- http://www.dawn.com/2011/03/19/angry-incidents-mar-australia-pakistan-match.html ('Angry incidents mar Australia Pakistan match')
- http://netindian.in/news/2011/03/20/00011907/yuvraj-scores-century-india-make-268-491-overs
- http://www.tata.com/aboutus/articles/inside.aspx?artid=NyGNnLHkaAc (Tata Code of Conduct)
- http://business-standard.com/india/news/tatas-didn/t-want-to-bribe-their-way-into-airline-biz-ratan/116029/on (Tatas didn't want to bribe their way into airline biz: Ratan)
- http://www.cathnews.com/article.aspx?aeid=14627 ('Mother Teresa inspired Steve Waugh')
- http://www.udayan.org/index.php?option=com_content&view=article&id=49&Itemid=55 ('Patrons of Udayan')
- http://www.rajasthantour4u.com/blog/index.php/2010/03/26/jamnalal-bajaj-the-world-famous-industrialist-born-in-sikar-rajasthan ('Jamnalal Bajaj—The World Famous Industrialist Born in Sikar, Rajasthan')
- http://wenku.baidu.com/view/91777b6c1eb91a37f1115c30.html ('The Rise and fall of Carly Fiorina—An Ethical Case Study' by Craig Johnson)
- http://jonathangifford.com/business-and-leadership/carly-fiorina-and-the-hp-compaq-merger/ ('Carly Fiorina and the HP Compaq Merger' by Jonathan Gifford)

Execution:

- http://www.kingcricket.co.uk/south-africa-choke-in-1999-world-cup-semi-final-against-australia/2007/09/21 ('South Africa choke in 1999 World Cup Semi Final against Australia' by King Cricket)
- http://www.cricketdiaries.com/2011/01/19/great-world-cup-matches-sri-lanka-v-south-africa-2003 ('Great World Cup matches: Sri Lanka versus South Africa, 2003')

- http://www.rentcell.com/Iridium.pdf ('Learning from Corporate Mistakes: The Rise and fall of Iridium' by Sydney Finkelstein and Shade H. Sanford)
- http://www.icmrindia.org/free%20resources/casestudies/Iridium1.htm ('Reviving Iridium: Iridium's failure')
- http://www.itsonlycricket.com/entry/2127/ ('Record of biggest partnerships in India vs Australia test matches')
- http://www.boeing-747.com/ ('Boeing 747')
- http://www.boeing-747.com/background.php ('Boeing 747')
- http://www.informationweek.com/news/internet/google/208400949 ('Google's Marissa Mayer Sides With Simplicity' by Thomas Claburn)
- http://www.justvirendersehwag.com/virender-sehwag-news/sehwag-praises-master-blaster ('Sehwag praises Master Blaster')
- http://www.indianexpress.com/news/i-can-watch-the-innings-a-hundred-times-sehwag/584554/2 (I can watch the innings a hundred times: Sehwag)
- http://www.arxmansports.com/?tag=One-Day-International ('VVS Laxman: The Saviour from Hyderabad')
- http://www.financialexpress.com/news/cricket-has-become-a-very-professional-and-thinking-game/88046/0 ("Cricket has become a very professional and thinking game")
- http://www.japan-101.com/business/just_in_time.htm ('Just in Time or JIT—Toyota's Manufacturing Technique')
- http://www.brighthub.com/office/project-management/articles/71540.aspx ('Real life examples of Successful JIT Systems' by Jack Wilson)
- http://www.gizmag.com/go/7494/ ('Learning from Dell—the faithful implementer of "Just In Time"' by Mike Hanlon)
- http://www.nifty-stuff.com/dell-case-study.php ('Dell a Case Study')
- http://www.inventorymanagementreview.org/justintime ('Inventory Management Review—McDonald's, A Guide to the benefits of JIT')

- http://worldacademyonline.com/article/16/324/jit_compared_with_traditional_manufacturing.html ('JIT compared with traditional manufacturing')
- http://hbr.org/1989/09/getting-control-of-just-in-time/ar/1 ('Getting control of Just-In-Time' by UdayKarmarkar)
- http://www.planetcricket.net/wordpress/2012/02/1861/the-curious-case-of-indian-cricket/ ('The curious case of Indian Cricket' by Fenil)
- http://www.ramint.gov.au/designs/purchase/mintissue.cfm ('Mint Issue: Archive')
- http://www.globaltimes.cn/NEWS/tabid/99/ID/667415/Microsoft-quarterly-earnings-beat-estimates.aspx ('Microsoft quarterly earnings beat estimates')
- http://www.agilent.com/about/companyinfo/history/ ('Company History')
- http://www.referenceforbusiness.com/biography/A-E/Barnholt-Ned-1943.html ('Ned Barnholt')
- http://people.forbes.com/profile/edward-w-barnholt/1388
- http://people.forbes.com/profile/william-p-sullivan/2183
- http://www.agilent.co.in/about/companyinfo/execs/bios/sullivan.html ('William P. (Bill) Sullivan')
- http://www.eyeflare.com/article/funny-airplane-announcements ('Funny airplane announcements')
- http://gosw.about.com/od/resortsandtours/a/swjokes.htm ('Southwest Airlines Jokes')
- http://avstop.com/history/historyofairlines/southwest.html ('History of Southwest Airlines')
- http://cooperativeintelligenceblog.com/2011/03/16/your-employees-are-your-competitive-advantage-really ('Your employees are Your Competitive Advantage, REALLY' by Ellendnaylor)

Innovation and Change:

- http://www.indobase.com/indians-abroad/sabeer-bhatia.html ('Indians Abroad')
- http://www.theresourcesolutions.com/topics/general_knowledge/who_is_the_founder_of_facebook.htm ('Who is the founder of Facebook?')
- http://inventors.about.com/od/fstartinventions/a/Facebook.htm ('Who invented Facebook?' by Mary Bellis)
- http://www.cse.iitb.ac.in/~venkat/mypage.html
- http://knowledge.wharton.upenn.edu/article.cfm?articleid=695 ('Lou Gerstner's Turnaround Tales at IBM')
- http://www.forbes.com/2002/11/11/cx_ld_1112gerstner.html ('How Lou Gerstner got IBM to dance' by Lisa Dicarlo)
- http://www.referenceforbusiness.com/biography/F-L/Gerstner-Louis-V-Jr-1942.html ('Louis V. Gerstner Jr')
- http://www.enotes.com/topic/Louis_V._Gerstner,_Jr. ('Louis V. Jr Gerstner')
- http://tech.fortune.cnn.com/2011/03/04/ibms-sam-palmisano-a-super-second-act ('IBM's Sam Palmisano: A super second act' by JessiHempel)
- http://news.cnet.com/IBM-On-demand-computing-has-arrived/2100-7339_3-5106577.html ('IBM: On-demand computing has arrived' by Stephen Shankland)
- http://www.businessinsider.com/how-steve-jobs-took-apple-from-near-bankruptcy-to-billions-in-13-years-2011-1?op=1 ('The amazing story of how Steve Jobs took Apple from near bankruptcy to Billions in 13 Years' by Alyson Shontell)
- http://www.guardian.co.uk/technology/2011/mar/28/ipad2-apple-demand ('iPAD 2 demand leaves Apple struggling' by Josh Halliday)
- http://www.businessinsider.com/blackboard/apple ('Apple')
- http://www.sify.com/sports/ashok-mankad-a-king-around-the-

circuit-news-columns-jehbDkahdjh.html ('Ashok Mankad, a "king" among the circuit' by PartabRamchand)

- http://www.guardian.co.uk/sport/2004/aug/23/cricket.comment ('Interview—Graeme Hick' by Simon Hattenstone)
- http://www.slideshare.net/gurjeit/worlds-biggest-brand-failures ('Brand Failures' by Matt Haig)
- http://www.icmrindia.org/free%20resources/casestudies/Marketing%20freecasestudyp1.htm ('Kellog's Indian Experience: A failed launch')
- http://www.chillibreeze.com/articles_various/what-not-to-do-when-launching-a-product-410.asp ('Revolutionary Products'—Launched and Lynched' by EshitaJayaswal)
- http://www.nytimes.com/2003/04/29/business/worldbusiness/29FAST.html?8hpib ('Tastes of India in U.S. Wrappers' by SarithaRai)
- http://www.indiamarks.com/guide/What-You-Can-and-Can-t-Get-at-McDonalds-India-/1739/ ('What you Can and Can't get at McDonald's in India' by Noreen)

Know your Market:

- http://cricketnext.in.com/news/ganguly-bhajji-avoided-2004-nagpur-test/53828-13.html ('Ganguly, Bhajji avoided 2004 Nagpur Test')
- http://cricketnext.in.com/blogs/sanjayjha/652/61794/what-really-happened-in-nagpur-test-2004.html ('What really happened in Nagpur Test 2004?' by Sanjay Jha)
- http://www.icmrindia.org/casestudies/catalogue/Business%20Strategy1/Business%20Strategy%20Hindustan%20Motors%20Struggle%20for%20Survival.htm ('Hindustan Motors' Struggle for Survival')
- http://www.authorstream.com/Presentation/bharatsoni007-250363-hindustan-motors-4928421-case-study-ppt-business-finance-powerpoint/ ('Hindustan Motors')

- http://boyracer.blogspot.in/2011/01/cars-that-wrote-indian-automobile.html ('Cars that wrote the Indian Automobile History' by DevFadia)
- http://www.wired.com/cars/futuretransport/news/2008/07/portfolio_0708 ('Southwest Airlines' Seven Secrets for Success' by Joe Brancatelli)
- http://fishtrain.com/2007/08/21/why-is-southwest-airlines-one-of-the-best-low-cost-airline/ ('Why is Southwest Airlines One of the Best Low Cost Airlines?' by Bimin Chan)
- http://www.espncricinfo.com/magazine/content/story/145850.html ('When Sunny spat the dummy' by Martin Williamson)
- http://www.cricages.com/cricket/indian-cricket/a-famous-victory-at-melbourne-after-a-near-walk-out/ ('A Famous victory at Melbourne after a near walk out' by J Venkatesh)
- http://www.dailyfinance.com/2011/10/26/why-amazon-doesnt-care-much-about-wall-street ('Why Amazon Doesn't Care Much About Wall Street' by Barbara Thau)
- http://www.sitepoint.com/jeff-bezos-gives-advice-on-long-term-success ('Jeff Bezos Gives Advice on Long Term Success' By Josh Catone)
- http://techcrunch.com/2011/07/27/amazons-market-cap-passes-100-billion/ ('Amazon's Market Cap passes $100 Billion' by LeenaRao)
- http://venturebeat.com/2011/09/09/jeff-bezos-long-term-amazon/ ('How Jeff Bezos' long term thinking paid off big for Amazon')
- http://www.linkedin.com/news?actionBar=&articleID=870286327&ids=dP8PdzwOc3sUb30Od3kNcP0Te2MMdP0Uc3gMdPwIej4Tc3gTdPsU&aag=true&freq=weekly&trk=eml-tod-b-ttle-4&ut=3Ir4EF52ucKkY1/
- ('DEAR AMERICA: It's Time To Say A Big 'Thank You' To Amazon' by Henry Blodget)

- http://www.martinfrost.ws/htmlfiles/oct2011/What-Went-Wrong-At-Eastman-Kodak.pdf ('What Went Wrong at Eastman Kodak?' by George Mendes)
- http://www.dailymail.co.uk/news/article-2098920/Bankrupt-Kodak-stop-making-cameras-invented-them.html ('Bankrupt Kodak to stop making digital cameras (even though it invented them)')
- http://www.forbes.com/2002/01/29/0129carpstrike_print.html ('Kodak's Carp Out of Focus' by DavideDukcevich)
- http://money.cnn.com/magazines/fortune/fortune_archive/2004/01/12/357932/index.htm ('Kodak: The CEO vs. the Gadfly After the film company announced plans to remake its business, one investor activist declared war. Did he overplay his hand?' by Joseph Nocera and Kate Bonamici)
- http://changethis.com/manifesto/41.02.SeducedSuccess/pdf/41.02.SeducedSuccess.pdf ('Seduced by Success' by Robert J. Herbold)
- http://articles.latimes.com/2011/dec/04/business/la-fi-hiltzik-20111204 ('Kodak's long fade to black' by Michael Hiltzik)
- http://www.mediajournal.org/ojs/index.php/jmm/article/viewFile/216/104 ('The Sony Corporation: A Case Study in Transnational Media Management' by Richard A. Gershon and Tsutomu Kanayama)
- http://wwww.post-gazette.com/pg/05180/530332-28.stm ('Sony's new CEO fights discord at rival units' by Phred Dvorak)
- http://www.businessmodelalchemist.com ('The Customer—Value Canvas V.0.8' by Alexander Osterwalder)

Traits for Success:

- http://www.mumbaimirror.com/index.aspx?page=article&sectid=59&contentid=201104112011041103463788026b6fda9 ('Sling along Malinga'by Joseph Koraith)

- http://www.husdal.com/2008/10/18/ericsson-versus-nokia-the-now-classic-case-of-supply-chain-disruption ('Ericsson versus Nokia—the now classic case of supply chain disruption')
- http://www.ftpress.com/articles/article.aspx?p=1244469 ('The Fire that changed an Industry: A Case Study on Thriving in a Networked World' by Amit S. Mukherjee)
- http://www.t20worldcup2012.in ('Yuvraj 6 sixes against Broad (England) 2007')
- http://www.espncricinfo.com/twenty20wc/content/story/311713.html ('Yuvraj was spurred by Flintoff')
- http://www.citigroup.com/citi/press/executive/100524a.htm (CEO VikramPandit: Responsible Leadership)
- http://www.mbarendezvous.com/successstory.php?id=38 ('Motivational Enzyme: MrVikramPandit')
- http://www.referenceforbusiness.com/biography/A-E/Engibous-Thomas-J-1953.html ('Thomas J. Engibous')
- http://money.cnn.com/magazines/fortune/fortune_archive/2004/02/09/360102/index.htm ('Toyota Global Body Shop: The Japanese automaker is putting the final touches on a new strategy: being able to build almost anything, anywhere' by Stuart F. Brown)
- http://casestudy.co.in/wp-content/uploads/2009/11/Oldsmobile_-A-tired-Brand.pdf('Oldsmobile: How the "King of Chrome" ended up on a scrap heap')
- http://www.forbes.com/lists/2011/10/billionaires_2011.html ('The World's Billionaires 2011')
- http://www.topz10s.com/top-10-ceo-of-india ('Top 10 CEOs of India')
- http://www.veethi.com/india-people/azim_premji-profile-25-23.htm ('AzimPremji Profile')
- http://www.jagsheth.net/opinion_wipro_azim.html
- http://greathumancapital.wordpress.com/category/leadership/
- http://www.mapsofindia.com/who-is-who/sports/mansur-ali-khan-pataudi.html ('Mansur Ali Khan Pataudi')

- http://www.goodlearners.net/ThomasEdison.html ('Thomas Edison: Genius is one percent inspiration 99 percent perspiration')

Teamwork:

- http://www.cata.ca/files/PDF/Resource_Centres/hightech/reports/studies/quebec-HPQ-merger.pdf ('The HP-Compaq Merger—A Hitech Giant or another merger fiasco' by Leo B., Hugo P., Hongqi H.)
- http://www.hp.com/hpinfo/newsroom/press/2001/010904a.html ('Hewlett Packard and Compaq agree to merge, creating $87 billion global technology leader')
- http://bendercon.wordpress.com/2009/04/24/hpcompaq-merger-harvard-business-case ('HP/Compaq Merger-Harvard Business Case' byJohn Bender)
- http://www.awpagesociety.com/images/uploads/HP-Compaq-case.pdf('The Hewlett-Packard and Compaq Merger: A Case Study in Business Communication' by Charlotte L. Hoopes)
- http://www.ciol.com/content/news/exeTrack/Portraits/2005/105121301.asp ('You (Indians) are all crazy' by PriyaPadmanabhan)
- http://www.bangalore.philips.com/news.asp
- http://www.espncricinfo.com/westindies/content/story/529493.html ('Gayle meets board chief but future remains unclear')
- http://www.icmrindia.org/casestudies/catalogue/Business%20strategy1/Business%20Strategy%20Leaving%20India%20The%20Peugeot%20Story.htm ('Leaving India: The Peugeot Story')
- http://www.automobileindia.com/auto-component-manufacturer/premier-auto.html
- http://www.expressindia.com/latest-news/When-fighter-Kumble-bowled-with-broken-jaw/380784/ ('When 'fighter' Kumble bowled with broken jaw')

- http://www.greatpersonalities.com/sachin-tendulkar/20.htm
- http://knowledgetoday.wharton.upenn.edu/2012/01/return-of-the-founder/ ('Return of the Founder')
- http://www.thermaxindia.com/about-us/heritage-and-values/founding-family.aspx ('Founding Family')
- http://articles.economictimes.indiatimes.com/2012-10-05/news/34279918_1_chairperson-meher-pudumjee-thermax-unrelated-businesses ('How a shareholder's letter to Anu Aga catalysed change at Thermax')
- http://www.my-wasimakram.blogspot.in/ ('Great Fast Bowler of The Century WasimAkram')
- http://www.wired.com/magazine/2010/03/ff_youtube_5secrets/all/1 ('5 Secrets of YouTube's success' by Wired)
- http://www.google.com/press/pressrel/google_youtube.html ('Google to acquire Youtube for $1.65 Billion in Stock')
- http://findarticles.com/p/articles/mi_m0NXD/is_2_15/ai_n30959641/ ('The rise and fall of Carly Fiorina: An ethical case study' by Craig Johnson)
- http://findarticles.com/p/articles/mi_m0NXD/is_2_15/ai_n30959641/pg_4/ ('The rise and fall of Carly Fiorina: An ethical case study' by Craig Johnson)
- http://wenku.baidu.com/view/91777b6c1eb91a37f1115c30.html ('The rise and fall of Carly Fiorina: An ethical case study' by Craig Johnson)
- http://www.carly-fiorina.com/hp-employees-on-carly-fiorina/gbook.php

Attitude:

- http://users.chariot.net.au/~byoung/waugh1.htm ('Tribute to Steve Waugh')
- http://www.nirma.co.in/genesis.htm ('Genesis')
- http://toostep.com/insight/success-story-of-nirma ('Success Story of Nirma' by SushantAwasthi)

- http://articles.economictimes.indiatimes.com/2011-04-03/news/29377296_1_mahendra-singh-dhoni-railways-job-sourav-ganguly ('Mahendra Singh Dhoni: From a "ticket collector" to Team India "World Cup winning" captain')
- http://news.bbc.co.uk/2/hi/south_asia/2107812.stm ('Top Indian Businessman dies')
- http://www.theage.com.au/technology/biz-tech/microsofts-evangelist-the-bizarre-behaviour-of-steve-ballmer-20090723-dtvk.html ('Microsoft's Evangelist: The bizarre behaviour of Steve Ballmer' by Asher Moses)
- http://www.thisismoney.co.uk/money/news/article-1714820/Forbes-Rich-List-2011-Worlds-100-wealthiest.html ('Forbes Rich List 2011: World's 100 Wealthiest')
- http://www.isixsigma.com/press-releases/robert-w-galvin-inducted-six-sigma-hall-fame ('Robert W. Galvin inducted into the Six Sigma Hall of Fame' by Jessica Harper)
- http://www.galvinpower.org/robert-galvin ('Robert W. Galvin')
- http://articles.economictimes.indiatimes.com/2011-04-08/news/29396834_1_anil-kumble-sehwag-cricket-field ('KapilDev, Anil Kumble on why it is ok to yell at juniors sometimes' by DibyenduGanguly)

Challenges of Success:

- http://blogs.wsj.com/autoshow/2009/06/01/general-motors-chapter-11-filing ('General Motors' Chapter 11 Filing' by Wall Street Journal Staff)
- http://www.telegraph.co.uk/finance/newsbysector/transport/general-motors/5421879/GM-files-for-Chapter-11-bankruptcy-protection.html ('GM files for Chapter 11 bankruptcy protection' by James Quinn)
- http://www.rediff.com/sports/sep/10a1.htm ('The Cricket Interview: LaxmanSivaramakrishnan')
- http://www.indianetzone.com/9/narendra_hirwani.htm ('NarendraHirwani, Madhya Pradesh Cricket Player')

- http://www.guardian.co.uk/sport/blog/2009/aug/19/rahul-dravid-vinod-kambli-career ('VinodKambli and Rahul Dravid: A Study of Potential versus Performance')
- http://www.livemint.com/2009/03/22232524/Long-before-Tata-Motors-there.html ('Long before Tata Motors, there was Sipani's Dolphin' by VenkateshaBabu)
- http://www.carazoo.com/article/0709200901/Car-Blasts-From-The-Past ('Car Blasts from the past')
- http://automotivehorizon.sulekha.com/suzuki-s-saga-of-success_newsitem_28 ('Suzuki's saga of success' by JayashankarMenon)
- casestudy.co.in/wp-content/uploads/2010/03/Mauruti-Case-Study.doc('MarutiUdyog Limited—Managing competition successfully')
- http://www.espncricinfo.com/magazine/content/story/149458.html ('How does it feel to drop the World Cup?')
- http://www.venturenavigator.co.uk/content/158 ('Digital Equipment Corporation—A Case Study')
- http://sloanreview.mit.edu/improvisations/2011/02/17/lessons-from-ken-olsen-and-digital-equipment-corp ('Lessons from Ken Olsen and Digital Equipment Corporation' by Martha E. Mangelsdorf)
- http://reviewessays.com/Business/Motorola-Analogue-Digital-Failure/37882.html ('Motorola Analogue / Digital Failure')
- http://mediacenter.motorola.com/content/Detail.aspx?ReleaseID=10662&NewsAreaID=2 ('Motorola announces Fourth Quarter and Full Year Financial Results')
- http://www.executiveforum.com/PDFs/syd_synopsis.pdf ('Why Smart Executives fail' by Sydney Finkelstein)

And finally, my own article:

- http://www.deccanherald.com/content/167103/management-lessons-learn-cricket.html ('Management Lessons to be learnt from cricket' by Dev Prasad)

A NOTE ON THE AUTHOR

Dev Prasad is an IT professional residing in Bangalore. He secured his degree in Electronics & Communication Engineering from Regional Engineering College (now NIT), Trichy, and done his MDP Program from IIM Bangalore. He has held senior management positions at various European and American Multinational Companies.

Though an engineer by qualification, he has a wide range of interests. These include reading, writing, travelling, photography, study of mythology and listening to music. He likes creative writing and has worked as a part time freelance copywriter for three years for many advertising agencies. He has written many poems, one of which was selected by International Poets Association, USA.

He is passionate about serving the society and has been associated with a few NGOs working for underprivileged children. He loves sports like cricket, badminton, table tennis and chess.

His debut book *KRISHNA: A Journey Through the Lands & Legends of Krishna* was long listed for 2010 Vodafone Crossword Award.

He can be contacted at dev.prasad63@gmail.com